Studies on the History of Papermaking in Britain

Alfred H. Shorter

Studies on the History of
Papermaking in Britain

Edited by
Richard L. Hills

VARIORUM

Published by VARIORUM
    Ashgate Publishing Limited
    Gower House, Croft Road,
    Aldershot, Hampshire GU11 3HR
    Great Britain

    Ashgate Publishing Company
    Old Post Road,
    Brookfield, Vermont 05036
    USA

ISBN 0-86078-386-3

British Library CIP data
    Shorter, Alfred H.
    Studies on the History of Paper-making in Britain
    - (Variorum Collected Studies Series; CS 425)
    I. Title II. Hills, R.L. III. Series
    676.0941

Library of Congress CIP data
    Shorter, Alfred Henry.
    Studies on the History of Paper-making in Britain/
    Alfred H. Shorter : edited by Richard L. Hills.
      p. cm. -- (Collected Studies Series; CS 425)
    ISBN 0-86078-386-3
    1. Paper-making - Great Britain - History. 2. Paper mills -
    Great Britain - History. I. Hills, Richard Leslie, 1938- .
    II. Title III. Series: Collected studies: CS425.
    TS1095.07S58 1993
    676'.0941—dc20   93-34844
                                     CIP

Printed by Galliard (Printers) Ltd
    Great Yarmouth, Norfolk, Great Britain

COLLECTED STUDIES SERIES CS425

CONTENTS

This volume contains xii + 348 pages

INTRODUCTION

Mrs. Shorter has very kindly given her permission for the publication of her late husband's articles on papermaking. We have been able to locate almost all the places which published them and have received their support to reprint them in the format in which they first appeared, with one exception, that of the Dixotype News on Hurcott Mill where we have been unable to locate a printed original. I would like to thank all those who have supported us in this way for it shows the value they attach to Dr. Shorter's work and that they too feel that publication is worthwhile.

Dr. Shorter was one of the pioneers of industrial history and approached it through his background of historical geography. This is reflected in his articles which are mainly concerned with the distribution of papermills in Britain. The research for these articles formed the basis not only for his doctoral thesis at the University of Exeter which was awarded this degree in 1954, but also for his two major books. The first was published in 1957 under the title, *Paper Mills and Paper Makers in England, 1495–1800*. It was Volume VI of the *Monumenta Chartae Papyraceae Historiam Illustrantia* series of the Paper Publications Society of Hilversum, Holland, the *series* which has formed such an important basis for the study of the history of papermaking and watermarks across Europe. Just how much of a pioneering study this was may not be immediately recognised. While there had been earlier books on specific topics like those of Thomas Balston on *William Balston, Paper Maker, 1759–1849* (1954) or of Joan Evans, *The Endless Web, John Dickinson & Co. Ltd., 1804–1954* (1955), Shorter's was the first general account of papermaking in Britain. It preceded Donald C. Coleman's *The British Paper Industry, 1495–1860*, which appeared the following year while Alistair G. Thomson, *The Paper Industry in Scotland, 1590–1860*, was not published until 1974. Even that classic, R.H. Clapperton, *The Paper-making Machine* was not published until 1967. Shorter's second book, *Papermaking in the British Isles, An Historical and Geographical Study*, was published posthumously in 1971 and brought the story more or less up to that date. Here it is the distribution of paper mills throughout the country which is examined, although some of the technical developments are discussed too. There is also *Water Paper Mills in England* published by the Society for the Protection of Ancient Buildings in 1966 as their pamphlet No. 9.

Therefore it may be questioned why we should be reproducing these articles, many of which were published over thirty years ago and some of which stretch back now for almost fifty years. One answer lies in the sole article we have not reprinted, for in *Devon and Cornwall Notes and Queries*, Vol XX, 1938, we can trace the start of Shorter's interest in papermaking. He wrote, "Since taking up the subject of the old-established industries of the South West, I have found references to the following Paper Mills which have existed at sometime in the county of Devon, and which no longer make paper". He listed fourteen mills and asked for more information about them. He was concerned to have details of "the origin of each mill, its history, the materials used at different times, the importance and scope of the trade, and the reasons for its decline or extinction". These questions we are still asking today and they were to form the basis of Shorter's research work which he started from his own base in the South West and broadened out until it covered almost the whole of Great Britain. Although the work had to be postponed for the duration of the Second World War, he picked it up again soon afterwards and we can see how it grew in the various articles on the counties of Devon and Cornwall. Rarely can the development of a person's interest and research be followed in this way.

I have grouped the articles into four sections. In the first are either the more general ones or those covering specific topics which do not have a geographical slant. Those placed at the beginning show his geographical interests, as can be seen in some of the titles, *Paper Mills on the Map, The Distribution of British Paper Mills in 1851*. However, our historian becomes involved in the changing names of mills and the periods in which they worked. In addition to their names, those mills functioning between 1816 and 1860 had a number allocated by H.M. Customs and Excise. Such a system, it might be thought, would solve the nomenclature problem; far from it, it only adds confusion, and we find Shorter wrestling with the problem in his articles, *The Excise Numbers of Paper Mills in England and Wales*. Then, if you start investigating what the mills actually produced, you will soon discover watermarked paper, hence *Watermarks in English Paper with Special Reference to the Nineteenth Century*. This covers the period after his first book and contains ones different from and more extensive than his second.

The next section contains those articles relating first to Devon and Cornwall in which, as I have mentioned earlier, we can see the origins of Shorter's work and which cannot be separated into their respective counties. Neither can those articles on Somerset and Dorset be divided so these four counties form a block together. The majority of all these articles were his earliest and here the foundations were laid. In the following section we pursue his treatment of papermaking county by county, arranged alphabetically. Most of these papers contain such information as he had been able to obtain on specific mills. While there is some duplication with his first book in the period up to 1800, many mills continued long after that and so here we can find details about the entire history of a mill with important facts not included in his second book. In fact, often it is only in these papers that we have the outline histories of very many paper mills in the British Isles. The final section covers the three remaining countries that make up the British Isles, Scotland, Wales and Ireland.

We can see a new approach to papermaking history in *The Provenance of Paper Used in Devon in the Late Eighteenth Century* and it is a pity that Shorter did not live to pursue this line of approach further. However his contributions to the study of the history of papermaking in these islands have been outstanding and formed the basis on which many later historians have been able to build. Among them I may mention Martin Tillmanns, *Bridge Hall Mills, Three Centuries of Paper and Cellulose Film Manufacture* (1978); Brian G. Luker, *Mill 364, Paper Making at St. Cuthberts* (1991); and John N. Balston, *The Elder James Whatman, England's Greatest Paper Maker (1702–1759)* (1992); to say nothing of the debt which the present editor owes. We hope that, by bringing together all of Shorter's articles, not only will his reputation be enhanced but that his scholarship will be made more widely available.

Mottram   RICHARD L. HILLS
April 1993

I

PAPER MILLS ON THE MAP

In the January number of this Journal, " Shadower " kindly referred to a research paper of mine, dealing with the earliest records of paper mills and paper-makers in Devon and Cornwall. This is part of a research scheme which I am developing as a survey of the distribution of the paper-making industry in the British Isles at various stages in its evolution. Although a professional geographer, I venture to hope that this work will be of interest and importance to paper-makers who would like to know more about the location of the industry in the past, as well as to students of historical geography in general.

From a study of a considerable variety of sources of information, I conclude that in many parts of our islands the number of paper mills which have worked at one time or another is very much larger than that of the mills now working. Two such areas are shown in my maps accompanying this article—Devon and North-East England. In some counties, paper-making has disappeared altogether ; my maps show the distribution of former paper mills in Cornwall, Norfolk and Suffolk, and other examples of such counties are Shropshire and several in Wales and Ireland. Other regions present a different story, particularly the great paper-making districts of Lancashire, Scotland, Kent, Buckinghamshire and Hertfordshire ; even in some of these, however, I have found references to the existence of the industry at places where it is not to be found to-day.

The changing map

A great deal of material on the subject of early paper mills in England was assembled by Mr. Rhys Jenkins, who published a distribution map (see *Collected Papers of Rhys Jenkins*, 1936). Local research may well reveal other early sites, and one of my tasks is to build up a series of maps of paper mills which existed during the eighteenth and nineteenth centuries. The number of mills which worked in the first half of the eighteenth century must have run into hundreds, but so far I have been able to establish the sites of only a few of them. During the

PAPER MILLS ON THE MAP

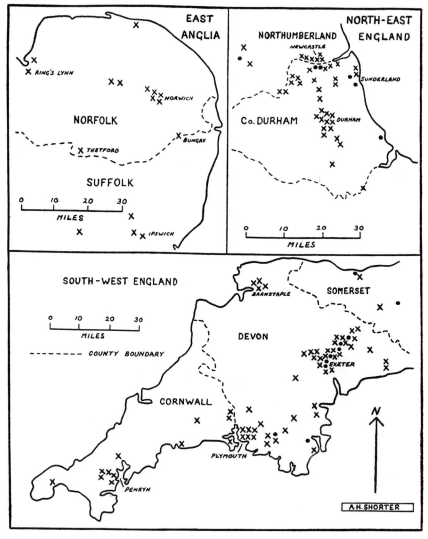

● PAPER MILLS STILL IN EXISTENCE AS SUCH
X PAPER MILLS CONVERTED, DERELICT OR
DESTROYED

course of that century, the growth of trade, industry and population, and the increased demand for paper, together with the rise in costs of importing paper from France, resulted in the establishment of many more paper mills and in the spread of the industry in Britain. For the early part of the nineteenth century, I have a great deal of information from the Excise Records (consulted in the Library of the H.M. Customs and Excise, London, by permission of the Librarian).

It seems that, in many areas, the number of paper mills increased up to the 1820's and '30's, with a decrease since that time. Computing totals from all my sources for Devon and Cornwall, I find the trend as follows : seventeenth century, two mills ; first half of the eighteenth century, eight ; second half of the eighteenth century, twenty-eight ; 1820's and 1830's, forty-nine ; 1850's, twenty-eight ; 1900, twelve ; now, eight. It is possible, however, that distribution and quantity maps will show something of a distinctive story for each region of the British Isles ; a series of such maps should help us to suggest geographical, historical and economic factors at work in the evolution of the industry. One fact that is illustrated on my maps, for example, is that paper mills were established in or near many of the old " regional capitals " of our country, e.g. Exeter, Plymouth, Durham, and Norwich. In such towns, the presence of raw materials, a considerable local market for the finished product, and good communications were important factors, but, of course, the nature and amount of water available must have been of great significance in the siting of all mills.

The aim of the study

To sum up—my survey should provide something of an historical atlas of paper mills in the British Isles. I also intend to construct maps to show the numbers of people employed in paper-making at various times in the different regions, sources of materials, trade and so forth. I have much local research on hand, attempting to identify the sites of mills of which I have only the names or localities. It would be of great assistance if paper-makers who have any kind of early record of their mills—and possibly also of " extinct " mills in their neighbourhood—would kindly communicate with me at the Geography Department, University College of the South-West, Exeter, where this research is at present centred. I should be very grateful for any help of this kind.

Photo: A. H. Shorter

Formerly a paper mill : Coosebean, near Truro, in
Cornwall.   The mill was the large two-storey building
in the back centre of the group.

Photo : A. H. Shorter

Working to-day : Head Weir Paper Mills, below
Blackaller Weir, on the River Exe at Exeter.

II

PAPER MILLS IN ENGLAND IN THE 1690's

The arrival of French refugee paper makers in England in the late seventeenth century led to the formation of the Company of White Paper Makers in 1686. Four years later the Company's charter was confirmed and prolonged by Act of Parliament, but their work ceased by 1697-8. From various statements made in support of the Company and on behalf of those who were opposed to their monopoly of the manufacture of high quality white paper, we learn that the Company had four or five paper mills in 1690 (increased to eight by 1697) and that there were about a hundred other paper mills in England.

Many years ago Mr. Rhys Jenkins made a very valuable contribution[1] to the history of English papermaking and compiled a map and a list which gave about forty per cent. of the mills which must have existed in 1690. Further research has established the locations of many more mills and has added a number of other possible sites. Most of the relevant dates and authorities have now been mustered[2], but information is still coming in. For example, Hampton Gay Mill (Oxfordshire), long known as a paper mill from 1803[3], has recently been identified as early as 1681[4]. Alton Mill (Hampshire), already known from 1759, may have been the mill at ,"Hoileton, near Southampton" mentioned in 1686[5].

One is so frequently asked about the early English paper mills that it now seems desirable to give a map and a revised list of mills in the 1690's. The mills which certainly or in all probability existed at that time are shown on the map by dots, and other possible sites[6] by circles. The dates given in the list are those of the earliest known references to a paper maker or a paper mill on each site. The numbers against the mill names are simply for use in referring to the map. In 1690 the Company of White Paper Makers probably held Up Mill (Hampshire) (95), a mill at or near Colnbrook (Buckinghamshire) (68), Byfleet (Surrey) (82) and possibly Alton (Hampshire) (90) and two mills at or near Plymouth (42 and 43). They later took over a mill at Dartford (Kent) (96) and they may have controlled Eynsford (Kent) (98).

List of Paper Mills in England in the 1690's

Berkshire: Sutton Courtenay, 1631 (51). East Hagbourne, 1690 (52). Sheffield, 1687/8 (53). Cookham, 1658 (54).

Buckinghamshire: Stowe, name Paper Mill Spinney (55). Great Brickhill, 1695 (56). West Wycombe, 1684 (57)[7]. Eight mills in the parish of High Wycombe in 1690 (earliest reference 1636) (58 to 65). Glory Mill, 1627 (66). Thorney, 1699 (67). Colnbrook, 1636 (68). Horton, 1635 (69). Wraysbury, 1605 (70).

Cambridgeshire: Dernford, 1664 (78).

Cheshire: Chester, 1696/7 (10).

Derbyshire: Duffield, 1700 (20).

Devon: Exeter, 1669 (40). Countess Weir, 1638 (41). Plymouth, 1683-4 (42, 43).

Durham: Chopwell, 1697 (1). Croxdale, 1678 (2). Hunwick, 1674 (3).

Essex: Chelmsford, 1686 (79).

Gloucestershire: Wick, 1639 (36).

Hampshire: Bentley, 1675 (89). Alton, 1686 (90). Bramshott, 1698/9 (91). Warnford, 1617 (92). Bedhampton, 1676 (93). Frog Mill, 1663 (94). Up Mill, 1686 (95).

Hertfordshire: Hatfield, 1680 (80). Sopwell, 1649 (81).

Kent: Dartford, 1679 (96). Dartford, 1588 (97). Eynsford, 1648 (98). Shoreham, 1690 (99). Sandling, 1671 (100). Sandling, 1700 (101). Turkey Mill, 1680 (102). Lower Tovil, 1686 (103). Upper Tovil, 1680 (104). Ivy Mill, 1685 (105). Little Ivy Mill, 1689 (106). Barton Mill, 1665 (107). Buckland, 1638 (108).

PAPER MILLS IN ENGLAND IN THE 1690'S

Lancashire: Cark, 1617 (6). Pincock, 1651 (7). Skelmersdale, field names Paper Mill Meadow (8). Farnworth Bridge, 1674 (9).

Leicestershire: Cossington, 1657 (23).

Middlesex: Harefield, 1641 (71). West Drayton, 1641 (72). Longford, 1641 (73). Poyle, 1636 (74). Stanwell, 1682 (75). Hounslow, 1636 (76). Tottenham, 1680 (77).

Nottinghamshire: Bulwell, 1674 (21). Lenton, 1699 (22).

Oxfordshire: Hampton Gay, 1681 (48). Eynsham, 1682 (49). Wolvercote, 1672/3 (50).

Shropshire: Great Bolas, 1665 (24, 25). Hanwood, name Paper Mill Coppice (26). Cound, 1655/6 (27). Coton Spring, 1686 (28). Langley, 1650 (29).

Somerset: Chewton Keynsham, 1678 (37). Wookey Hole, 1610 (38). Dulverton, name Paper Mill Cottages (39).

Staffordshire: Rugeley, 1612 (30).

Surrey: Byfleet, 1673 (82). Cobham, 1687 (83). Stoke, 1679 (84, 85). Godalming, 1625 (86). Catteshall, 1692 (87). Eashing, 1658 (88).

Warwickshire: Perry Barr, 1648 (31, 32).

Westmorland: Ambleside, 1681 (4). Milnthorpe, 1700 (5).

Wiltshire: Longdean, 1635 (44). Bemerton, 1554 or 1569 (45). Salisbury, 1686 (46). Nunton, 1666 (47).

Worcestershire: Hurcott, 1630 (33). Beoley, 1645-50 (34). Hewell, 1645 (35).

Yorkshire, North Riding: Thornton le Dale, 1680 (11, 12).

Yorkshire, West Riding: Thorp Arch, 1683 (13). Ryther, 1684 (14). Holmfield, name Paper Mill Field (15). Monk Bretton, 1666 (16). Owlerton, 1689 (17). Brightside, 1699/1700 (18). Norton, 1656 (19).

PAPER MILLS IN ENGLAND IN THE 1690'S

REFERENCES

1. R. Jenkins, Paper-Making in England, 1495-1788, in *Collected Papers*, 1936.
2. A. H. Shorter, *Paper Mills and Paper Makers in England 1495-1800*, The Paper Publications Society, Hilversum, Holland, 1957, especially Appendix B.
3. The paper mill is mentioned in the Notes by William Balston, 1803, *Papers from Springfield Mill*, Kent. Information from Mr. Thomas Balston.
4. In 1681 a grist mill was leased to John Allen of Hampton, paper maker, at a rent of £9 a year; the mill was to be used only for papermaking. Information from Dr. R. P. Beckinsale, University of Oxford, quoting *Barry Mss.*, Bodl. doc. 24.
5. On April 24, 1686, Denis Manes, a Protestant refugee paper maker from Angoulême, wrote, "I have been in prison eleven months at Caen for trying to send three paper makers to some works I have with Messrs. Cardonnel, Dupin, Gruchy at Hoileton, near Southampton." A. T. Hazen, Eustace Burnaby's Manufacture of White Paper in England, *Papers of the Bibliographical Society of America*, 48, 1954, p. 328, quoting *H.M.C., Downshire Mss.* 1924. It is possible that this reference should be connected with Up Mill, South Stoneham, near Southampton, which was held by the Company of White Paper Makers, but I can find no local name there like "Hoileton." The name sounds suspiciously like Alton, but that place is some 25 miles from Southampton.
6. The evidence for these possible sites is given in A. H. Shorter, *op. cit.*, p. 38 and Appendix B. The sites include five places where "Paper Mill" is part of a local name but where no references to paper makers are known, and seven places where paper makers are recorded before A.D. 1700 but no reference to a paper mill has been found.
7. On the map the mills in Buckinghamshire Nos. 57 to 70 and in Middlesex Nos. 71 to 76 have had to be massed in one group, the scale being too small to show the numbers separately.

PAPER MILLS IN ENGLAND IN THE 1690'S

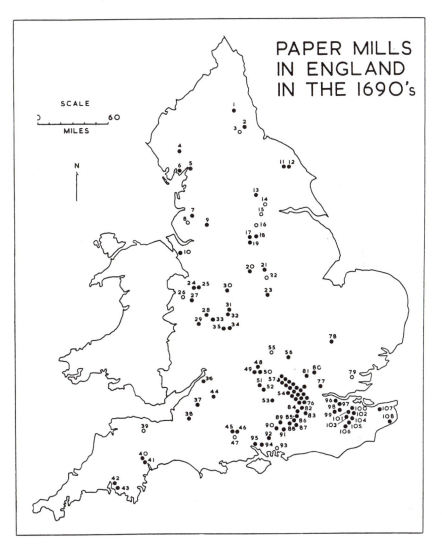

PAPER MILLS
IN ENGLAND
IN THE 1690's

III

PAPER MILLS IN ENGLAND
IN THE 1820s

One of the chief reasons why the period chosen
for consideration in this paper is of considerable
interest to students of the history of paper-
making in England is that during the 1820s the
number of paper mills at work in that country
reached its peak. By way of introduction to this
period, brief reference may be made to the rise
and fall in the number of paper mills in England
from the seventeenth to the nineteenth century.
Throughout that time the paper-making industry
was growing, and the total number of mills
used by paper makers ran into many hundreds.

We can trace the trends in the numbers of
paper mills from several important sources from
about 1690 onwards. Whereas in 1690[1] there
must have been approximately 100 to 110 paper
mills in England, in 1712[2] the Excise authorities
gave the totals of paper makers in "England,
Wales and Berwick upon Tweed" as 209, and in
Scotland 7. By 1738[3] the number of paper mills
in England and Wales had increased to 278, of
which three-fourths were used for the manufacture of coarse paper. There is no other official
statement as to the number of mills later in the
eighteenth century, but for the years from 1785
onwards[4] there is a list of the numbers of
licences granted to paper makers each year, from
which it is clear that by 1800[5] the total number
of paper mills in England and Wales must have
been about 410.

In 1816, 522 licences were granted to paper
and board makers, and the numbers rose still
higher during the 1820s. In 1825 there were 602
and in 1829 (the peak year) 643; thereafter the
numbers generally declined, and in 1841, for
example, there were only 370 licences. Although
there is no complete list of the numbers of paper

PAPER MILLS IN ENGLAND IN THE 1820'S

mills at work each year during the period 1816—1851, there is no doubt that they corresponded reasonably closely with the numbers of licences which were issued. Fortunately many Excise records of the period have been preserved[6], including "General Letters" and amendments, which give the names of paper makers and mills, each distinguished by an Excise Letter or Number. By the Act of 58 Geo. 3, c. 65 (1818) the numbering of all premises which were subject to Excise duties was made statutory, but the Excise authorities had already compiled and issued a list of paper makers and mills with Letters or Numbers. From this list, dated 8th October, 1816, we learn that there were some 21 board makers in the London area (each of these was distinguished by an Excise Letter — A to V) and that the paper and board mills which were then at work in England and Wales were numbered up to 489. It will be seen that the total of 510 is just a little short of the number of licences recorded for the year 1816—522 .

The practice of allocating Excise Numbers to paper and board makers continued up to 1851. Many amendments to the lists issued in 1816 and in later years were necessary, for many entirely new mills were established, changes occurred in the tenure of paper and board mills, and mills started up again after periods "off work". In some cases a completely new Excise Number was given to the mill concerned, in other cases a Number which had become disused because of the cessation of work (temporarily or permanently) at one mill was allotted to another mill. The highest Excise Number ever allotted to an English paper mill (No. 694) had been reached by 1832; as there were so many mills going out of work at and after that time, it was not necessary to create new Excise Numbers, and old disused Numbers were allotted to mills which were either completely new or were re-starting work.

In 1851 a list of paper mills was compiled for a "Return to an Order of the Honourable

PAPER MILLS IN ENGLAND IN THE 1820'S

House of Commons, dated 13 June 1851"[7]). Although a few paper mills which must have been in existence in England at that time were for some reason omitted from the list (they were probably not actually at work at the time the Return was compiled), there is no doubt that the totals given in the Return may be used for a comparison with those given by the Excise authorities in 1816 and other years. In 1816 there were between 510 and 522 paper mills and board factories at work in England and Wales; in the Return of 1851 the total for England is 296, and for Wales 8.

The various figures quoted earlier in this paper show that there was a steady increase in the number of paper mills in England throughout the eighteenth century and that the peak was reached in the 1820s. By that time paper-making machines[8] were being installed in many mills, and steam-engines were being substituted for water-wheels in mills and factories of many kinds. The effects of these changes on the paper-making industry and on its geographical distribution became more and more marked from about 1830. Larger paper mills, equipped with machines and steam-engines, were able to compete for markets much more effectively than the small vat mills driven by water; where they were near the ports, towns, industrial districts and good communications by land and water, they were much better placed than the small mills in rural districts. Thus from about 1830 can be traced not only a marked decrease in the total number of mills at work, but also a general geographical contraction of the paper-making industry.

The distribution map shows the paper mills which existed in England at any time between 1817 and 1832. Thus it covers the peak period in terms of numbers of mills and licences issued to paper makers, and it gives a fair representation of the geographical distribution of paper mills in England just before the general geographical contraction set in. The chief source from which the map has been compiled is the Excise Letters

PAPER MILLS IN ENGLAND IN THE 1820'S

PAPER MILLS IN ENGLAND IN THE 1820'S

of the period 1817—1832, but in order to identify the sites of individual mills many other sources have been used, especially maps and Directories of the 1820s.

541 paper mills are marked on this map. Each dot indicates the site of a paper mill which is recorded during the period 1817—1832; a dash indicates a mill of which no record has been found within that period, but of which there is evidence both before and after it. The distribution shown on this map reflects two very marked features of the geography of paper-making in England from the eighteenth century and into the nineteenth. One is the very wide dispersal of the industry, and the other is the marked concentrations of paper mills in certain areas, for example to the north-west (the Wye Valley of Buckinghamshire and the valleys of the Chess and Gade in Hertfordshire) and south-east (the Maidstone district) of London. The geographical background of these distributions in the eighteenth century has been analysed elsewhere[9], and in so far as many of the small rural mills were concerned, the distribution in 1817—1832 reflects many of the features of the earlier century. The really great changes in distribution had not yet occurred — the elimination of many small mills (especially remote water-driven vat mills), the geographical and economic concentration of paper-making into generally fewer and larger mills, and the appearance of more mills in certain well-favoured industrial and trading areas such as Lancashire and North Kent. These and many other changes are part of the story of the paper-making industry in England from the 1830s to the present day.

PAPER MILLS IN ENGLAND IN THE 1820'S

NOTES

[1]) For a discussion of the number and geographical distribution of paper mills in England circa 1690, see A. H. Shorter, Paper Mills and Paper Makers in Eng= land, 1495–1800, The Paper Publications Society, Hilversum, 1957, pp. 34–38.

[2]) Reply of the Excise Commissioners, 25 July 1712, to an inquiry arising from a Treasury Minute, 23 July 1712, in Treasury Minute Book, XIX, 242. Excise and Treasury Correspondence, 1693/4–1721/2, 62.

[3]) Excise and Treasury Correspondence, 1715/6–1745, 245–7.

[4]) British Parliamentary Papers, Reports from Commis= sioners (1857), IV, First Report of the Commissioners of Inland Revenue, 177, Appendix No. 30, lxix.

[5]) The number of licences granted in 1800 was 417.

[6]) These records are in the Library of H. M. Customs and Excise. I am grateful to the Librarian, Mr. R. C. Jarvis, for his kind help in my research work on these records, and to the Commissioners of Customs and Excise for their permission to use information from their archives in this paper.

[7]) This was a "Return of the Number of Paper Mills at present in work in England, Wales, Scotland, and Ireland, distinguishing the number in each country; also the Number of 'Beating Engines' at Present at work in each Mill and the Number at present silent. Ordered by the House of Commons to be printed 27 February 1852". House of Commons Papers, Session of 1852, Vol. 51, No. 128. For an analysis of the geographical distribution of these mills see A. H. Shorter, The Distribution of British Paper Mills in 1851, in The Paper Maker, CXXI, 1951, pp. 416–423.

[8]) The first paper=making machine was set to work in Frogmore Mill, Hertfordshire, in 1804. In 1820 the out= put of hand=made paper in the United Kingdom was still greater than that from machines, but in 1830 the output of machine=made paper was more than double that from vats. A. D. Spicer, The Paper Trade, 1907, App. IX.

[9]) A. H. Shorter, Paper Mills and Paper Makers in England, 1495–1800, The Paper Publications Society, Hilversum, 1957, pp. 74–9.

The list of paper mills in 1851 reveals also that there were many quite small mills with less than six beating engines each; some indeed had only one or two. Many of these small mills have gone out of production.

Sixthly, we note the consequent change in the balance of the distribution of the paper mills. In 1851 the leading positions in England in terms of numbers of mills were held by Yorkshire (36), Kent (33), Buckinghamshire (23), Lancashire (22), Devon (21) and Durham (14). Today, the order is Lancashire, Kent, Yorkshire, Buckinghamshire, Devon and Somerset.

Some old-established mills omitted

Finally, there are some obvious omissions of old-established mills from the 1851 list, and presumably this can only mean that at the time the Return was compiled these mills were not at work: e.g., Bathford in Somerset, Chaps in Wiltshire, Wolvercote in Oxfordshire, Frogmore in Hertfordshire, Alton in Hampshire, Chartham in Kent, and Langcliffe in Yorkshire. All these old mills are still working except Alton. The Isle of Man and the Channel Isles, where there were paper mills in the nineteenth century, are not mentioned in the list.

These seven observations have, of course, to be set against the historical background of the paper industry as a whole. In 1851 the Excise duty on paper was still in force. The number of paper-making machines in use was constantly increasing and the number of vats declining. Output and demand were both rising, yet in 1851 the problem of raw materials must have been looming large, for the age of esparto and woodpulp was yet to come. Many British paper-makers successfully overcame the difficulties and problems of the 1850's and 1860's. In these days of another crisis as regards raw materials for the paper industry one wishes even greater success to the paper-makers during the years ahead.

The following list gives, under each Collection of Excise, the names of the paper mills (col. 1), re-grouped by counties (col. 2), and the number of beating engines at work (col. 3) and silent (col. 4) in 1851.

THE DISTRIBUTION OF PAPER MILLS IN 1851

England and Wales
Barnstaple Collection

1	2	3	4
Blatchford	Devon	2	
Playford	,,	2	
St. Decumans	Somerset	5	

Bath

Catherine	Somerset	1	
Henley	,,	2	
Lower Wookey	,,	6	1
Wookey Hole	,,	2	
Calstone	Wiltshire	1	
Longdean	,,	1	
Widdenham	,,	1	

Bedford

Apsley	Hertfordshire	10	
Croxley	,,	11	2
Hamper	,,	6	
Home Park	,,	12	
Nash	,,	11	
Two Waters	,,	4	
Bowden	Buckinghamshire	3	
Claptons	,,	14	
Glory Moor	,,	10	1
Loudwater	,,	6	
,,	,,	4	
,,	,,	5	
Lower Bledlow	,,	2	
Lower Marsh	,,	8	
,,	,,	4	
Lower Saunderton	,,	2	
Rye	,,	2	
Wooburn	,,	11	

Bristol

Cheddar	Somerset	1	1
,,	,,	2	1
North Wick	,,	1	
Golden Valley	Gloucestershire	2	1

Cambridge

Sawston	Cambridgeshire	2	2
St. Neots	Huntingdonshire	4	

Canterbury

Buckland	Kent	4	
Bushy Rough	,,	2	2
Cheriton	,,	2	
Crabble	,,	3	
Hinksden	,,	1	
Little Chart	,,	2	
River	,,	6	2
Spring Gardens	,,	5	

THE DISTRIBUTION OF PAPER MILLS IN 1851

	Chester		
Cefnybedd	Denbigh	3	
Morda	Shropshire	1	
Westonrhyn	,,	1	
	Cornwall		
Kennal Vale	Cornwall	3	
	Cumberland		
Branthwaite	Cumberland	2	
Egremont	,,	3	2
Kirkoswald	,,	2	
Ulverston	Lancashire	5	
	Derby		
Dunsley	Derbyshire	2	
Duffield	,,	1	
Darley	,,	6	
Masson	,,	2	2
Peckwash	,,	16	2
Epperstone	Nottinghamshire	4	
Kings	Leicestershire	2	
	Dorset		
Witchampton	Dorset	3	
	Durham		
Ayres Quay	Durham	5	
Butterby	,,	2	
Ford Farm	,,	11	
Hett	,,	2	
Langley	,,	11	
Moorsley Banks	,,	3	
Relly	,,	3	
Whitehill	,,	2	
Richmond	Yorkshire	14	
Yarm	,,	4	
	Essex		
Greenstead Green	Essex	2	
	Exeter		
Bridge	Devon	9	
Cullompton	,,	2	1
Colyton	,,	2	
Countess Weir	,,	2	4
Exwick	,,	2	
Hele	,,	16	
Huxham	,,	4	
,,	,,	2	
Head Weir	,,	4	1
Langford	,,	1	1
Stoke Canon	,,	9	
Kensham	,,	11	
Trews Weir	,,	5	1

THE DISTRIBUTION OF PAPER MILLS IN 1851

	Gloucester		
Postlip	Gloucestershire	5	
	Grantham		
Houghton	Lincolnshire	2	
	Halifax		
Bradley	Yorkshire	2	1
Booth Wood	,,	2	1
Dean	,,	4	3
Firth House	,,	3	
Goose Eye	,,	2	
Ingrow	,,	2	2
Skipton	,,	2	1
	Hampshire		
Barford	Hampshire	1	
Bramshott	,,	1	
Standford	,,	1	
Catteshall	Surrey	4	
Chilworth	,,	3	1
Chilworth Pond	,,	4	3
Eashing	,,	5	
Sickle	,,	1	1
Iping	Sussex	7	1
West Ashling	,,		2
	Hereford		
Cleobury	Shropshire	2	
Ludlow	,,	1	
Cone	Gloucestershire	6	
Rowley	,,	1	
Itton Court	Monmouthshire	1	
Lady	,,	8	2
Lark	,,	1	
Linnet	,,	4	2
Whitebrook	,,	1	
	Hertford		
Stratford	Essex	3	
Standon	Hertfordshire	1	1
	Hull		
Ellerburn	Yorkshire	3	
Stepney	,,	4	
	Isle of Wight		
Romsey	Hampshire	1	
West End	,,	1	

THE DISTRIBUTION OF PAPER MILLS IN 1851

	Lancaster	
Burneside	Westmorland	4
Cowanhead	,,	4
Waterhouse	,,	4
Hollins	Lancashire	22
Matshead	,,	2
Oakenclough	,,	8
Over Darwen	,,	4

	Leeds	
Cut Side	Yorkshire	2
Dock Street	,,	4
East Morton	,,	7
,,	,,	10
,,	,,	2
Hunslet	,,	14
Hirst	,,	2
Otley	,,	11
Pool	,,	3
Weetwoodside	,,	4
Wood	,,	2
Woodside	,,	2
,,	,,	2

	Lichfield		
Birmingham	Warwickshire	1	
,,	,,	1	
,,	,,	1	
,,	,,	6	
,,	,,	1	
,,	,,	2	
,,	,,	1	
,,	,,	1	
Tamworth	Staffordshire	8	4
,,	,,	3	3

	Lincoln	
Ordsall	Nottinghamshire	2
Retford	,,	2

	Lynn	
Lynn	Norfolk	2
Lyng	,,	2
Thetford	,,	3

THE DISTRIBUTION OF PAPER MILLS IN 1851

	Manchester		
Belmont	Lancashire	8	
Bridge Hall	,,	34	
Creams	,,	15	
Collyhurst	,,	3	
Eagley Bridge	,,	2	
Halshaw Moor	,,	36	
Hall i' th' Wood	,,	3	
Heap Bridge	,,	7	
Kearsley	,,	24	
Lomax Bank	,,	2	
Reddish	,,	3	1
Springfield	,,	18	
Shuttleworth	,,	8	
Smedley	,,	4	
Throstle Nest	,,	15	
Woolfold	,,	6	
Charlestown	Derbyshire	8	
,,	,,	5	3
Diggle	Yorkshire	2	6
	Newcastle		
Dilston	Northumberland	2	
Haughton	,,	8	
Scotswood	,,	12	
,,	,,	4	2
Warden	,,	6	1
Fellingshore	Durham	4	
Jarrow	,,	10	1
Lintzford	,,	7	
New Stourbridge	,,	4	
Shotley Grove	,,	20	2
Urpeth	,,	4	
	Northampton		
Rush	Northamptonshire	2	
Cotton	,,	1	
Yardley	,,	1	
Wansford	,,	1	
	Northwich		
Folly Grove	Cheshire	2	
Mill Bank	,,	5	
Worthington	Lancashire	6	
	Norwich		
Bungay	Suffolk	1	
Lower Sheringham	Norfolk	1	
Norwich	,,	2	
Taverham	,,	5	

THE DISTRIBUTION OF PAPER MILLS IN 1851

	Oxford		
Deddington	Oxfordshire		1
Ensham	,,		4
Hampton Gay	,,	6	
Hinksey	,,	1	
Newton	,,	1	
Sandford Ferry	,,	6	
Widford	,,	6	
Weirs	,,	2	
Quenington	Gloucestershire	4	
	Plymouth		
Aller	Devon	1	1
Ivybridge	,,	2	
,,	,,	6	
Kilbury	,,	2	
Lee	,,	2	
Tuckenhay	,,	5	
Danescombe	Cornwall	1	
Tamar	,,	1	
	Reading		
Arborfield	Berkshire	2	
Bagnor	,,	3	
Cookham	,,	6	
Colthrop	,,	6	1
Hagbourn	,,	2	
Sutton	,,	6	
Sheffield	,,	4	6
Temple	,,	6	
Shiplake	Oxfordshire	2	
Bourne End	Buckinghamshire	3	
,,	,,	3	3
,,	,,	1	1
,,	,,	3	2
Cliveden	,,	9	
Marlow	,,	3	
Taplow	,,	4	
Wyrardisbury	,,	7	
Poyle	Middlesex	7	2

THE DISTRIBUTION OF PAPER MILLS IN 1851

	Rochester		
Basted	Kent	5	
Bearsted Spot	,,	1	
Darenth	,,	2	
Dartford	,,	4	
Eynsford	,,	1	
East Malling	,,	4	
,,	,,	5	
Footscray	,,	4	
Great Ivy	,,	6	
Hawley	,,	3	
Hayle	,,	2	
Loose	,,	2	
Otham	,,	1	
New	,,	1	
Hampton	,,	1	
Pauls Cray	,,	3	
South Darenth	,,	8	
St. Mary Cray	,,	11	
Springfield	,,	8	
Shoreham	,,	1	
Sundridge	,,	1	
Snodland	,,	4	
Tovil	,,	5	
Turkey	,,	10	
	Salisbury		
Bulford	Wiltshire	1	
Downton	,,	3	
Clatford	Hampshire	1	1
Down	,,	1	2
Laverstoke	,,	1	2
	Shrewsbury		
Tibberton	Shropshire	2	
	Sheffield		
Damflask	Yorkshire	1	
Ecclesfield	,,	4	
Friars	,,	1	
Lewden	,,	1	
Olive	,,	1	
Owlerton	,,	1	
Rivelin	,,	1	
Storrs	,,	1	
Spring Grove	,,	1	
Bank Vale	Derbyshire	4	
Greenhouse	,,	1	
Whitehall	,,	8	

THE DISTRIBUTION OF PAPER MILLS IN 1851

	Staffordshire		
Alton	Staffordshire	3	1
Cheddleton	"	1	
Ivy House	"	1	
Newcastle-under-Lyme	"	4	
Winkhill	"	2	2
	Stourbridge		
Hurcott	Worcestershire	2	
	Suffolk		
Bramford	Suffolk	2	
Melford	"	1	
	Surrey		
Bois	Buckinghamshire	4	
Thorney	"	3	
Weirhouse	"	2	
Carshalton	Surrey	3	
Esher	"	10	3
Wandsworth	"	3	1
Woking	"	4	
Drayton	Middlesex	1	
Twickenham	"	2	
Loudwater	Hertfordshire	7	
Solesbridge	"	4	
Sarrat	"	7	
	Sussex		
Chafford	Kent	4	3
Sharps	Sussex	1	
	Wales, East		
Golden Grove	Breconshire	1	
Llangrwyney	"	1	
	Wales, North		
Afonwen	Flintshire	3	
Greenfield	"	5	
Wheeler	Denbighshire	3	
	Wales, West		
Haverfordwest	Pembrokeshire	2	
Millbank	"	4	
	Worcester		
Beoley	Worcestershire	1	
	York		
Bishop Monkton	Yorkshire	2	
Thorp	"	1	

THE DISTRIBUTION OF PAPER MILLS IN 1851

	London, South	
Bermondsey Wall	London	2
Grove, Great Guildford Street	,,	2
Mansfield Street	.,	1

	Scotland	
	Aberdeen	
Stoneywood	Aberdeenshire	14
Mugiemoss	,,	12
Waterton	,,	4
Peterculter	,,	12

	Ayr	
Overton	Renfrewshire	9
Strath	Ayrshire	1
Dalmenie	,,	8

	Dumfries	
Dalbeattie	Dumfries	1

	Edinburgh	
Kinleith	Midlothian	0
Woodhall	,,	4
Kates	,,	8
Balerno	,,	6
Balerno Bank	,,	4
West Colinton	,,	6
Mossy	,,	3

	Glasgow	
Millholm	Lanarkshire	5
	,,	1
Dalsholm	,,	7
Woodside	,,	9
Kelvindale	,,	9

	Haddington		
Polton	Midlothian	10	
Kevock	,,	4	3
Springfield	,,	14	
Lasswade	,,	6	
Newbattle	,.	5	
Portobello	,,	4	
Esk	,,	14	
Valleyfield	,,	21	
Dalmore	,,	7	
Chirnside	Berwickshire	2	1
Bleachfield	,,	2	1
Mill Bank	,,	2	1

THE DISTRIBUTION OF PAPER MILLS IN 1851

	Linlithgow		
Herbertshire	Stirling	6	
Carrongrove	,,	1	
New	Linlithgow	1	
Grange	,,	1	
Carriden	,,	3	
New Calder	Midlothian	1	
Peggys	,,	2	
Caldercruix	Lanarkshire	8	
Moffat	,,	5	
	Montrose		
Bullionfield	Forfar	4	2
	Stirling		
Crook of Devon	Fife	1	
Auchmuty	,,	5	
Balbirnie	,,	4	
Leslie	,,	4	
Rothes	,,	10	
Airthrey	Stirling	2	
	Ireland		
	Belfast		
Carnanee	Antrim	2	
Milltown	,,	6	1
Derriaghy	,,		1
	Coleraine		
Dunadry	Antrim	2	
Antrim	,,	3	
	Cork		
Transtown	Cork	1	
Dripsey	,,	1	
Towerbridge	,,	2	
	Dublin		
Ballyboden	Dublin	1	
,,	,,	1	
Boldbrook	,,	1	
Harolds Cross	,,	3	1
Templeogue	,,	2	1
Old Bawn	,,	3	1
Killeen	,,	2	2
Drimnagh	,,	1	
Golden Bridge	,,	2	2
Great Newtown	,,	1	
Edmondstown	,,	1	1
Kilternan	,,	1	1

THE DISTRIBUTION OF PAPER MILLS IN 1851

	Galway		
Galway	Galway	2	
	Limerick		
Six Mile Bridge	Clare	1	
	Londonderry		
Donemara	Tyrone	1	
	Naas		
Clondalkin	Dublin	9	1
Salmon Leap	,,		2
Saggart	,,	15	
	Newry		
Fartlaghan	Tyrone	2	1
Roan	Armagh	2	

NOTE.—Many mill names in the list are spelled differently from the present or usual form, which I have given wherever possible.

V

PAPER MILLS:
THEIR GEOGRAPHICAL
DISTRIBUTION IN BRITAIN

THE distribution of the British papermaking industry today shows several clusters of mills within regions of high density of population and also a wider scatter both in these regions and in rural districts. The distribution is remarkably wide and its origins are complex. It can only be accounted for by considering a great variety of factors which have affected the industry at different stages in its history. Some of these factors are outlined in this article.

A considerable proportion of the sites of British paper mills at work at the present time are the residue of a much larger number of sites which were first used for paper making before 1800. In that year (immediately before the introduction of the Fourdrinier machine and the spread of the use of the steam engine in the industry) there were probably about 500 paper mills in the British Isles, the great majority being quite small with only one or two vats each. Some mills were situated in remote valleys in rural areas, others were on riverside sites in or near towns, but whatever the other advantages of situation may have been, the principal value of such sites for papermaking lay in the strength and reliability of the streams for the development of power and in the quantity and cleanliness of the water for the process. As many suitable sites were available, the industry from its early days became widely scattered; by 1800 papermaking was carried on in every English county except Rutland and Huntingdon.

EARLY CONCENTRATIONS IN FAVOURED AREAS

Here and there mills were rather more concentrated in valleys which were specially suitable not only because of their physical character but also because of their proximity to a principal source of rags and other materials and to important markets for paper. The clusters of mills in the southern valleys of Buckinghamshire and Hertfordshire and in the Maidstone district of Kent were the most remarkable concentrations, closely linked with the city and port of London. The mills near Exeter formed one of several other noteworthy clusters; in that area there was a focus of trade in the city and also a local encouragement to paper makers in that large quantities of press or glazed papers were required in the Devonshire woollen trade. Concentrations of paper mills were not, however, confined to England; there were, for example, many mills in the valleys near Edinburgh and in the Dublin district. The distribution of mills in Scotland was not so wide as that in England, because the density of population over a large part of the country was so much lower, but even so there were a number of scattered mills. Ireland, too, had several mills in remote localities. In Wales most of the old paper mills were in the comparatively thickly populated northern and southern counties.

ASCENDANCY OF MACHINES OVER VATS

Although there were before 1800 a few large manufacturers of paper, many of the mills were run by small proprietors who had been attracted to papermaking by the increase in the demand for all kinds of paper in the eighteenth century; and the chief means by which production could be increased were to add a vat to a mill which already existed or (more commonly) to start a new one- or two-vat mill. As these trends continued in Britain generally down to the 1820's and 1830's, more and more mills were set up; but from that time the geography of papermaking began to undergo a series of marked changes, one of the first and chief causes of which was the success in a competitive age of those mills in which papermaking machines and steam engines were installed and which became larger and more economic producers. After about 1830 many vat mills ceased work; and, in turn, other small out-of-date mills began to close as firms using

PAPER MILLS: THEIR GEOGRAPHICAL DISTRIBUTION IN BRITAIN

**THE LOCATION OF PAPER AND BOARD MAKING ACTIVITY
IN BRITAIN.** The differences in dot sizes—based on the number of papermaking
machines in a particular town or area—give some indication of relative importance.

newer equipment, methods and materials, and taking
advantage of better geographical situtions, proved the
most effective in competition. During the late nineteenth
century, and indeed until well into the twentieth, many
machine mills closed; a large proportion of the casualties
were small and remotely situated one-machine mills and
mills producing common papers. Thus there was a great
reduction in the total number of paper mills; the earlier
scatter underwent a severe contraction, and the ancient
clusters thinned out, as in the Wye Valley of Buckinghamshire. Although a number of long-established mills
survived independently, the industry gradually tended to
become more concentrated economically and geographically; larger firms appeared and more groups and combines
were formed, in some of which, however, both old and
new mills might be found.

A DIVERSITY OF LOCATION, PRODUCT AND PLANT

Thus there is considerable variety among the mills which
have survived on sites which were first used for paper-
making earlier than about the 1830's. In England, the
residue includes not only mills in rural areas, ranging
from Fourstones (Northumberland) to Stowford (Devon),
but also a number of old-established mills in or near
towns, e.g. the Head Weir Mills at Exeter. There is also
great variation in size, equipment and products, extend-
ing from the few mills where hand-made paper is still
produced, as at Hayle (Kent), through several one-
machine mills, e.g. Witchampton (Dorset), to larger (and
in some cases specialized) mills on or adjacent to old sites,
e.g. Glory Mills (Buckinghamshire). When one views the
modern spread of Colthrop Mills (Berkshire), it is not
easy to appreciate that the first paper makers on the site
(in 1744) were working only two vats in water mills.

The present distribution of papermaking in Britain is
also remarkable for the widespread residue of a considerable number of machine mills which were set up during
the last 40 years of the nineteenth century, a period which
opened with the abolition of the Excise duty on paper and
which saw great changes in the materials used in the

industry. The factors which affected the choice of sites for many of the present mills which have survived from that period (and for others which were not so successful) were in certain ways different from those which had been important in earlier times. The primary factor common to all periods was, of course, the availability of an abundant supply of water suitable for the papermaking-techniques of the time. But new mills no longer needed to be tied to streams, water could be obtained from deep wells, and even the qualities of the water available locally could be improved by various processes. The locational factors which now carried more weight included (1) the attractions of a well-populated industrial or commercial region, (2) proximity to a coalfield or a point where coal could easily be imported, (3) facilities for the importation of the newer materials (esparto and wood pulp) in bulk and for exporting the finished products, (4) nearness to a river or the coast for the convenient disposal of effluent, and (5) good communications.

THE SITUATION IN SCOTLAND

In Scotland most of the mills set up during this period were within the well-populated region from Glasgow and Renfrew in the west to Fife and Midlothian in the east, and they had almost all the above factors in their favour. This emphasized the high degree of concentration in the Scottish papermaking industry which had been aided by the industrialization of the lowland region and the growth of such industries as linen and chemicals. The high reputation for the manufacture of medium- and good-quality printing papers which Scotland already had in the first half of the nineteenth century has since been considerably enhanced, notably in the field of fine printings and writings and in esparto papers generally. The Scottish industry is also remarkable for the very wide range of papers which are now produced.

In England, a large proportion of the new mills of the period were in the north-west, especially in Lancashire, but by no means all of these were successful. Elsewhere in England, we find several mills whose sites testify to the operation of most of the important factors during this period; examples are Rawcliffe Bridge (Yorkshire) and the Hendon and West Hartlepool Mills (Co. Durham). In Wales the Ely Mills (Cardiff) and the Oakenholt Mills (Flint) were founded during this time. Here and there we find single instances of British mills having been placed not in an industrial area or near a port, but close to important lines of communication, as at Creech St. Michael (Somerset).

THE PRESENT PATTERN

During the present century it has not been necessary to establish so many new paper mills in Britain; for one thing, many firms wishing to expand in order to meet new and increasing demands have been able to modernize and to add new buildings on or near existing sites, and for another, a new mill is so very much bigger than the typically small mill of long ago. A remarkable development has taken place in modern times along the lower Thames and at Aylesford and Kemsley Mills, on sites which further demonstrate the value of most of the factors mentioned in connection with the previous period. Elsewhere, a number of board and paper mills have been placed near large towns, e.g. the paper mills at Keynsham near Bristol, and others were sited close to navigable water, e.g. Ellesmere Port (the Mersey and the Manchester Ship Canal) and Selby (Yorkshire).

The variety of British mills has been further extended by the addition of new sites in south Wales, e.g. Bridgend. A very interesting recent development has been the siting of a wood pulp mill at Sudbrook (Monmouthshire) and the planning of pulp and paper mills near Fort William in the Scottish Highlands.

VI

THE EXCISE NUMBERS OF PAPER MILLS IN ENGLAND AND WALES

Most of us who are interested in the history of the British papermaking industry are aware that for many years there were Excise duties on paper and boards made in this country, that these duties were abolished in 1861, and that during the time when the duties were in force each paper mill and board mill bore, for official purposes, an " Excise Number." Among the mills which are now at work there are many which were established before 1861; these are still widely known by their old Excise Numbers as well as by the names of the firms and mills. Little is generally known, however, about the history of the allocation of these Numbers to individual mills, and the chief purpose of this contribution is to throw a little light on how the Numbers were allotted by the Excise authorities during the first half of the nineteenth century. As far as I am aware, the records in the library of H.M. Commissioners of Customs and Excise were first systematically searched for evidence relating to the British papermaking industry in 1947, when I was granted permission to extract any relevant information for my study of the historical geography of the industry. I gratefully acknowledge the kind help given me by Mr. R. C. Jarvis, Librarian, H.M. Customs and Excise. I am indebted to the Commissioners for their permission to use and to publish information from their records.

By way of introduction, brief reference must be made to the Excise duties themselves and to the Excise records dating from the time before there is any reference to the Excise Numbers and Letters. The first duty on paper to be managed by the Excise after the Restoration, became effective in 1712, and over the 150 years which followed the duties were from time

to time increased, extended and modified. At the out-
set of my inquiry I hoped that among the Excise
records covering that long period there would be
found not only many references to individual British
paper makers and paper mills but also lists of the
mills which would provide the necessary information
for the compilation of maps showing the geographical
distribution of the papermaking industry during
successive periods of the eighteenth and nineteenth
centuries. Among the variety of interesting Excise
documents are some which refer to the administration
of the duties on paper, and others which mention
individual makers or mills, but the earliest lists of
paper mills (by number and name, or locality) and
paper makers date only from the year 1816.

Information about the Excise system of control over
papermaking is available from various sources, including the "Instructions to be observed by the
Officers in the Country, employed in charging the
Duties on Paper" (1781). It is clear that the Excise
authorities had to obtain details of all the paper mills
in the kingdom; Article II of the "Instructions"
reads "You must take care that every maker of paper
in your division give notice in writing at the next
Excise-Office, of their respective names and places of
abode, and of every workhouse, storehouse, room and
other place; and also of all the mills, vats, presses,
utensils, and other vessels intended to be used in the
making, drying, keeping of paper, etc. which notices
or entries must be attested, copied, filed and described,
as directed in the Excise instructions . . ." The 23
Articles of the "Instructions" are followed by
a specimen entry and the method of book-keeping involved; most of the details in this specimen refer to
a paper maker named Anthony Johannet at a two-vat
paper mill at "Ensford" (Eynsford, Kent). The
actual entries made by the Excise officers relating to
the hundreds of paper mills in the kingdom must have
been destroyed long ago; what a quarry of information they would have been for historians today!

We can well understand not only the complaints of
the paper makers about the imposition and the burden
of the duties but also their irritation at the system of

control to which they were subjected, in which various local difficulties arose. Among the petitions of individual paper makers is one from Henry Fletcher of Duffield Mill, Derbyshire, who claimed redress in that his paper mill was badly damaged by a fire which resulted from the carelessness of an Excise officer who was inspecting the paper at the mill by candlelight[1]. The various petitions to have the duties reduced or removed include one from eight representatives[2] appointed by a General Meeting of the Paper Makers of Great Britain; the signatories include James Whatman (of Turkey Mill, Kent) and Joseph Portal (of Laverstoke Mill, Hampshire). In these and other references of the eighteenth century, there is no reference to either the makers or the mills by Excise Numbers.

Although we have no official list of mills before 1816, we can trace the increase in the total number of mills from four principal sources between 1690 and 1785. Whereas in 1690[3] there must have been approximately 100 to 110 paper mills in England, in 1712[4] the Excise authorities gave the totals of paper makers in England, Wales and Berwick-upon-Tweed as 209, and in Scotland 7. (These figures probably refer to the actual numbers of paper mills.) In 1738[5] the Excise authorities stated that there were 278 paper mills in England and Wales, of which three-fourths were used for the manufacture of coarse paper. For the years from 1785 onwards[6] there are statements of the total numbers of Excise licences granted to paper makers each year, from which it is clear that by 1800 the total number of paper mills in England and Wales must have been about 410. None of these sources refers to the Excise Numbers of mills and in no case is there a list of mills or makers. Thus in attempting to identify the English paper mills which existed before 1816 I had to turn to a prolonged search of sources other than those of the Excise. As a result of my systematic search of the fire policies of the Sun Insurance Office, Ltd., eighteenth century newspapers and other sources[7], the great majority of paper mills in England up to 1816 have now been identified.

THE EXCISE NUMBERS OF PAPER MILLS IN ENGLAND AND WALES

In view of the fact that so many Excise documents in the form of lists of paper makers and mills and of records of the production of individual mills in the eighteenth century have been destroyed, it is indeed fortunate that there are in the library of H.M. Customs and Excise copies of lists and amendments (in the form of General Letters or Orders, manuscript and printed) which give the names of paper makers and the Excise Numbers, names or localities of their mills during the period 1816-1851.

By the Act of 58 Geo. 3. c.65 (1818) the numbering of all premises which were subject to Excise duties was made statutory, but the Excise authorities had already compiled and issued a list of paper makers and paper mills, each distinguished by a Letter or Number, in 1816. This list is preceded by a letter signed by W. Wardley, Excise Office, London, and dated 8th Oct., 1816, which reads as follows:—

" The Commissioners order, that the Paper Mills and Pasteboard Manufactories enumerated in the following List, be distinguished on the Entry Papers, delivered to the respective Traders, agreeably to the Directions of the first Section of the Act of the 56 Geo. 3ᵈ Cha.103, by the Letter or Number therein prefixed to each, and that whenever a new Paper Mill or Pasteboard Manufactory is erected, the proper Supervisor state that Circumstance, and request Information as to what Letter or Number is to be used to distinguish the same."

In accordance with these and later instructions, many amendments became necessary, for after 1816 many entirely new mills were established, changes occurred in the tenure of paper and board mills, and mills started up again after periods " off work." In some cases a completely new number was given to the mill concerned, in others a number which had become disused because of the cessation of work at one mill was allotted to another mill. The necessary amendments were sent out from the Excise Office to the Collections of Excise in the form of General Letters and Orders, and this practice continued up to 1851. England and Wales were given one series of Letters and Numbers, but an entirely separate series of Numbers was given to the Scottish mills, and another series to those in Ireland. In 1851 a list of paper mills (arranged under the headings of the Collections of Excise) which gave the number of beating engines at work and silent in each mill was compiled for a " Return to an Order of the Honourable House of Commons, dated 13 June 1851[8]." For references to individual paper mills or lists of mills in the United Kingdom after that time, we have to turn to Directories of Paper Mills and Paper Makers, newspapers, the records of papermaking firms, and other sources.

For the official purposes of the Excise authorities in charging and collecting the duties which from time to time were imposed on many commodities, each country of the United Kingdom was divided into a number of fairly large areas, which in turn were split up into smaller units. In England and Wales, which were usually listed and treated together in the Excise returns and statistics, a distinction was drawn first between the " London Establishment " of Excise and the " Country Establishment." The latter was divided into about 60 " Collections " (of which some 56 are represented in the Excise list of paper mills and board manufactories in 1816, discussed below). Each Collection was divided into Districts, and the further sub-divisions were known as Divisions and Rides, the last being the areas in the country surveyed by the individual officers of the Excise.

Most of the Collections, with which we are chiefly concerned here, bore the name of a town or county, but it is obvious that the boundaries of many of these Excise areas did not coincide with those of cities, counties and so on. The exact limits of the Collections cannot be traced from the information given in the Excise Letters which refer to paper mills. It would be misleading as well as inaccurate to insert conjectural boundaries of all the Collections on a distribution map of paper mills in 1816.

The Excise General Letter of 8th Oct., 1816, lists the paper mills and board manufactories in England and Wales in accordance with the major divisions of the country mentioned above. At the head of the list comes the London Establishment; this dealt with a comparatively small area, in and around the city. In 1816 there were no paper mills within the boundaries of this area. There were, however, some 21 board makers (comprised of 19 manufacturers of pasteboard and two sheathing board makers) lettered A to V, excluding J, and beginning with A. Joseph Reynolds........Pasteboard maker........Chancery Lane.

This is followed by the Country Establishment of Excise, sub-divided into these Collections: Barnstaple, Bath, Bedford, Cambridge, Canterbury, Chester, Cornwall, Coventry, Cumberland, Derby, Dorset, Durham, Essex, Exeter, Grantham, Gloucester. Halifax, Hants., Hereford, Hertford, Hull, Isle of Wight, Lancaster, Leeds, Lichfield, Lincoln, Liverpool, Lynn, Manchester, Marlborough, Northampton, Newcastle, Northumberland, Northwich, Norwich, Oxford, Plymouth, Reading, Rochester, Salisbury, Salop, Sheffield, Somerset, Stafford, Stourbridge, Suffolk, Surrey, Sussex, Uxbridge, Wales East, Wales North, Wales West, Wellington, Whitby, Worcester, York.

This general arrangement of Collections alphabetically and the numbering of paper mills in one complete series right through the Collections meant that in this list in 1816 the paper mills which happened to be in the Barnstaple Collection at that time came at the head of the list, followed by those in the Bath Collection and so on. Here are the details of the first two Collections:—

Barnstaple Collection

	Paper Maker	
1. John Waycott	Paper Maker	Moretonhampstead
2. William Drake	do.	Four Mills
3. —. Godfrey	do.	Marsh Mill
4. Messrs. Kingwell & Hayes	do.	Oakford
5. Philip Rock	do.	Playford Mill

Bath Collection

6. Thomas Bevan	Paper Maker	Bitton Mill
7. James Bryant	do.	Compton
8. Charles Gumm	do.	Herriotts
9. John Gillings & Co.	do.	Cheddar
10. George Emery	do.	Banwell
11. Giles Hall	do.	Rickford
12. Thomas Kendall	do.	Northwick
13. Henry Garner, Senr.	do.	Weaverne
14. Henry Garner, Junr.	do.	Chap's Mill*
15. Thomas Bevan	do.	Slaughterford
16. Stephen & Daniel Bearer	Paper and Pasteboard Makers	Longdean
17. Messrs. Cottle & Ward	Pasteboard Maker	Doncomb
18. Geo. Yeeles & Jno. Midhurst	Paper Maker	Bathford*
19. Henry Garner	do.	Widdenham
20. Jno. Bally, Wm. Allen & Geo. Steart	do.	Montalt
21. Thomas Bevan	do.	Catherine Mill

(A star * indicates a mill which is still working in 1958 and which has the same Excise Number as it had in 1816; this also applies in the extracts given below. A cross † indicates a mill which is still working in 1958 but whose number was changed at some date after 1816.)

It will be seen from the above extract that the Excise Letter gives no information about machines, vats or other equipment at the various mills, or about the numbers employed or the quality of the products (except to distinguish broadly between the makers of paper and boards). The numerical arrangement had nothing to do with the relative size, importance or age of the mills, but followed solely from their situation within the Collections which were arranged alphabetically.

The following further extracts from the list, which altogether comprises about 500 entries, have been selected because in most cases they refer to mills which are still working in 1958 and will thus be of particular interest to present day paper makers.

(Where it is necessary for the purposes of identification, I have added the name or locality of the mill in parentheses.)

Cambridge Collection

			Paper Maker	
25.	Richard Macanzie Bacon	...		Sawston*

Canterbury Collection

			Paper Maker	
27.	Thomas Horn	...	Paper Maker	Buckland*
29.	William Phipps & Sons	...	do.	Crabhole* (Crabble)
33.	George Pike	...	do.	Chartham*
35.	Edward Paine	...	do.	Ford Mill*

Dorset Collection

			Paper Maker	
72.	William Burt	...		Witchampton*

Exeter Collection

			Paper Maker	
94.	Edward Pim	...		Exeter* (Head Weir Mill)

Gloucester Collection

			Paper Maker	
103.	Nathl. Lloyd & Co.	...		Postlip†

Halifax Collection

106.	George Woods	...	Paper Maker	Langcliff Mill†
116.	Joshua Dyson	...	Pasteboard Maker	New Mill†

Hull Collection

			Paper Maker	
156.	Robert Smithson	...		Stepney*

Lancaster Collection

			Paper Maker	
161.	James Evans & Co.	...	Paper Maker	Waterhouse*
162.	Michael Branthwaite	...	do.	Cowanhead*
163.	William Bateson	...	do.	Oakenclough*

Leeds Collection

			Paper Maker / Pasteboard Maker	Mill
174.	William Garnett	...	Paper Maker	Otley*
175.	Michael Nicholson	...	do.	Pool*
176.	Michael Nicholson & Co.	...	do.	Pool
185.	Thomas Lockton	...	Pasteboard Maker	Pool

Lichfield Collection

188.	Messrs. Fowlers	...	Paper Maker	Alders Mill†

Liverpool 2nd Collection

213.	James Greaves	...	Paper and Pasteboard Maker	Millbank*

Manchester Collection

222.	Joseph Bealy	...	Paper Maker	Creams*
482.	Elizabeth Crompton	...	do.	Colly Hurst*

Northumberland Collection

248.	Robert Rumney	...	Paper Maker	Warden† (Fourstones Mill)

Oxford Collection

264.	James Swann	...	Paper Maker	Wolvercote†

Plymouth Collection

272.	Francis Fincher	...	Paper Maker	Ivybridge† (Stowford Mill)

Reading Collection

No.	Paper Maker		Mill
282.	Messrs. Hepper & Hicks ... : ...	Paper Maker	Taplow*

(It is believed that the present Jackson's Lower and Hedsor Mills are on the sites of two of the following four mills.)

No.	Paper Maker		Mill
284.	Eady Wildman ... ... :	do.	Bourne End
285.	Richd. & Wm. Lunnon ... :	do.	do.
286.	William Pegg ... ... :	do.	Green (Eghams Green)
287.	Harry Pegg ... ... :	do.	do.
293.	Hannah & John Wickwar ... :	do.	Colthrop*

Rochester Collection

No.	Paper Maker		Mill
298.	Messrs. Balston, Gaussen & Bosanquet	Paper Makers	Springfield*
300.	Messrs. Finch Hollingworth & Thos. Hollingworth ... ... :	do.	Turkey Mill*
310.	John Green ... ... :	do.	Hayle*
311.	John Pine ... ... :	do.	Tovil* (Lower Tovil)
312.	Messrs. Ruse, Turner & Welch ... :	do.	Tovil* (Upper Tovil, Tovil Mills)
316.	Thomas Fielder ... ... :	Paper Maker	Snodland*
323.	John Buttanshaw ... ... :	do.	Roughway†
329.	Charles Cripps ... ... :	do.	Paul's Cray† (Cray Valley Mill)
334.	Edward Smith ... ... :	do.	Milton* (Sittingbourne)

Salisbury Collection

No.	Paper Maker		Mill
337.	Messrs. Portal & Bridges ... :	Paper Maker	Laverstoke*
342.	Edward Jones ... ... :	do.	Romsey† (Abbey Mills)

Somerset Collection

No.	Paper Maker		Mill
364.	Joseph Coles ... ... :	Paper Maker	Lower Wookey* (St. Cuthbert's Paper Works)
366.	Golding & Snelgrove ... :	do.	Wookey Hole*

Stourbridge Collection

No.	Paper Maker	
372.	Robt. Vaughan Brook	Hurcott*

Uxbridge Collection

No.	Paper Maker	
401.	Henry Fourdrinier	Two Waters* (Frogmore Mill)
402.	Jno. Dickinson & Geo. Longman	Nash Mill*
403.	ditto	Apsley Mill*
414.	John Hay	Lower Marsh* (Wycombe Marsh Mills)
424.	George Harrison	Wooburn* (Soho Mills)
426.	Freeman Gage Spicer & Stepn. Spicer	Upper Glowry* (Glory Mills)
427.	ditto	Loudmoor Water* (Hedge Mill)
428.	ditto	Loudmoor Water* (Snakeley Mill)
430.	Richard Plastow	Loudwater*

Wellington Collection

No.	Paper Maker	
450.	Elizabeth Dart	Longmoor* (Higher King's Mill)
455.	John Dewdney	Heald† (Devon Valley Mill, Hele)
456.	John Mathews	Bridge* (Silverton Mills)
457.	Daniel Cragg	Stoke* (Stoke Canon)
462.	William Wood	St. Decuman's*

York Collection

No.	Paper Maker	
478.	Ralph Lomas	Bishop Monkton†

THE EXCISE NUMBERS OF PAPER MILLS IN ENGLAND AND WALES

All the paper mills and board manufactories which are listed in the Excise General Letter of 8th Oct., 1816, have been marked on the distribution map showing England and Wales. A dot indicates a paper mill, a stroke a board maker's establishment, and— in the case of only a few mills—a dot with a stroke through it refers to a place where papermaking and boardmaking were being carried on in the same mill. It will be appreciated that a great deal of work has had to be done in order to locate those mills which ceased work many years ago, especially those which closed down shortly after 1816.

In some cases the Excise list merely gives the name of the place or district and indeed in a few cases only "Paper Mill"; in others the mill name is given, but some of these names have changed since 1816. The old name of Mill No. 456, for example, was Etherleigh or Elleris (Bridge) and in the 1816 list it is simply recorded as Bridge; for many years, however, this factory has been known as the Silverton Paper Mills, of Reed & Smith, Ltd. (The Bridge refers to the site on the River Culm; Silverton Railway Station is close to the mill, and the village of Silverton is about two miles away.)

Many sites have been identified from a search of old maps and local sources, and in the case of mills which have long since ceased to make paper it is not always easy to recognise the site. A number of these mills have had diverse fates. For example, none of the five mills which were in the Barnstaple Collection of Excise in 1816 (they were all in Devon) has survived as a paper mill. The original Mill No. 1 (Town Mills, Moretonhampstead) no longer exists. A saw mill now occupies the site of Four Mills (near Crediton) and Marsh Mill (in the parish of Newton St. Cyres) is a corn mill. Oakford Mill (in the parish of Upton Pyne) has gone, but the main building of Playford Mill (near Barnstaple) is still standing.

Perhaps two of the most interesting features of the geographical distribution of the mills in 1816 are the concentrations (for example, in the Wye Valley of Buckinghamshire, the Maidstone district and around Exeter) and the wide dispersal of paper-

THE EXCISE NUMBERS OF PAPER MILLS IN ENGLAND AND WALES

making, from Cornwall to Northumberland and from Norfolk to Pembrokeshire; nearly every English county is, in fact, represented in the list of paper mills at work in the late eighteenth and early nineteenth centuries. This wide distribution meant that paper mills were to be found in most of the Collections of Excise; these did not correspond to the counties, however. The map does not attempt to show the boundaries of the Collections, but it does indicate, in the case of South-West England, how these boundaries not only cut across the counties but also went through clusters of mills in some areas. In 1816 the Cornish paper mills were divided between the Cornwall and Plymouth Collections, and those in South Devon, between Plymouth and Exeter. The Barnstaple Collection extended almost to Exeter, and the mills in and near Exeter were divided between the Barnstaple Exeter and Wellington Collections. The Bath Collection included paper mills in North Somerset, South Gloucestershire and North-West Wiltshire, while the Somerset Collection only had those near Wells and Stoke St. Michael.

After 1816 many changes took place. For one thing, the boundaries of some of the Collections were changed from time to time; in some cases this meant that a paper mill was transferred from one Collection to another. Mill No. 222 (Creams Mill), for example, was in the Manchester Collection in 1816, in Halifax in 1836 and in Wigan in 1839. From time to time also, Collections other than those given in the 1816 list come into the story of the paper mills, examples are Bristol and Wigan. The practice of allotting Letters to manufactories within the London Establishment was abandoned about 1820, numbers being used instead. Thus the Excise Number 1, which had been held by the mill at Moretonhampstead in 1816 and 1817, was in 1822 borne by a manufactory in Baldwin's Gardens, London.

In the 1816 list the Excise Numbers go up to 489; it was probably the original intention to set down a strictly numerical order of mills, but even by the time the Letter of 8th Oct., 1816, had been finally prepared for issue, some changes had been made. In

THE EXCISE NUMBERS OF PAPER MILLS IN ENGLAND AND WALES

CORNWALL

PLYMOUTH EXETER

BARNSTAPLE WELLINGTON SOMERSET

BATH

English an

THE EXCISE NUMBERS OF PAPER MILLS IN ENGLAND AND WALES

elsh mills, 1816

that list Nos. 37 and 38, for example, have no entry of a paper maker or paper mill against them. There were, too, some insertions: in the Manchester Collection, for example, the Mill No. 482, Collyhurst, was quite out of numerical order, and in the Halifax Collection Mill No. 489 came between Mills Nos. 111 and 112. After 1816 there were so many changes that it is not easy to follow the story of all the mills through the various Excise Letters containing amendments.

Generally speaking, most of the changes in, and additions to, the Excise Numbers, were necessary because of (1) the establishment of new paper mills, (2) the application of the duties to various kinds of board factories, many of which were short-lived and (3) the cessation of work (temporary or permanent) for various reasons at many mills. The records would have been easier to follow if the Excise authorities had decided that from the very first list of numbers in 1816 any new mill or manufactory would be given an entirely new number and that once a number had been used it would never be given to any other mill or factory. But, of course, it was not for them to forecast what the trends in the paper industry would be. In fact, they not only added a great many new numbers, some of them to entirely new mills and others to old mills which resumed work after an idle period, but they also began to re-use numbers which had been borne by mills which ceased work temporarily or permanently, and several of these, too, were given to mills which were either new or were resuming work.

Taking the new numbers first, and recalling that the highest number in 1816 was No. 489, we find that much higher numbers were quickly reached, and that among the paper mills still working in 1958 there are several whose numbers recall the allocation of these high numbers to what were, at the date stated, entirely new mills. Examples are Springfield (Lancashire), No. 521 in 1821; Home Park, No. 614 in 1825; Sandford, No. 621 in 1827; Ivy House, No. 630 in 1829; Lomax Bank, No. 677 in 1832; and Kearsley, No. 682 in 1832. It appears that for a short time about 1832, Tuckenhay Mill, which has usually borne the number 267, was allotted No. 694, and that this was the highest number given by the Excise authorities to any paper or board mill in England and Wales.

There are very many examples of the re-allocation of " old " numbers; for instance, Horton Kirby Mill in 1832 bore the number 87, which in 1816 had been borne by Little Baddow Mill, Essex, a mill which had ceased work by 1832. Hele Mill, which had been No. 455 in 1816, has. been No. 431 since 1822. Alders Mill bore the number 188 from 1816 to 1832, but by 1838 this had been changed to 196. The St. Paul's Cray Mill, which was No. 329 in 1816, has been No. 587 since 1832. Many such changes came about after the mill in question had been " off work " for a time because of some accident (as at Hele after a fire in 1821) or other cause, which in some cases was followed by a change of proprietor (as at St. Paul's Cray).

A glance at any recent Directory of Paper Mills or Paper Makers in England shows that there is a great variety of numbers borne by mills today; earlier in this discussion it was demonstrated that many of these are indeed old Excise Numbers allotted to the mills in question at various dates before the Excise duties were abolished in 1861. But what of the other numbers?

It appears that some of the new mills established after 1861 assumed old and disused Excise Numbers, or at least followed the Excise idea of having a mill number. Presumably, the firms concerned were perfectly entitled to do this; as the duties were no longer in force, the Excise authorities would not object, and it would be a good idea to have a distinctive number for a new mill. This seems to have been so in the case of the paper mill which was established as The Ettrick Forest Mill at Dartford in 1862; in The Paper Mills Directory for 1860 there is no mention of a Mill No. 1, but in the 1866 edition that number appears in the entry of The Dartford Creek Paper Co., Ltd. The old number 483, which as an Excise Number had been borne by a paper mill at Smedley (Manchester) from 1816 to 1838, was assumed by the mill at Stalybridge from about 1896.

THE EXCISE NUMBERS OF PAPER MILLS IN ENGLAND AND WALES

Some mills which were founded after 1861 have long been known by a distinctive trade number which is obviously not of Excise origin; examples are Broad Dumers (888) and Withnell Fold (3009). On the other hand, many of the paper and board mills which began work after about 1870 never took a number at all, and the practice of assuming numbers ceased many years ago.

REFERENCES

[1] The petition refers to Duffield Mill in 1740; the tenant was Thomas Steer. Excise and Treasury Correspondence, 1715/6-1745, 324.

[2] This petition was presented in 1765. Excise and Treasury Correspondence, 1763-8, 134-5. For evidence suggesting the connection of the representatives with certain paper mills in England, see A. H. Shorter, Paper Mills and Paper Makers in England, 1495-1800, The Paper Publications Society, Hilversum, 1957, p.64.

[3] For a discussion of the number and geographical distribution of paper mills in England circa 1690, see A. H. Shorter, op.cit., pp. 34-8.

[4] Reply of the Excise Commissioners, 25 July 1712, to an inquiry arising from a Treasury Minute, 23 July 1712, in Treasury Minute Book, XIX, 242. Excise and Treasury Correspondence, 1693/4-1721/2, 62.

[5] Excise and Treasury Correspondence, 1715/6-1745, 245-7.

[6] British Parliamentary Papers, Reports from Commissioners (1857), IV, First Report of the Commissioners of Inland Revenue, 177, Appendix No. 30. lxix.

[7] The results of these searches were first presented in A. H. Shorter, The Historical Geography of the Paper-making Industry in England, thesis for the Degree of Ph.D., University of London, 1954. For details of the identification and tenure of individual paper mills up to 1800, see A. H. Shorter, Paper Mills and Paper Makers in England, 1495-1800, Appendix B.

[8] This was a "Return of the Number of Paper Mills at present in work in England, Wales, Scotland, and Ireland, distinguishing the number in each country; also the Number of 'Beating Engines' at Present at work in each Mill and the Number at present silent. Ordered by the House of Commons to be printed 27 February 1852." House of Commons Papers, Session of 1852, Vol. 51, No. 128. For an analysis of the geographical distribution of these mills see A. H. Shorter, The Distribution of British Paper Mills in 1851, in The Paper Maker, CXXI, 1951, pp. 416-423.

VII

WATERMARKS IN ENGLISH PAPER
PART I
(with special reference to the early nineteenth century)

The collection and study of watermarks can lead to interesting and valuable contributions to the history of papermaking. For various reasons, many historians and others have had to grapple with the problems of identifying the makers and dates of manufacture of the paper in books and documents, and in many cases they have found the watermarks in the paper to be of some assistance in their task. Although there have been many articles and books written about watermarks, it is only comparatively recently that a start has been made on the systematic task of indentifying by paper maker and mill some of the great number of marks which were used by English paper makers between the 1490's (when John Tate of Sele Mill, Hertford, employed the device of an eight-pointed star within a double circle) and the 1860's, after which time the identification of makers and mills is comparatively easy because of the availability of the *Paper Mills Directory* and the *Directory of Paper Makers.*

As long ago as 1796, the Reverend S. Denne wrote a short illustrated paper (*Observations on Paper-Marks*) in *Archaeologia,* but this had little to do with English watermarks. During the nineteenth century there were probably a number of paper makers who in order to make a comparative study of the qualities of the sheets of paper, collected specimens of watermarked papers from other mills, and there were certainly people who were sufficiently interested in either the history of papermaking or the subject of watermarks generally to make a collection of tracings or of the marks themselves, in the sheets or cut out, filed and mounted. I am grateful to W. & R. Balston, Ltd., for allowing me to study some of the watermarked papers in the Balston files at Springfield Mill (Kent), which is an example of a paper maker's collection. As an example of a manuscript work dealing with the history of paper and including illustrations of watermarks, there is E. J. Powell's *A Treatise of Paper Making*, 1868 (which I consulted by kind permission of the Honorary Librarian, The Constitutional Club, London). There is in the possession of the Technical Section of the British Paper and Board Makers' Association at Kenley, a collection of watermarks in a book described on a catalogue slip therein as I. (or J.) Hewlett, 1378 *Varieties of Paper Marks*, 1879[1]. In cases where complete double or single sheets of paper have been preserved (as in the collection at Springfield Mill) the watermarks and countermarks can be studied in relation to the size and quality of the paper. In Hewlett's collection, however, many watermarks have been cut from the sheets and mounted by the collector, so that one is able only to study the marks themselves.

Among the works of the twentieth century which are of importance to the student of English watermarks, mention must be made first of the books by Churchill[2] and Heawood[3], both of which are now well known. Churchill's illustrations include a number of English marks, and he gives a list of British makers and mills, with dates; one of his principle sources consisted of papers and watermarks in the possession of the B.P. & B.M.A. He does not, however, give a map or details of location of every mill, and his list of names is clearly not derived wholly from watermarks. He suggests that certain English names of the eighteenth century appear to be those of " merchants or manufacturers with works abroad "; it is certain, however, that the names concerned are those of English paper makers or stationers who had an interest in the English paper industry during the eighteenth century. Heawood's monumental work contains a very useful introduction to the study of watermarks, and he gives over 4,000 illustrations, with sources. The arrangement of his collection is not by periods or countries, but by the subjects of the marks—many different figures, Britannias, coats of arms and so on. Several British watermarks are to be seen in his collection, but he could suggest only a few identifications of English paper makers and mills.

More recently, Mr. Thomas Balston[4] has given a most valuable survey of the Whatman watermarks and countermarks; almost all the other English marks which I have been able to trace up to the year 1800 have now been recorded and illustrated[5], but I am sure that in due course more examples will be found. I shall be very pleased to receive (at the University of Exeter) tracings of, or information about, English watermarks which have not yet been recorded or identified, and to help to assign them to makers and mills. So far there are very few watermarks which can be definitely identified as those of English makers and mills up to the year 1700. They are those of Tate (1490's), Spilman at Dartford (1588-1626)[6], Eustace Burneby[7] (letters E B, probably at a mill in South Buckinghamshire or West Middlesex, *circa* 1675-7), Thomas Quelch at Wolvercote Mill (letters T Q, *circa* 1680-5), Denis Manes at Plymouth (royal coat of arms with letters D M underneath, *circa* 1690), Thomas Meale at Eynsham, Oxfordshire (letters T M. *circa* 1692-3), and the Company of White Papers (the word Company, *circa* 1695-8) whose identified mills were at South Stoneham (near Southampton), Dartford and at or near Colnbrook[8].

Much of the printing paper which was probably made in England in the early eighteenth century has no watermark. But as the English manufacture of white paper began to improve and extend, more makers started to use watermarks; at Postlip Mills, for example, the name of the paper makers (Durham) and various devices were used, including one—incorporating the rose and thistle—which appears to commemorate the union of England and Scotland in 1707. Several English makers began to employ marks which had been, or were being used by continental makers, and these included the horn, Pro Patria. the Lion Passant, fleur-de-lis, Strasbourg Arms and Britannia.

Some used a shield incorporating the horn, fleur-de-lis or bend, some (for example, William Jubb of Ewell Mill, Surrey) added a bell, and several of the leading makers included in their watermarks the initials of at least one well-known Dutch paper maker—Lubertus van Gerrevink (L V G). The use of A R and G R with a crown also became more widespread; it has sometimes been suggested that papers watermarked thus were intended for official use, but it is reasonably certain that they were more widely employed.

During the late eighteenth century the watermarking of good quality paper became much more common in England, especially because of the provision by Act of Parliament in 1794[9] that no drawback of Excise duty was allowable on exportation except on papers which had the date of manufacture in the sheet. As many makers were already using, or began to insert, their initials or names in the watermarks, there was by 1800 a considerable variety of marks in the English " white " industry. Although by an Act of Parliament in 1811[10] the regulation of 1794 in respect of the date of manufacture was revoked, the practice of watermarking dates continued for many years afterwards. The watermarks of English makers of the nineteenth century (eventually including many from both vat and machine mills) cover a very wide range. In the early 1800's the continuation of watermarking practice from the eighteenth century is clear; initials, names, dates, shields and other devices were used and, as time went on, many more makers inserted the name of their mills. In papers which, by the latter part of the nineteenth century, were marked with the name of the firm and mill, identification is quite straightforward. An example is before me as I write: this is a double page of *The Times* for August 20, 1898. One of the long margins of the page is fully watermarked, in letters half an inch high, WRIGLEY & SON MAKERS, and the other long margin BRIDGE HALL MILLS. (These mills, near Bury, Lancashire, were in the hands of the Wrigley firm up to about 1925).

WATERMARKS IN ENGLISH PAPER

REFERENCES

[1] I am indebted to Mr. Francis Bolam, Secretary of the Technical Section, for permission to consult this work and to trace watermarks therein.

[2] W. A. Churchill, *Watermarks in Paper in Holland, England. France, etc., in the XVII and XVIII centuries and their interconnection,* 1935.

[3] E. Heawood, *Watermarks, mainly of the 17th and 18th centuries.* The Paper Publications Society (General Editor. E. J. Labarre), Hilversum, Holland, 1950.

[4] *James Whatman, Father and Son,* 1957 (previously published in serial form in *The Paper Maker*).

[5] A. H. Shorter, *Paper Mills and Paper Makers in England. 1495-1800.* The Paper Publications Society, 1957. See especially Appendixes C and D and the reproductions of 217 watermarks.

[6] See *The Dartford Paper Mills,* published by The Wiggins Teape Group, 1958.

[7] See A. T. Hazen, *Eustace Burnaby's Manufacture of White Paper in England,* Papers of the Bibliographical Society of America, 48 (1954), 324.

[8] These watermarks, and the authorities for associating them with the particular mills, are given in A. H. Shorter. *op. cit.,* especially Appendixes B and C.

[9] 34 G.III, c.20.

[10] 51 G.III, c.95.

IDENTIFICATIONS

The examples of English marks given below are a very small selection from those which can now be identified by makers and mills, but they serve to illustrate the variety of watermarks and counter-marks which were used in this country during the early nineteenth century. Some of these marks have had to be taken from single sheets or pieces of sheets of paper; they do not, therefore, necessarily illustrate the *whole* of the watermark or countermark.

Nos. 1 a, b, c; 2 a, c; 3 a; 4 a, b; and 10 are from I. Hewlett, 1378 *Varieties of Paper Marks*, 1879; by permission of Mr. Francis Bolam, Secretary of the Technical Section, British Paper & Board Makers' Association. Nos. 8 a and c are from papers in the files of the Technical Section; also by Mr. Bolam's permission. Nos. 2 b, d; 3 b; 6 a and 9 are from the collection of Mr. E. J. Labarre, The Paper Publications Society, Hilversum, Holland (by his permission), and Nos. 5, 6 b, 7 and 8 b are from papers at Springfield Mill (Kent), with the sanction of W. & R. Balston Ltd., and Mr. Thomas Balston.

Note — The watermark illustrations in this article are half original size.

1. Initials of maker

R B

1830

(a) Maker—Richard Barnard.

Mill—Eyehorne Street, Hollingbourne, Kent.

Source of name of maker and mill—*Excise General Letter,* 28th November, 1832.[1]

E P

1811

(b) Maker—Edward Paine

Mills—Ford Mill and Conyer Mill, Kent.

Source of name of maker and mills — *Excise General Letter,* 8th October, 1816

1. Initials of maker (cont.)

O & P
1803

(c) Makers—Hugh Oxenham and John Pim.
Mill—Countess Weir, Devon.
Source of name of makers and mill—*Excise General Letter,* 8th October, 1816.

S EVANS & Co
1845

(b) Makers—Samuel Evans & Co. (Samuel Evans, William Evans and Joseph Humphries).
Mill—Darley (Derbyshire)
Source of name of makers and mill—*Excise General Letter,* 28th, November, 1832.

2. Name of maker

J CRIPPS
1805

(a) Maker—James Cripps.
Mill—St. Pauls Cray, Kent, or Dulcote, Somerset.
Source of name of maker and mill—*Letter* dated 1st October, 1803 (papers from Springfield Mill, Kent,' wherein James Cripps is mentioned as a Master Paper Maker (at St. Pauls Cray), or *Apprenticeship Books* (Public Record Office, I.R.1), 71/120, wherein James Cripps is mentioned as a paper maker at Dulcote in 1803.

J GREEN
1815

(c) Maker—John Green.
Mill—Hayle (Kent).
Source of name of maker and mill—*Excise General Letter,* 8th October, 1816.

2. Name of maker *(cont.)*

G PIKE
1810

(d) Maker—George Pike.
Mill—Chartham (Kent).
    Source of name of maker and mill—*Excise General Letter,*
8th October, 1816.

3. Name of maker and mill or district

EDW.(D) PAINE
LITTLECHART
1810

(a) as for 1 (b).

R TURNER
CHAFFORD MILL

(b) (date of document, 1836).
Maker—Richard Turner.
Mill—Chafford (Kent).
    Source of name of maker and mill—*Excise General Letter,*
28th November, 1832.

4. Name of mill

DE MONTALT MILLS
BATH, 1811.

(a) Makers—John Bally, William Allen and George Steart.
Mill—De Montalt Mills (Somerset).
    Source of name of makers and mill—*Excise General Letter,*
8th October, 1816.

JOHN HAYES
1807

IVY MILL
1809

5. Horn

Maker—John Hayes.
Mill—Rush Mill, Northampton.

Source of name of maker and mill — *Excise General Letter*, 8th October, 1816.

(b) Makers—Thomas Smith and Henry Allnutt.
Mill——Great Ivy Mill (Kent).
Source of name of makers and mill—Loose *Rate Book*, and *Excise General Letter*, 8th October, 1816.

GATER RUSE-& TURNERS

1827   1805

6. Fleur-de-lis (cont.)

(b) Makers — Joseph Ruse, Richard Turner and Thomas Turner.

Mill—Upper Tovil (Kent).

Source of name of makers and mill — *London Gazette*, 2nd September, 1815.

R & T

6. Fleur-de-lis

(a) Makers—John and Edward Gater.

Mills—Frog Mill and West End (Southampton).

Source of name of makers and mills—*Excise General Letter*, 28th November, 1832.

J LARKING

J BATES
1813
"

8. **Britannia**

Left

(a) Maker—John Bates.

Mill—Wycombe Marsh (Buckinghamshire).

Source of name of maker and mill—*General Meeting of Master Paper Makers*, 13th June, 1803 (papers f r o m Springfield Mill, Kent), and *Sun Fire Insurance Policy No. 33801*, 24th November, 1724.

7. **Bend (Strasbourg Arms)**

Maker—John Larking.

Mill—East Malling (Kent).

Source of name of maker and mill—*Letter*, 30th April, 1801 (papers from Springfield Mill, Kent).

RADWAY 1818

L 1 & D 1809

8. Britannia (*cont.*)

(c) Maker—Joshua C. Radway. Mill—Quenington (Gloucestershire).

Source of name of maker and mill—*Excise General Letter*, 8th October, 1816.

Right

(b) Maker—Possibly William Balston (note the letter B in the watermark), making paper for the firm of Longman and Dickinson. (George Longman and John Dickinson were stationers in 1807.[3] Shortly afterwards they were in partnership as paper makers at Apsley and Nash Mills, Hertfordshire.[4])

Mill—Possibly Springfield (Kent).

Source of name of maker and mill — Thomas Balston. *William Balston Paper Maker*, 1954.

H WILLMOTT
1809"

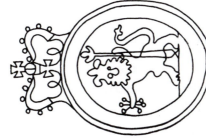

9. Lion.

Maker—Henry Willmott.

Mill—Shoreham (Kent).

Source of name of maker and mill — *London Gazette*, 12th January, 1813.

---

10. Name of size or type of paper

FOOLS CAP
1815
W

Maker and mill unknown.

REFERENCES

[1] I am indebted to **Mr. R. C. Jarvis**, Librarian H.M. Customs and Excise, and to the Commissioners of Customs and Excise, for permission to quote from the *Excise General Letters*.

[2] Quoted by kind permission of W. & R. Balston, Ltd., and Mr. Thomas Balston.

[3] *Sun Fire Insurance Policy* No. 809738, 9th November, 1807. I acknowledge with thanks the permission of the Sun Insurance Office, Ltd., to quote their policies.

[4] *Excise General Letter*, 8th October, 1816.

VIII

PAPER-MOULD MAKERS IN ENGLAND

During the long period when the whole, or the greater part of the English papermaking industry was based upon vats, large numbers of moulds must have been made for the hundreds of paper mills which were at work. From newspaper advertisements in the eighteenth and early nineteenth centuries, it appears that the stock of moulds carried in a one-vat mill may have been anything up to fifty pairs. The earliest full account I have of the equipment of a one-vat mill in England is of a white paper mill which was built at Huxham (Devon) in or about the year 1703; there were nine pairs of moulds with two deckles each and seven pairs with three different deckles[1]. A notice of a sale at Mr. Austin's (a paper maker at North Mill, Bledlow, Buckinghamshire) mentions eight pairs of paper moulds[2]. At the Bagnor paper mill (Berkshire), the "implements in trade" of Joseph Wells, a bankrupt, deceased, included 21 pairs of moulds of different sizes[3]. In 1811 the utensils in a paper manufactory at Core's End (Buckinghamshire) included about fifty pairs of moulds[4].

The outlay on moulds, a most essential part of the handmade paper maker's equipment, must have been considerable, especially for the comparatively large-scale manufacturers of white paper, and frequent replacements would be necessary. Mr. Thomas Balston states that in the eight years 1780-7 eighty new pairs of moulds were required by Whatman and that during that period the expenditure on wire, moulds and deckles was about £460[5].

Where were moulds made for English paper makers? In the course of searching for information about paper makers and mills, I have noted several references to wire workers who had a connection with paper makers and to the specialised craft of mould making. A wire worker named William Leach, near the Market Place in Devizes (Wiltshire), delivered paper from the warehouse of William Coles, paper maker, and also acted as a collector of rags— he gave ready money for any quantity of rags within fifteen or twenty miles of Devizes[6].

The craft of mould making was carried on in many different localities. As we might expect, many of the mould makers were to be found at the centre of districts where there were numerous paper mills. Here are a few examples. About the year 1800 at least twenty mills were at work within five miles of Maidstone[7], and mould makers of Maidstone and Loose (nearby) are recorded in the eighteenth and early nineteenth centuries. Owen Mackentee was a mould maker at Maidstone in 1795[8], and for a time he was in partnership with John Green the younger[9]. William Harris, paper mould maker, was buried at Loose in 1757[10]; he may have been an ancestor of the Thomas Harris who made all the moulds for Whatman during the period 1780-7[11], and of the William Harris of Ivy Street who was following the same trade in 1813[12]. At least 28 paper mills were working in the Wye Valley of Buckinghamshire — from West Wycombe down to Bourne End and Hedsor—about the year 1800[13]. In 1794 John Rutt was a mould maker in the Wycombe district[14], and in 1810 he and John Revnell, described as paper mould manufacturers of Wooburn Moor (which is near Glory Mills), dissolved their partnership[15]. About the same time, Henry Brewer was a paper mould maker at Chesham Bois[16], amid a smaller group of mills in the Chess Valley[17]. Evidence has been found of some fourteen paper mills in south-east Lancashire during the last quarter of the eighteenth century[18], and in this area George Lownds was a paper mould maker at Manchester in the 1790's[19].

There were also mould makers in certain districts where although the paper mills were fewer and more scattered, several existed within a reasonable distance of the premises of a mould maker. William Smith was a paper mould maker at Stoke, near Guildford

(Surrey[20]); in that district about six paper mills were at work in the early nineteenth century[21]. Other examples are J. Everett, at Newbury (Berkshire[22]), John Gauthern, at North Newton (Oxfordshire[23]), and Thomas Findley, at Gateshead (Co. Durham[24]). In some cases the mould maker's principal connection was probably with one comparatively large paper-making firm in the district; an example is Joseph Hughes, of Winchcombe (Gloucestershire[25]), who may have supplied the moulds for the Postlip Mills nearby.

Paper moulds were also made in several of the large cities. In London, for example, Robert Everitt, of Tooley Street, was a paper mould maker[26], and James Butler, wire weaver and sieve maker, of 2 Saffron Street, Great Saffron Hill, advertised "all sorts of wire work" for paper mills[27]. In the 1770's, Ann Fowler had a wire work and paper mould manufactory in Redcliffe Street, Bristol[28].

PAPER-MOULD MAKERS IN ENGLAND

REFERENCES

1. Advertisement in the newspaper *Post Man*, May 16-18, 1706.
2. *Jackson's Oxford Journal*, January 25, 1777.
3. *Reading Mercury and Oxford Gazette*, March 19, 1792.
4. The notice advertises the sale of the property of Mr. (probably William) East, who was leaving the Fuller's Mill at Core's End. *Reading Mercury and Oxford Gazette*, September 16, 1811.
5. T. Balston. *James Whatman Father & Son*, 1957, pp. 60-2.
6. *Gloucester Journal*, April 4, 1738.
7. A. H. Shorter. *Paper Mills and Paper Makers in England, 1495-1800*, The Paper Publications Society, Hilversum, Holland, 1957, pp. 184-196.
8. *Sun Fire Insurance Policy* No. 636823, January 23, 1795.
9. Their partnership was dissolved in 1802. *London Gazette*, November 20, 1802.
10. *Loose Parish Register*.
11. T. Balston. *op. cit.*
12. *Loose Parish Register*, Baptisms.
13. A. H. Shorter, *op. cit.*, pp. 132-144.
14. J. Parker. *Early History and Antiquities of Wycombe*, 1878, p. 75.
15. *London Gazette*, July 21, 1810.
16. He was bankrupt in 1811. *London Gazette*, May 26, 1811.
17. A. H. Shorter, *op. cit.*, pp. 130-2 and 177-8.
18. *Ibid.*, pp. 202-6.
19. *Universal British Directory of Trade, Commerce and Manufacture*, circa 1791, 3, p. 827.
20. *Sun Fire Insurance Policy* No. 799155, January 20, 1807.
21. A. H. Shorter, *op. cit.*, pp. 238-240.
22. *Universal British Directory of Trade, Commerce and Manufacture*, circa 1791, 4, p. 80.
23. In 1786 there was a notice to paper makers that William Gauthern, who had served his time and worked with his uncle John Gauthern of North Newton for more than fifteen years, had moved to Birmingham to follow the trade of paper mould making. *Gloucester Journal*, June 5, 1786.
24. *Heworth Parish Register*, 1808 and 1812.
25. *Universal British Directory of Trade, Commerce and Manufacture*, circa 1791, 4, p. 770.
26. *Sun Fire Insurance Policy* No. 535956, October 15, 1787.
27. *Reading Mercury and Oxford Gazette*, June 9, 1806.
28. *Felix Farley's Bristol Journal*, May 27, 1775.

IX

EARLY STEAM-ENGINES IN BRITISH PAPER MILLS

In his book *William Balston Paper Maker,* Mr. Thomas Balston describes the plans for the establishment of Springfield Mill, Kent, and (p. 39) mentions that there is a local tradition that William Balston's steam-engine at that mill was the sixth to be erected in a paper mill. Mr. Balston gives the localities of three paper mills which had steam-engines before Springfield's was installed; these were near Hull, near Aberdeen, and at the Neckinger in Bermondsey, London. Where were the others? According to the evidence given below, there were certainly two, and possibly three other paper mills which had steam-engines by 1806, the year when Springfield was ready for work. All six mills will now be briefly considered in chronological order of the evidence which relates to steam-engines therein.

1. As Mr. Balston states, in the year 1786, Boulton, Watt & Co. supplied a 10 h.p. engine of the Sun and Planet type to Howard and Houghton's mill at Wilmington, Sutton in Holderness, near Hull. In 1787 the paper mill, including the steam-engine, was insured by John Howard, esquire, of Hull[1]. The paper makers were Thomas Houghton the elder and younger, who unfortunately went bankrupt in the following year[2].

2. In 1802 Messrs. Harrison and Pearson of Crane Street in the City of Chester, iron founders and paper makers, insured their foundry and paper mill engine house with ware room over in one building, their stock and utensils therein and the steam-engine therein[3]. Assuming that it was used for working the paper mill, this may have been one of the earliest steam-engines installed in English paper mills in the nineteenth century.

EARLY-STEAM ENGINES IN BRITISH PAPER MILLS

3. Mr. Balston states that in 1802 a 20 h.p. engine of the same type as that at Wilmington, near Hull, was supplied by the same firm to Brown. Chalmers & Co., of Aberdeen. In 1803 Messrs. Brown, Chalmers & Co., of Ferryhill, near Aberdeen, paper makers, insured their steam and paper engine house under one roof, and the steam engine[4].

4. In 1803 the Tyne Steam Engine Paper Mill, near Newcastle upon Tyne, the property of Messrs. Shaftoe. Hawkes and Read, was destroyed by fire[5]. This mill was on the Durham bank of the Tyne, on a site known as Fellingshore, or Heworthshore[6].

5. The paper mill at Thames Bank (near Neat House, a mile from Westminster Bridge), "recently employed in the Straw Paper Manufactory" was for sale in 1804[7]. The brochure of the sale mentions " a compleat steam engine of eight horse power " and " a steam engine of eighty horse power, universally acknowledged to be the most compleat and substantial that ever was made, costing six thousand pounds[8]."

6. An advertisement of the sale of all the machinery and equipment of the Neckinger Paper Mill, Bermondsey, mentions a steam-engine with two boilers of 24 h.p.[9] The Neckinger and Thames Bank Mills were worked by Matthias Koops & Co., who must have installed the steam-engines by 1802; in that year the firm ran into difficulties, and in October it was resolved at a general meeting of the proprietors of the Thames Bank Straw Paper Manufactory that no money should be paid on account of debts thereafter contracted, or " credit given to or delivery of goods on account of the said concern[10]."

EARLY-STEAM ENGINES IN BRITISH PAPER MILLS

REFERENCES

1. *Sun Fire Insurance Policy* No. 533943, 6th Aug., 1787. I am grateful to the Sun Insurance Office Ltd., for their kind permission to quote from their fire insurance policies.
2. *London Gazette*, 29th Nov., 1788.
3. *S.F.I.P.* No. 728044, 15th Jan., 1802. The paper makers were George Harrison and Joseph Pearson, whose partnership was dissolved in 1812. *London Gazette*, 30th June, 1812.
4. *S.F.I.P.* No. 753169, 16th Sep., 1803. The plant of this mill—the Devanaha Paper Mill at Craighy Ferryhill—was purchased by the paper makers at Culter Mills in 1808. A. Dykes Spicer, *The Paper Trade*, 1907, p. 224.
5. *Jackson's Oxford Journal*, 31st Dec., 1803. In a notice of dissolution of partnership in 1808, the firm is given as R. Shafto Hawks and E. Reed. *London Gazette*, 24th May, 1808.
6. A. H. Shorter, *Paper Mills and Paper Makers in England, 1495-1800*. The Paper Publications Society, Hilversum, 1957, p. 160.
7. *Felix Farley's Bristol Journal*, 18th Aug., 1804.
8. D. Hunter, *Papermaking, The History and Technique of an Ancient Craft*, 1957, pp. 355-6.
9. *Reading Mercury and Oxford Gazette*, 20th Oct., 1806.
10. *London Gazette*, 19th Oct., 1802.

X

The Distribution of Paper-making in Cornwall in the Nineteenth Century.—Although the predominant occupation of mining is the best-known of the industries of Cornwall, there have been manufacturing concerns of some small importance in certain localities of the county. There is now but little trace of these minor industries, e.g. woollen goods and paper, and the conditions under which they sprang into activity are not now clearly known ; but it is likely that at the end of the eighteenth century (the period of the working-out of the early phases in the " Industrial Revolution " in other parts of the country) people like millers, farmers and small-scale manufacturers were seeking new opportunities, and that the making of paper offered possibilities. In some cases old mills were taken over or converted, in others new buildings were erected on newly-chosen sites. While there are but few clues as to the originators of the small, but interesting, industry of paper-making in this part of England, fragments of information exist from which it is possible to piece together a tolerably continuous story. The mills and their history have been largely forgotten, and they are usually merely mentioned in the various County Histories and Directories. These, of course, are neither infallible nor detailed, and the writer is fully conscious of the limitations of such sources, and of the need for further information, wherever it can be found.

The map shows the distribution of paper mills which have existed at some time in the county, and reveals that seven localities were concerned. In spite of a long search, no evidence which would suggest the presence of paper mills in other parts of Cornwall has been discovered by the present writer. The geographical distribution of the mills suggests the factors which were at work in the origin of the industry. A principal requirement in the early days of the industry in this country was a regular flow of water, preferably clear, down a somewhat steep slope—a supply which would thus be available for the paper-making process and for power. This requirement is fulfilled in many parts of Cornwall, since the rainfall is almost everywhere over thirty inches annually and well distributed throughout the year, so that this consideration does not appear to have affected greatly

3   THE DISTRIBUTION OF PAPER-MAKING IN CORNWALL

the distribution of the mills within the county.

The questions of a market for the finished products and of labour supply were probably of great importance. The mills of Kennall Vale, Ponsanooth, Penryn, Truro and Liskeard were situated in districts where mills of several kinds were in action, and were thus in " manufacturing centres " on a small scale. Labour supply here, and in the Penzance and Calstock districts, too, was most probably cheap and relatively abundant.

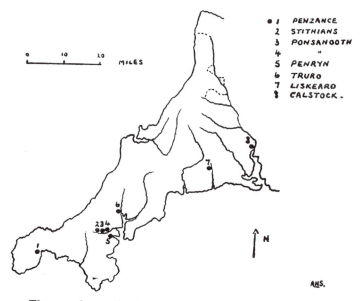

The northern districts of Cornwall were rather sparsely populated and could probably be well supplied with paper from Plymouth and Barnstaple, where, according to Rhys Jenkins (1), paper mills were working in the eighteenth century. In the West, however, were the relatively thickly-peopled coastal and mining areas, and here the towns of Truro, Falmouth, Penryn, Camborne, Redruth and Penzance had to be supplied. The Bodmin—St. Austell district, too, could easily be furnished with paper from the western mills, and much of the interests of the population of that district were bound up with the exploitation of the china-clay. In

(1)   Paper-making in Devon. " Devon & Cornwall Notes & Queries ", 8, 1914–15, pp. 119–121.

the West, at any rate, a local market seems to have been assured for papers for wrapping, writing and printing, and, in connection with this, one may perhaps note the fact that in 1828 (2), of the three newspapers published (weekly) in Cornwall, two were issued in Truro and the other in Falmouth.

The materials used for the manufacture of paper were most probably rags collected locally, the straw of the oat, waste paper, and perhaps sailcloth. Some of the paper was exported, and some sent to the London market, but so far there is little evidence to say how this was done. The mills at, or near, good ports—Penryn is the best example—had the advantage of easy export, but it is difficult to say whether the coming of the railway helped the industry very much. It did not save it from ultimate extinction, since the mills were too small and isolated to compete successfully with the bigger concerns growing up in other parts of the country at the end of the nineteenth century.

Although Cooke (3) declared that, if further enterprise were forthcoming in Cornwall, " the manufacture of paper . . . (among other things) . . . might be conducted with almost certain success ", we have no record of the establishment of a paper mill after the date of his writing, and the work of the oldest mill probably goes back at least to 1800. Polwhele (4) notes paper mills " in the neighbourhood " of Penryn, and Gilbert (5) mentions their existence in the same town. From his further description one might surmise that this activity was not very much older than the date of his work (6) : " to the ancient manufacture of poldavies, Penryn has added the flourishing concerns of mustard-making, twine-spinning and paper-making ". Pigot (7) notes paper-making near Penryn, and Drew (8) speaks of " manufactories for paper ". Penaluna (9) and Cooke (10) mention these,

(2)   " A Topographical and Statistical Description of the County of Cornwall ". G. A. Cooke. 1828. p. 111.

(3)   ibid., p. 110.

(4)   " History of Cornwall ". R. Polwhele. 1806. Book III, Chap. VII.

(5)   " An Historical Survey of the County of Cornwall ". C. S. Gilbert. 1817. Vol. II, p. 786.

(6)   ibid., Vol. I, p. 338.

(7)   " Directory of Devon and Cornwall ". 1822-3. p. 192.

(8)   " History of Cornwall ". Drew. 1824. Vol. II, p. 290.

(9)   " The Circle, or Historical Survey of Sixty Parishes and Towns in Cornwall ". Wm. Penaluna. 1819. p. 199.

(10)   op. cit., p. 149.

5 THE DISTRIBUTION OF PAPER-MAKING IN CORNWALL

too, and the latter says that they were for "writing and packing paper". Robson (11) refers to "some paper manufactories" there. Some of these notes on mills "near" Penryn may include those at Ponsanooth, but the paper mill at Penryn was probably as old as these references.

"Stationary" is included in a list given (12) of the exports to Portugal and Spain from Falmouth, so that it is quite likely that paper was sent abroad from Penryn as early as 1819. Penaluna (13) says that paper was exported from Penryn, and Lewis (14), in a discussion of the trade of the town, lists paper among its manufactures and implies that it was exported thence. In 1844 (15) there is a statement of the varied and prosperous activities there: "manufactories for paper, woollen cloth, gunpowder, paint and arsenic works, corn mills and breweries". In 1850 (16), a note says that there was "no manufacture of any importance, but several good breweries and grist and paper mills". Paper is mentioned in 1868 (17), and an important entry (18) shows that the manufacturer (James Mead, of Commercial Road, Penryn) had steam mills for the manufacture of "straw paper, large quantities of which are almost weekly sent to London", and that "the material used is the straw of the oat, and the fabric is complete and perfect". Apparently Mead owned the mill in 1873 (19), and until 1897 when, we read, his mill was producing "straw paper" (20). Thereafter we find

(11) "Commercial Directory of the Western Counties". 1838. p. 41.
(12) Penaluna, see (9) above.
(13) "Survey of the County of Cornwall". Penaluna. 1838 ed., Vol. I, p. 218.
(14) "Topographical Dictionary of England". S. Lewis. 1842. Vol. III, p. 491.
(15) Pigot's "Royal National and Commercial Directory and Topography of Devon and Cornwall". 1844. p. 26.
(16) "Gazetteer of the World". A. Fullarton & Co. c. 1850. Vol. X, p. 842.
(17) "The National Gazetteer". 1868, Vol. III, p. 138.
(18) "Parochial History of the County of Cornwall". Lake. 1868. Vol. II, p. 89.
(19) "Post Office Directory". 1873. p. 978.
(20) Kelly's "Directory of Cornwall". 1897. p. 239.
Further reference to the mill occurs in:
"Royal County Directory of Devon and Cornwall". J. & G. Harrod & Co. 1878. pp. 892 and 894.
"A Geographical Dictionary or Gazetteer of Cornwall". 1884. p. 88.
Kelly's "Directory of Cornwall". 1893.
"A Compendium of the History and Geography of Cornwall". Rev. J. J. Daniell. 1894. p. 397.

no mention of the mill, and paper-making seems to have ceased about the same time at this place and at Stithians. According to local information the mill reverted to the production of flour, and was active until quite recently (September, 1937). The photograph (c) was taken just before the mill was demolished in connection with road-widening schemes.

The district around Penryn aroused the enthusiasm of Cooke (21) and his description of the water supplies of the area is worth quoting : " on the western side of the town the lands are high and rather barren ; from these issue several streams of water which amply supply the inhabitants. One of these streams, flowing with rapidity over some huge masses of stone, forms a singular cascade, and with its accompaniments of cottages, and wheels driven by it, enlivens the scene with much picturesque beauty ". In Kennall Vale there was a stream with power to supply a number of small manufactories, and Pigot (22) gives the names of Dunstan and Jenkins as paper-makers at Ponsanooth, near Penryn. According to Drew (23), the river here worked a " large paper manufactory " and we know that in 1827 (24) a " brown " and a " white " mill had been put up for sale at Ponsanooth, but later evidence of the industry at this place is lacking.

The Ordnance Survey Map, 1809 edition, shows the Kennall Mills near Stithians, but gives no clue as to their function, and the credit for the establishment of the paper industry at this place seems to be due to a William Tucker. In 1817 (25) there is a record of " extensive paper mills " near Penryn, " belonging to Mr. Tucker " who in 1822 (26) is given under the heading of Budock, where he probably lived. The mill seems to have prospered, together with others, for in 1819 (27) the extensive paper manufactory at Stithians produced " every kind of paper ", and in 1822

(21)   op. cit., p. 149.
(22)   1822–3 ed., loc. cit.
(23)   op. cit., Vol. II, p. 621.
(24)   " Royal Cornwall Gazette ".   12th May, 1827.
(25)   " The Gazetteer of the County of Cornwall ".   Truro.   1817.
(26)   Pigot.   1822–3 ed., loc. cit.
(27)   Penaluna.   1819 ed., p. 237.

THE DISTRIBUTION OF PAPER-MAKING IN CORNWALL

(a) COOSBEAN MILL.

(b) MILL AND LEAT,
COOSBEAN.

(c) OLD PAPER MILL,
PENRYN.

CORNISH PAPER MILLS.

(28) the "woollen cloth, paper . . . manufactories in the neighbourhood" gave employment to a "great number of hands". Drew (29) says that gunpowder mills had been erected in Kennall Woods "within these few years" and that "a paper mill has also been established in the same wood by Mr. Tucker". Kennall Vale had become a veritable hive of industry, and Drew, commenting on the number of mills in the locality, said that the river, which worked thirty-nine water-wheels in the five and a half miles of its course, at Kennall thus worked "an extensive paper manufactory". Penaluna (30) described the Kennall Wood paper mills as "extensively worked", and the actual site (above the Kennall gunpowder mills) is mentioned in Lewis (31). Pigot for (32) 1844 lists Tucker as a paper-maker here, but by 1852–3 (33) the mill had passed into the ownership of Williams and Powning. It is mentioned in the 1856 Directory, in 1868 (34), was in their hands in 1872 (35) and in the 1873 Directory (36) is listed under the firm of W. S. Williams and Co. In the last reference W. S. Powning is given as a paper merchant in Truro. Mention of the mill occurs in 1883 (37), 1884 (38) and 1889 (39), when it had changed hands to E. D. Polkinhorn ; he is mentioned in connection with a water mill, but a small paper mill at Stithians is quoted. In 1893 (40) and 1894 (41) the mill is listed, and these are the last records of paper-making at Kennall. Of three mills situated together, the old paper mill fell into ruins and the other two have been used as corn mills. According to local information, the lowest mill was once used for paper-making, but apart

(28) Pigot. loc. cit. (7) above.
(29) loc. cit. (23) above.
(30) op. cit., 1838 ed., Vol. II, p. 225.
(31) op. cit., Vol. IV, p. 194.
(32) p. 28.
(33) Slater's "Royal National and Commercial Directory and Topography". Cornwall. 1852–3. p. 37.
(34) "The National Gazetteer". 1868. Vol. III, p. 543.
(35) Lake (see 18 above). 1872 ed., Vol. IV, p. 183.
(36) loc. cit.
(37) Kelly's "Directory of Cornwall", p. 1,163.
(38) "A Geographical Dictionary or Gazetteer of Cornwall". 1884. p. 182.
(39) Kelly's "Directory of Cornwall". 1889, p. 1,160.
(40) Kelly's "Directory of Cornwall". 1893, p. 1,441.
(41) Daniell. op. cit., p. 223.

8 THE DISTRIBUTION OF PAPER-MAKING IN CORNWALL

from the doubtful reference to it as the small paper mill
(see above) there is no definite record to substantiate this.
In the other mill, however, one can see the huge power-wheel,
scraps of the machinery, and the air-drying loft. (Photographs (e) and (f) show the two mills.)

Evidence is scant concerning a paper mill at Penzance
which is mentioned by Penaluna in 1819 (42), Cooke (43)
and Robson (44), who gives the name of a paper manufacturer
as Benjamin Downing of Clarence Street. The fortunes of
this mill did not prosper, according to Richard Edmonds
(45)—the district " does not contain any factory, with the
exception of a small paper manufactory recently recommenced, in which only six individuals are occasionally
employed ". By about 1850 there were, according to the
Gazetteer of Fullarton (46), " no manufactures in the
district ", and in a Directory of 1864 (47) Downing is listed
as a printer.

Of greater importance was the paper mill at Coosbean,
near Truro, a settlement which now consists of two mills,
three houses and farm buildings. (Photograph (d).) The
mill is shown on the Ordnance Survey Map, 1809 edition,
and this was probably the large building (Photographs (a)
and (b)) which, according to the present owner, has been
used as a corn mill for the past twenty years and had been
a flour mill for forty years before that period. In the course
of digging on the farm land, traces of extensive water pipes
have been found, and these may have provided an auxiliary
water supply for the mill mentioned, or they may have
worked a mill in another building close by. The present
wheel can develop 23 horse power, and a supply from a small
tributary stream may have been necessary in summer.
Penaluna (48) mentions a paper mill in the neighbourhood

---

(42) Penaluna. 1819 ed.
(43) op. cit., p. 196 (see 2 above).
(44) op. cit., pp. 44 and 46 (see 11 above).
(45) " A Statistical Account of the Parish of Madron, containing
the Borough of Penzance ", etc. July, 1839. Vol. I of " Cornish
Pamphlets and Tracts ".
(46) op. cit., Vol. X, p. 844.
(47) " Directory of Penzance ". C. Coulson. 1864. p. 84.
(48) 1819 ed., p. 244.

THE DISTRIBUTION OF PAPER-MAKING IN CORNWALL

(d) COOSBEAN SETTLEMENT.

(e) LOWER MILL,
KENNALL VALE.

(f) OLD PAPER MILL,
KENNALL VALE,
STITHIANS.

CORNISH PAPER MILLS.

of Truro, and Pigot in 1822–3 (49) refers to the Coosbean Mill. The names of Magor, Turner and Plummer are given as paper-makers at that mill, which was probably the " large paper mill, in which ten tons of paper are manufactured weekly ", which was working in 1838 (50). Pigot (51) in 1844 lists Truro's manufactures of carpets, coarse woollens and paper, and in 1852 (52) paper is again mentioned ; but after that date the mill is not listed.

In the East of the county, Liskeard and Calstock are included in Gilbert's list of paper manufactories (53). This is the only reference to Calstock, but the mill at Liskeard is named on the 1809 edition of the Ordnance Survey Map of Cornwall, is mentioned by Penaluna (54), is listed in a Gazetteer of about 1850 (55) and in 1868 (56) was grouped among the principal manufactories of the town. According to Lake (57), however, " between Moorswater and Looe Mills there was as recently as 1824 a paper manufactory ; it was afterwards converted into a grist mill ". Allen (58) quotes Stockdale's " Excursions in Cornwall "—" there is a paper mill in the vicinity, but it does not greatly affect the place ", and also notes that the mill has been converted to a grist mill. There is not much evidence to say at what date this occurred.

Until 1881, there is little definite information about the numbers employed in the industry in Cornwall. The failure of small mills and the extensive use of machinery had very much reduced the " great number of hands " of 1822 (59), for in 1881 (60) the numbers employed in manufacturing paper were only six males and nine females, and in 1891 (61) nine males and twelve females. In 1901 (62) only one paper

---

(49)   op. cit., p. 200.
(50)   Penaluna. 1838 ed., Vol. II, p. 255.
(51)   op. cit., p. 2.
(52)   Slater. op. cit., p. 2.
(53)   op. cit., Vol. I, p. 338.
(54)   " Survey of Cornwall ". 1843 ed., Vol. II, p. 29.
(55)   op. cit., Vol. VIII, p. 756.
(56)   " The National Gazetteer ". Vol. II, p. 612.
(57)   op. cit., 1872 ed., Vol. III, p. 156.
(58)   " History of the Parish of Liskeard ". J. Allen. 1856. p. 373.
(59)   See note (7) above.
(60)   Census for Cornwall. 1881. p. 204.
(61)   „   „   1891.
(62)   „   „   1901. p. 55.

manufacturer is recorded. Competition from better-placed and better-equipped mills probably accounted for the cessation of the industry in Cornwall, a county in her position in relation to quick transport to the markets of the industrial areas and of London less fortunate than Devon, where paper-making still survives in places relatively accessible from the main arteries of commerce.

The writer wishes to express his best thanks to Miss D. W. Davey, B.A., for all her very kind help, especially in photography.

XI

The Paper-making Industry near Barnstaple.—
The small industries, past and present, of the Barnstaple
district are of unusual interest. Among other manufactures,
woollens, lace, earthenware, iron, furniture, gloves and
paper have been important, and they reflect the wealth
and importance of the borough as a port and a centre for
markets and supplies.

The three paper mills which have worked near Barnstaple
are the exceptions (1) to the statement that the paper-
making industry in Devon was confined to the south and east
of the county, where many paper mills started after the
decline of the Devon woollen industry. Near Barnstaple
there were good supplies of water for power and for use in
the mills, and streams at or near Pilton, Marwood and Shirwell, were used. There was probably a cheap labour supply,
especially after the woollen industry had collapsed, and the
men and women worked long hours. The " raw materials "
used were linen rags, gunny bagging, hemp, old sailcloth
and waste paper. The last was probably obtained from
shopkeepers in the area in part-exchange for supplies of
new papers. Some export of the finished product was possible
by sea, and later via the railway.

A paper mill is mentioned as early as 1759 (2), but the
site is not given. During the nineteenth century, three
paper-making " factories " were at work, and these were
called " Blatchford " near Shirwell, " Blakewell " near
Marwood, and " Playford " at Pilton. When paper-making
ceased, the mills were converted to other uses. The mill
at Blakewell suffered a fire in 1867, and later was used as
a grain mill. Blatchford mill was adapted to a similar use,
and the Pilton mill became a saw-mill.

Wm. Thorne, who constructed the North Devon Railway,
seems to have taken a hand in paper-making, and was listed
as a paper manufacturer in 1830 (3). Gribble (4) makes
no mention of paper mills, but two mills are given in works

---

(1) In White's " History and Gazetteer of Devon ", 1878 ed.,
p. 1,048, mention is made of a paper manufacturer at Hartland.
A resident ?
(2) Brice's " Gazetteer ". Vol. 1, p. 138.
(3) Pigot's " Directory of Devonshire ". (1830 ed.), p. 183.
(4) " Memorials of Barnstaple ". J. B. Gribble. 1830.

of 1842 (5) and 1850 (6).   One paper mill is mentioned in 1844 (7) and 1852-3 (8), and probably belonged to a Wm. List.   He is mentioned in 1856 (9) and 1857 (10), and as owner of the Blatchford mill, in 1866 (11) and 1873 (12). In this last year he was killed in the machinery, and the mill passed to other owners.   We read of it again in 1889 (13), owned by Abbott and Co., and in 1897 (14) owned by W. Smith.

In 1889, Jabez Penny started to manufacture paper at the Pilton mill, and it worked until 1906 (15).   The mill lease was not renewed after that date.   These small mills would find it very difficult to compete with the much larger mills then being set up much nearer the great industrial districts and markets of our land.

Each mill probably never occupied more than a dozen hands.   A former employee at the Blatchford mill remembers that only four hands were employed in his day.   Some of the other paper mills in Devon were equally small—that at Huxham, for example, was worked by the owner and his family, and produced only about two tons of paper per week.

The types of papers produced at the mills near Barnstaple were mainly " browns " and white-brown wrappers, and the markets for these were mainly local.   At Blatchford, grey and " royal " papers were made.   Some paper was exported, and this is mentioned in 1850 (16) and 1860 (17) and the Playford papers were sent far afield, even to Yorkshire, at the end of last century.   The paper-bag branch of the industry was specially profitable, and the mill also produced some carpet felt.

I should like to acknowledge my gratitude to Miss D. Drake, and to Mr. A. H. Slee, for their kind help.

(5)   " Topographical Dictionary of England ". S. Lewis. 1842, p. 153.
(6)   " History and Gazetteer of Devon ".   White.   1850 ed., p. 568.
(7)   Pigot's " Royal National and Commercial Directory of Devon-shire ".   1844 ed., pp. 8 and 13.
(8)   Slater's " Royal National and Commercial Directory and Topography ", Devonshire.   1852-3, pp. 10 and 16.
(9)   " Post Office Directory of Devon and Cornwall ".   1856, p. 463.
(10)   " Directory and Gazetteer of the County of Devon ".   M. Billing.   1857, p. 244.
(11)   " Post Office Directory of Devonshire ".   1866, p. 1,234.
(12)   „   „   „   1873, p. 615.
(13)   Kelly's " Directory of Devonshire ".   1889, p. 843.
(14)   „   „   „   1897, p. 1,052.
(15)   " Devon Trades Directory ".   1906-7, p. 40.
(16)   See (6) above, p. 569.
(17)   Stewart's " North Devon Handbook ".

XII

PAPER-MAKING IN DEVON AND CORNWALL.

A COMPREHENSIVE study[1] of the early distribution of paper mills in this country has shown that, up to the end of the seventeenth century, most of them were situated in the Home Counties, and near the larger centres of population in some other counties. There were, for example, paper mills in Staffordshire, and near Cambridge ; others were in Wiltshire—at Yatton Keynel (which could supply Bristol), and at Bemerton, near Salisbury ; in Hampshire—at Laverstoke and Southstoneham, near Southampton ; and in Devon—at Plymouth. The mills in Wiltshire and Hampshire were, it seems, "independent" clusters, and Dorset has had only one paper mill, at Witchampton. The paper-making industry in Somerset has been dealt with already[2] ; some of the mills in that county have had connections with those in Devon, especially as some of the latter depend on imports of fuels and raw materials via the Somerset ports of Watchet and Bridgwater, and as the continued prosperity of not a few of the mills in both counties is probably very much influenced by their position near the main railway (G.W.R.) system to Bristol and London.

The industry in Devon and Cornwall seems to have been inspired from Plymouth, and so grew in the eighteenth and nineteenth centuries that at least 37 mills have been occupied at some time during that period by paper-makers ; but of this number only nine are now at work. The great reduction in the number of mills and the reliance of several of the survivors on "extra-regional" control have meant that the circumstances of the origin of the mills have been almost forgotten, and there is a great lack of evidence about this, and about their history. This is true of the existing mills, as well as of those which are derelict and which have been destroyed or converted.

---

[1] " Paper-making in England, 1495-1788." RHYS JENKINS. The Library Association Record. Sept., 1900—April, 1902.
[2] By W. W. JERVIS and S. J. JONES. *Geography*. Vol. XV. 1929-30. P. 625.

PAPER-MAKING IN DEVON AND CORNWALL

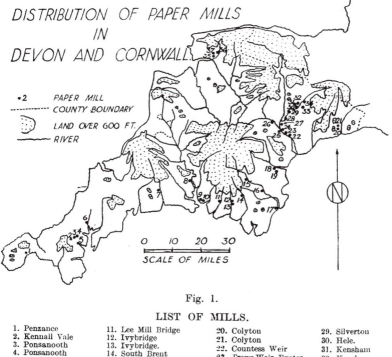

Fig. 1.

LIST OF MILLS.

1. Penzance	11. Lee Mill Bridge	20. Colyton	29. Silverton
2. Kennall Vale	12. Ivybridge	21. Colyton	30. Hele.
3. Ponsanooth	13. Ivybridge.	22. Countess Weir	31. Kensham
4. Ponsanooth	14. South Brent	23. Trews Weir, Exeter	32. Kensham
5. Penryn	15. Buckfastleigh	24. Head Weir, Exeter	33. Langford
6. Coosbean, Truro	16. Tuckenhay, Totnes	25. Exwick	34. Cullompton
7. Liskeard	17. Dartmouth	26. Newton St. Cyres	35. Pilton
8. Calstock	18. Bradley, Newton	27. Stoke Canon	36. Shirwell
9. Plymouth	Abbot	28. Huxham	37. Marwood
10. Plymouth	19. Aller, Newton Abbot		

FACTORS IN THE DISTRIBUTION OF THE MILLS.

The distribution map (Fig. 1) shows that, with the exception of those near Barnstaple, the mills have been situated in the south and east of Devon, and the south of Cornwall. This is the tract of land which almost always has been relatively rich in agriculture, pasture and mineral development ; its villages and towns have been relatively prosperous, and have had varied manufactures. The best systems of communications have taken their course through these favoured districts, and overseas contacts have been fostered by maritime activities along a coast of long, branching and sheltered inlets. The population map (Fig. 2)[3] reflects the importance of this part of the

---

[3] For this map the writer is deeply indebted to the industry of Mr. E. T. WOODLEY, B.Sc., Dept. of Geography, University College of the South-west of England, Exeter.

region at the beginning of the nineteenth century, and its advantages were undoubtedly major factors controlling the distribution of the paper-making industry ; but it is necessary, first, to discuss other considerations.

One of the primary requirements of the industry was an abundant supply of clean water for the processes, and, in the early days, for power. There are to be found in all parts of the two counties conditions which meet this requirement. An annual rainfall of over 30 inches is assured, and this, together with the broken character of the countryside, means

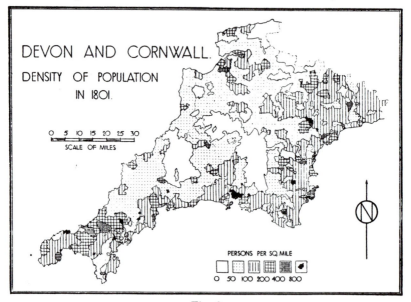

Fig. 2.

that the water supply in many valleys is fairly regular, and also powerful. Much of the water drains from uplands of granite, sandstone, or metamorphics, and is thus soft, or of only moderate hardness. At present, in the industry in Devon, the only difficulties which are experienced are the peaty character of some of the river water which drains off Dartmoor, and the " sludge " and poor summer flow which affect the Culm and the Exe. These difficulties can be overcome, however, and some mills derive additional supplies of water from powerful wells and springs.

The distribution and character of the water supply in the two counties did not of themselves determine the sites of the mills ; there is an abundant supply in several districts where paper-making has never been tried.

PAPER-MAKING IN DEVON AND CORNWALL

Another requirement was raw materials. In the early days of the industry these consisted mainly of rags, waste-paper, sailcloth, ropes and straw. The port of Exmouth imported " paper-stuff " from Portsmouth and Plymouth,[4] but there were local supplies of materials in the South-west. Linen rags and waste-paper were collected locally, often by shopkeepers under a system of part exchange for new supplies of paper from the mill-owner : ship's canvas and ropes were used in mills near the ports, and in some places in Cornwall fine oat straw was employed.

It is often rather loosely stated that many paper mills arose in various parts of the country where the old woollen industry had flourished. It is important to remember, in this connection, that woollen rags were of no use to the paper-makers unless the latter manufactured felt, too. In Devon some of the mills had housed a fulling industry, but the principal connection between the paper and declining woollen industries seems to have been that when the woollen trade had become but a shadow of its former prosperous self,[5] manufacturers and farmers turned to other enterprises in which the mill buildings and power and the local labour supply could once more be used. The paper-making industry in the South-west is much older than this decline in the manufacture of woollens, a decline which came at the end of the eighteenth century, but at least one of the fulling mills[6] was converted for paper-making, and others were on the sites of fulling or grist mills. A mill near the Head Weir (Exeter) is marked as a fulling mill on maps of Exeter from as early as 1744.[7]

Undoubtedly paper-making, in areas formerly important for their output of woollen goods, might be considered as a possible " paying proposition," for there would be ready at hand a supply of power, buildings, labourers both willing and cheap to hire, a considerable local market, and possibilities for developing an export trade. Advertisements in Exeter newspapers at times tried to prove these advantages,[8] but in some villages where one might expect to find traces of the industry, good alternatives were present ; in mid- and east Devon, enterprise developed the manufacture of silk or lace (as at Tiverton, Ottery St. Mary and Honiton), and any number of smaller concerns.

All the requirements noted above were present in the localities which came to be of importance in the paper-making industry. Some

[4] WOOLMER'S *Exeter and Plymouth Gazette.* 4/Feb. and 29/July, 1815.
[5] " Industry, Trade and People in Exeter, 1688-1800." W. G. HOSKINS. 1935. See especially Chap. III.
[6] " A History of Bradninch." C. CROSLEGH. 1911. P. 305.
[7] " The Early Printed Plans of Exeter, 1587-1724." K. M. CONSTABLE, M.A. Transactions of the Devonshire Association. 1932. Vol. LXIV. Pp. 455-473.
[8] WOOLMER. 23/Dec. 1813.

PAPER-MAKING IN DEVON AND CORNWALL

of the mills were situated near ports—Exeter, Barnstaple, Dartmouth, Plymouth, Penryn and Penzance ; most of these were also market towns, and Newton Abbot and Colyton were market centres, too. Many were to be found in villages and towns where the woollen industry had formerly been the principal concern—Cullompton, Bradninch, Buckfastleigh and Totnes, as well as Exeter and Barnstaple, are examples ; some were established in districts such as Kennall Vale and Ponsanooth, where there were several mills already occupied in diverse manufactures.

Thus the industry in every case was started in districts where the population was already numerous. Its story is one of individual, and often sporadic, attempts. From the scanty references to them, dating from the early years of last century, the existence of some mills seems to have been very short-lived, and their size quite small.

The Development of the Industry.

It is fairly clear that Huguenot refugees, for example the de Portals, and Germans, for instance Spilman, played an important part in establishing the industry in various parts of the country, and in the case of Devon the earliest record of paper-makers found so far refers to a Dennis Manes, a refugee, and dates from shortly before 1684. He had " kept a manufacture of paper in France, and was forced to leave it because of his religion," and had already settled in or near Plymouth. where he had two paper mills.[9] These mills seem to have persisted in the manufacture of paper in the eighteenth century, as leases of a paper mill in Plymouth date from 1710 and 1779,[10] and there was a rental of another in 1777-8.[11] In 1816 there is mention of only one and the greater part of its output of brown paper was " sent to London for exportation."[12] In 1814[13] paper-making was listed as one of the principal trades in the town, but it must have ceased shortly afterwards. The Mill Bay Mill, which ceased to produce paper in 1811, was for sale in 1815,[14] and this confirms the impression that post-war depressions had brought about a state of " stagnation of commerce "[15] in the area.

Despite the early establishment of mills in Plymouth, some of the supplies for other districts in Devon were imported through Exeter, and other ports, and an example given by Hoskins[16] is an import

[9] " Paper-making in Devon." RHYS JENKINS. Devon and Cornwall Notes and Queries. 8. 1914-15. (Quoting Register of the Privy Council.)
[10] Plymouth Municipal Records. ED. WORTH. 1893. P. 284.
[11] Town Rental of 1777-8, in the Muniment Room, Plymouth.
[12] BURT's " Review of Mercantile Interests in Plymouth." 1816. P. 196.
[13] " History of Plymouth." L. JEWITT. 1873. P. 634.
[14] WOOLMER. 23/Dec. 1815.
[15] WOOLMER. 24/Aug. 1816.
[16] op. cit. P. 108 and pp. 171-2.

PAPER-MAKING IN DEVON AND CORNWALL

from Southampton in 1700. But in the second half of the eighteenth century several paper mills were at work in the county. Rhys Jenkins[17] has shown that at this time the general condition of the industry in this country was relatively flourishing ; a turning point in its history was reached when Whatman exported paper to the Continent from 1775 onwards, and the Society of Arts had already given an impetus to the production of high-class papers by granting premiums and medals, while the progress of industrialisation in many parts of the country meant a large demand for wrapping papers. It is difficult to say how far each mill in the South-west was affected by these considerations ; in general, it may be said that although a few mills maintained a fairly continuous manufacture of high-class hand-made papers, some came later in an attempt to create a specialised product and market. Most mills in the region seem to have produced the lower grades, principally wrappers, at some time in their history.

After Plymouth the oldest mills were at Barnstaple, where one is mentioned in 1759[18] ; Bradninch (the Hele Mill, which was started in 1767 and which has worked fairly continuously, and the Kensham Mills) ; Countess Weir, about 1780 being the date of starting[19] ; Newton Abbot in 1790 (according to the original deed, in the possession of the present owner of the Bradley Mill) ; and Colyton which was mentioned in 1796.[20] Then in the 1820's, there come references to about 30 mills, so it is possible that, in addition to those just mentioned, one or two began to make paper earlier than the nineteenth century.

Near Barnstaple three paper factories worked during last century, one of which was probably that mentioned in 1759. Gribble,[21] the local historian, does not refer to paper mills, so that activity may have been intermittent ; one mill was burned down in 1867. The types of paper manufactured were mainly brown and white-brown wrappers and sugar-bag papers and the market for these was mainly local, with some export trade. Each mill provided work for only a few hands, and at the Playford Mill, which ceased work in 1906, and about which most is known, these were employed in making paper and felt, and large quantities of paper-bags were produced. Up to the end of last century there was a considerable demand, and to maintain his trade the manufacturer had to import some varieties not made by himself. Large consignments of paper were sent to Exeter, Bristol, Taunton and other Somerset towns, and even as far North as York. This mill shut down, it is said, because the miller

[17] op. cit. (1) above.
[18] BRICE's " Gazetteer." 1759. P. 138.
[19] "Devon and Cornwall Notes and Queries." 15. P. 153.
[20] Letter of 1/Jan., 1796, from John Rennie to James Watt, Jr. Information from Mr. Rhys Jenkins.
[21] " Memorials of Barnstaple." J. B. GRIBBLE. 1830.

could neither modernise his plant at a time when new machinery was rapidly being introduced in larger mills elsewhere, nor renew his lease.

At Colyton paper was made at two mills in 1820,[22] and work continued there in one until 1889.[23] This was a period of varying fortunes, for in 1842[24] the manufacture of paper, while being " the principal branch," was on a reduced scale, " there being but one establishment, in which 10 persons are employed." In 1860,[25] however, a " record " piece of paper measuring 21,000 feet long by 6 feet 3 inches wide was produced at Colyton.

In Moore's " History of Devonshire " (1829) three mills at Bradninch, and mills at Huxham, Stoke Canon, Countess Weir and Exeter are noted. There were other mills in this district about this time, as the evidence which follows shows, but the story of this cluster of factories is one of vicissitudes. Several of them suffered very much from fires, which were the curse of many a Devon village with thatched houses huddled together. All the mills have had several changes in ownership, and a number of names of undaunted managers and paper-makers who have been concerned with one or more of the mills in the district stands out.

Most of these mills were near the Culm or the Exe. There were two paper-makers at Cullompton in the 1820's ; and there is a reference[26] to Langford, probably to the mill on the Weaver. The Higher King's Mill seems to have made paper fairly continuously since about 1820. At Bradninch the Hele Mill was founded on the site of grist mills, and the old fulling and manor grist mills at Kensham were converted, too. According to Simpson's " Survey," in 1788, " only the common shop-papers " were made at these two last ; the mills " answered extremely well," and all three in 1842[27] occupied 60 to 70 people. Later a series of fires ruined the Kensham Mills, which were not used after the disasters of 1890 and 1892.

At Huxham there was a small mill where paper was made for a period of 60 years, from 1829 at least, and the mills at Silverton and Stoke Canon have been producing paper since the 1820's ; the latter providing work for about 30 persons in 1842,[28] as compared with about 60 to-day. The Tithe Map of 1842,[29] for the parish of Newton St.

---

[22] PIGOT's " Royal National and Commercial Directory." Devon. c. 1830. P. 189.

[23] KELLY's " Directory of Devonshire." 1889. P. 843.

[24] " Topographical Dictionary of England." S. LEWIS. 1842. P. 658.

[25] " Paper-making in Devonshire." H. R. WATKIN. " Devon and Cornwall Notes and Queries." 11. 1920-21. P. 33.

[26] W. WHITE's " History and Gazetteer of Devonshire." 1850 ed. P. 290.

[27] S. LEWIS. op. cit. Vol. I. P. 335.

[28] ibid. Vol. IV. P. 204.

[29] Consulted in the Diocesan Registry, Cathedral Close, Exeter.

Cyres, shows " Paper Mills " at Lower Marsh, and this seems to explain the reference to the working of the " Marsh Mills " near Exeter at an earlier date.[30]

In Exeter the Head Weir Mill had been converted for paper-making at the end of the eighteenth century, and has kept going despite numerous fires and changes in ownership. Trews Weir Mill was adapted from a short-lived cotton factory in 1838, and has made mainly brown, and occasionally news, papers. The mill near Countess Weir, which at one time employed about 50 people, and made esparto papers, closed about 1884.

The Exwick paper mill had been converted from a " shamoy " factory,[31] and was working for a few years prior to the fire of 1809.[32] It was revived later, and produced mainly brown papers, until it had to close down about 1868. When all the Exeter mills were at work, paper-making must have ranked high in the city's list of occupations, and in 1838[33] was placed second in importance to serges in its exports. In that entry 21 printers are listed, and since the demand was considerable, Exeter had a number of warehouses where the paper from the surrounding mills was stored.[34]

Near Newton Abbot there were two mills. The Bradley Mill produced paper intended for local consumption, including high-class grades for printing : this mill was burned down in 1860. The Aller Mills also were working in 1830, according to Pigot,[35] and are last-mentioned in 1870,[36] when there was an advertisement of hand-made writing paper ; in 1842 Lewis[37] mentioned that about 20 persons were employed.

There is brief reference to a paper mill at Warfleet, a " short distance from the town " of Dartmouth, in 1823.[38] The millowners at Tuckenhay, Totnes, have a sheet of paper made in the mill in 1809, and paper has been a principal product since the 1820's. The Tithe Map of the parish of South Brent, of date about 1840,[39] shows a paper mill to the west of the village ; no details of its activities are yet available. Further along this tract of land, Ivybridge, it seems, had

---

[30] PIGOT. 1822-3 ed. P. 220.

[31] WOOLMER. 12/July. 1817.

[32] " Exeter Itinerary and General Directory." T. and H. Besley. 1831. P. 39.

[33] ROBSON's " Commercial Directory of London and the Western Counties." 1838. P. 9.

[34] WOOLMER. 12/Oct. 1816.

[35] Ed. of c. 1830. P. 225.

[36] " Torquay, Newton Abbot and District Directory, 1869-70." Publ., J. W. Hill and Co. P. 54.

[37] op. cit. Vol. II. P. 606.

[38] PIGOT. 1822-3 ed. P. 211.

[39] Consulted in the Diocesan Registry, Cathedral Close, Exeter.

two paper mills in 1853,[40] and two are marked on the O.S. six-inch map ; the lower mill shut down about 1895. There was a " white " paper mill in Ivybridge in 1816,[41] and the entry of 1809[42] probably refers to the same. The Stowford Mill continues to make high-grade papers.

Mills at Lee Mill Bridge, further west, are mentioned in connection with paper in 1850,[43] and coarse paper seems to have been turned out on a considerable scale until the cessation of activity there in 1906. It is said that the substitution of steam for sail in the port of Plymouth had meant that the supplies of old canvas and rope on which the mills relied had become increasingly difficult to obtain.

The origin of the industry in Cornwall is not yet clearly known, but enterprise was probably inspired by the developments of the eighteenth century elsewhere. The districts where mills were established were the relatively thickly populated parts of the county. The northern districts were sparsely peopled in comparison, and the east and the north could be supplied from Plymouth and Barnstaple, as well as from the short-lived mills at Liskeard and Calstock. In the west of the county a local market seems to have been assured in the mining and coastal districts, and the towns of Truro, Falmouth, Penryn, Penzance and Redruth-Camborne were part of it. Here, too, labour was probably cheap and willing, and, in some districts, used to industrial conditions. But the industry persisted only in the Penryn area, where one factor of importance may have been that export was relatively easy through Falmouth, which was an important packet station.

Polwhele[44] noted paper mills " in the neighbourhood " of Penryn, and these may have been at Ponsanooth or Penryn itself. It is not certain whether this locality was the first in which paper mills were set up in Cornwall, but it soon became important. Penaluna[45] says that paper was exported from Penryn and Falmouth to Portugal and Spain, and the mill at Penryn seems to have worked continuously until the end of the century. Its last owner used oat straw for raw material, and sent large quantities of paper almost weekly to London.[46]

---

[40] SLATER'S " Royal National and Commercial Directory and Topography." 1852-53. P. 91.

[41] See Note ([12]) above.

[42] Plymouth Municipal Records. ED. WORTH. 1893. P. 284. Lease No. 549.

[43] " History and Gazetteer of Devonshire." W. WHITE. 1850 ed. P. 557.

[44] " History of Cornwall." 1806. Book III. Chap. VII.

[45] " The Circle, or Historical Survey of Sixty Parishes and Towns in Cornwall." 1819 ed. P. 199 ; and the 1838 ed., " Survey of the County of Cornwall." Vol. I. P. 218.

[46] " Parochial History of the County of Cornwall." LAKE. 1868 ed. Vol. II. P. 89.

PAPER-MAKING IN DEVON AND CORNWALL

Pigot[47] gives the names of two paper-makers at Ponsanooth, and in 1827[48] a " brown " and a " white " mill were put up for sale there. Further up the valley the Kennall Vale Mill commenced to produce "every kind of paper" about 1816,[49] and continued to work until 1894.

The small mill at Penzance, first mentioned by Penaluna in 1819, does not seem to have been successful, for in 1839[50] the district had a " small paper manufactory," recently recommenced, in which only six people were employed ; work had ceased there by 1850. There was a larger paper mill near Truro, mentioned by Penaluna,[51] in which 10 tons of paper were manufactured weekly,[52] and which worked until about 1852. Mills were probably tried at Calstock, to which only one reference has been found, dating from 1817.[53] The mill near Liskeard was in existence at the same time, and as late as 1868[54] paper-making was included in a list of the principal manufactures of that town : but it is clear that the industry had ceased there before that time.[55]

THE " DECLINE " OF THE INDUSTRY.

At the end of the nineteenth century[56] there were very few employed in paper-making in Cornwall. The Census for 1891 gives only nine males and 12 females, and in 1901 no employees were recorded. The industry had perished in the county, and its ultimate cessation may be traced to one main cause, whereas in the case of the Devon mills a number of contributory factors seems to have been potent. Cornwall is even more isolated than Devon from the main arteries of commerce and the markets of the Metropolis and the industrial areas of this country. This isolation prevented the mills, small and of local importance as they were, from competing with larger and better-placed mills, which could use wood pulps and power on a large scale, and were probably able eventually to capture even the local markets. The railway did not help much, apparently, and probably another adverse factor was the decline in the prosperity of Cornwall's mining industry.

---

[47] 1822-3 ed. P. 192.
[48] " Royal Cornwall Gazette." 12/May. 1827.
[49] PENALUNA's " Survey." 1819 ed. P. 237.
[50] " A Statistical Account of the Parish of Madron, etc." R. EDMONDS. July. 1839.
[51] 1819 ed. P. 244.
[52] PENALUNA's " Survey." 1838 ed. Vol. II. P. 255.
[53] " An Historical Survey of the County of Cornwall." C. S. GILBERT. 1817. Vol. I. P. 338.
[54] " The National Gazetteer." 1868. Vol. II. P. 29.
[55] " History of the Parish of Liskeard." J. ALLEN. 1856. P. 373.
[56] A full account of the history of the mills in Cornwall is given in " Devon and Cornwall Notes and Queries." Vol. XX. Part 1. Jan., 1938. P. 2-10. " The Distribution of Paper-making in Cornwall in the Nineteenth Century." ALFRED H. SHORTER.

PAPER-MAKING IN DEVON AND CORNWALL

In Devon a number of mills ceased to work because of local circumstances ; for example, fire or the cessation of the supplies of a special material, like ship's canvas, put an end to the activities of some. But some which started in the eighteenth or the early nineteenth centuries (and were probably very small) ceased work in the 1820's, or thereabouts. This setback seems to have been caused by the advent of the paper-making machine, and general post-war depressions helped ; but it was not to be expected that all these mills could make a large profit out of such a small-scale and secondary industry. Some persisted, even with the hand-making processes, and only one or two, e.g., Trews Weir, started later than this period. The coming of the railway to the South-west seems to have produced no extension of the industry, and may even have contributed to the decline. In Cornwall the two mills which survived longest were not on the main railway system ; but in Devon most of the mills at present working are very near it, and it now seems to be one of the few factors helping them (see Fig. 3).

In 1856[57] the numbers employed in Devon were 665, but this figure was easily surpassed by those for other industries in the county, including lace, gloves, woollens, furniture, tanning and rope-making. Some mills ceased work between 1856 and 1871, but in the latter year[58] the totals employed in paper-making were 415 men and 334 women, while in 1881[59] 415 men and 369 women were occupied, so that apparently the trade of individual mills had increased. The use of machinery was concentrated in large mills, which continued to grow, whereas small mills ceased work. In the Exeter area the increased demand for paper-making machinery had resulted in an Exeter firm's making this a special line,[60] but the industry experienced a decline from the 1890's until the early years of this century, as a result of factors both extra-regional and local. Nevertheless, the 1901 Census showed that the numbers employed were probably maintained at a steady level—in that year 452 men and 337 women. The " decline " was more apparent than real. There were fewer mills, but more people employed in them. An opinion of the state of the local industry in 1907, however, was that it was in a sad plight— " the present condition of the paper-manufacturing business is about as bad as it can possibly be unless it ceases to exist." [61]

---

[57] " Post Office Directory of Devon and Cornwall." 1856. P. 2.
[58] " History and Gazetteer of Devonshire." W. WHITE. 1879 ed. P. 26.
[59] Census for the South-western Counties. P. 196.
[60] KELLY'S " Directory of Devon and Cornwall." 1883. P. 731.
[61] Transactions of the Devonshire Association. 39. 1907. P. 176-7.

PAPER-MAKING IN DEVON AND CORNWALL

PRESENT CONDITIONS.

The mills now left working have expanded, and despite the series of booms and setbacks, during and after the Great War, have maintained their position. The numbers employed in 1931, according to the Census for that year, were 419 men and 198 women, and the figures of to-day supplied by the managers of the mills show a considerably higher figure.

Competing in a very wide but exceedingly keen trade, the owners of the mills have had to seize whatever chances have been presented. Many changes in the types of paper produced have been made, and the papers now manufactured in Devon are of a great variety. Ivybridge works for a general market in writing papers and for special Government orders ; Buckfastleigh produces coloured printing papers ; and Totnes is the sole survivor of the old hand-made paper firms : it relies on the excellent water supply close at hand, and makes small quantities of high-grade writing papers from best-quality white rags. The Exeter mills make relatively cheap lines : Trews Weir, brown wrappers ; Head Weir, boards and pastings ; Stoke Canon, envelopes, cartridges and boards. The Silverton and Hele Mills produce a variety of high-class writing and printing papers, and the mill at Cullompton makes coloured papers for printing.

The trade of the mills is difficult to summarise, but several of them send from 50 to 80 per cent. to London, 10 to 25 per cent. to Bristol, and 10 to 20 per cent. to the Midlands, all mainly by rail. A small proportion of the trade is local, as, nowadays, sales are for the most part arranged through agents in London and the Provincial towns. Some of the mills export a little writing paper via London, principally to the Dominions (especially Australia and New Zealand), France and South America, and these mills now have the advantage of main road and rail transport to the Metropolis, whereas formerly the goods had to be carried slowly by road to the little outport of Exeter, Topsham. In general, however, it remains true that the costs of long-distance transport are keenly felt by all the mills.

As regards raw materials, there have been great changes in the types used. Waste-papers, however, are still widely utilised, and some mills take advantage of the road-transport services to London, whence the lorries can bring a return cargo of this cheap material. One mill—Totnes—still obtains best-quality rags from France and the North of England, as well as locally. Esparto is used at the Silverton Mill, and is imported from Oran and Melilla via the little port of Watchet, which is also responsible for the import of pulps from Norway, Sweden and Finland. These materials have replaced stuffs like hemp, rope and canvas, which were used in the Exeter area until the turn of the century ; but waste-paper has come to be the principal

100

PAPER-MAKING IN DEVON AND CORNWALL

Fig. 3.

item in the materials used in the mills where the cheaper grades are made.

Another great change, as compared with last century, is that only a small amount of water-power is now used. Some mills find that the water-power available in the winter months eases the burden of running costs ; but coal is now imported, mainly from South Wales via Bridgwater (except in the case of Ivybridge, which gets its coal via Plymouth to some extent).

PAPER-MAKING IN DEVON AND CORNWALL

Some of the machinery is old, but has been altered very much to keep it up to modern requirements. Some of the machinemen and foremen have been imported from Scotland or other paper-making areas. While a tribute is due to the tenacity of Devonian industry, undoubtedly the wide experience of these men, and of the mill-owners and managers, has helped a great deal to keep the mills going in economic and geographical circumstances which are now by no means the best. Fuel and transport costs are now high ; the area no longer has any great advantage in cheap labour, since rates of wages are standardised ; and although some of the mills maintain a high reputation in certain " lines," it is difficult to say to what extent further specialisation would help, for the largest and most successful mills produce a variety of papers. This year (1937) has seen a considerable boom, but the uncertainty of its duration is a disturbing feature in a county where the industry now depends so much for its success on outside factors.

———

The writer wishes to express his best thanks to his kind friends for their help in connection with this work—especially to Miss D. W. Davey, B.A., for her aid in Cornwall ; Mr. C. W. Bracken, M.A., for information about the Plymouth Mills ; Miss D. Drake and Mr. A. H. Slee, B.A., for their work in locating and describing the Barnstaple mills ; Mr. J. Horsburgh and Mr. Rhys Jenkins, for many suggestions ; and the owners and managers of all the working and derelict mills which they have allowed him to explore. This acknowledgment in no way attributes the responsibility for the writer's views to his friends.

XIII

Paper-Mills in Devon and Cornwall.—In three contributions
to Vol. XX of this magazine,[1] I attempted to throw a little light on the
historical geography of the paper-making industry in the two counties.
My work on the subject was interrupted by the war, but sufficient has
now been done to reveal its skeleton. At this stage in the investigation,
a brief survey may be of interest to readers, some of whom may be able
to assist me from their knowledge of the localities concerned.

Like many other counties, Devon and Cornwall formerly had paper-
mills in a number of districts from which the industry has vanished.
As with Shropshire,[2] all paper-making in Cornwall ceased many years
ago. Devon has relatively few mills working now, and it is a long time
since a new paper-mill was started. We have none of the enormous mills
to be found in some of the ports and large industrial regions of the
country, and the working mills have survived in long-established paper-
making centres.

In the early stages of the industry, many of the mills were, of course,
quite small, producing common papers by the " vat " or " hand " method
to meet mainly local requirements. Up to the eighteenth century, French
papers may be said to have dominated the market, but in that century
the number of paper-mills in Britain greatly increased, the chief reasons
being the growth of population and trade, and—from various causes—
the rising cost of imports from France. Devon and Cornwall offered
considerable facilities for the establishment of the industry : abundant
and reliable supplies of suitable water (a primary requirement of the
paper-maker both for the manufacturing process and for power), cheap
labour, many ports for the import of rags and other raw materials, a
relatively large population and markets near at hand.

The map accompanying this article shows large areas in the two
counties which, apparently, have never had paper-mills, the most extensive of such regions being the moorlands, the Culm plateau, and mid-
Devon and North Cornwall generally. In the latter areas, the nature
of the water supply and inaccessibility were probably strong factors
but, as I have suggested elsewhere,[3] a distribution-map of paper-mills
at work in the early nineteenth century can be reasonably well correlated
with a population-density map of Devon and Cornwall for that time.
Bearing these factors in mind, we see that most of the early paper-mills
were started in or near (*a*) the largest towns, which were also ports,
with marked concentrations in the Exeter and Plymouth districts ;

[1] " The Distribution of Paper-making in Cornwall in the Nineteenth Century,"
pp. 2–10. " Paper-mills in Devon," pp. 34–5. " The Paper-making Industry
near Barnstaple," pp. 56–7.

[2] L. C. Lloyd, " Paper-making in Shropshire," *Trans. Shropshire Archaeological
Society*, XLIX, 1937–8, pp. 121–187.

[3] " Paper-making in Devon and Cornwall," *Geography*, XXIII, 1938, pp. 164–176.

PAPER MILLS IN DEVON AND CORNWALL

(*b*) other ports, e.g. Fowey ; (*c*) country towns, e.g. Colyton, Moreton-hampstead. Some were placed in rather remote valleys, e.g. Shaugh.

Several paper-mills were set up in similar localities in the early nineteenth century and, from time to time, attempts were made to attract paper-makers to other places, e.g. Ashburton.[4] The number of paper-mills at work in Devon and Cornwall at any one time seems to have reached its peak in the 1830's. In some cases, regional factors must have influenced their history, e.g. the state of the mining industry in relation to the mills in West Cornwall. But in the course of last century, larger factors adversely affected the small mills far away from the bigger centres of industry and from the important markets for paper. The introduction of the paper-making machine, with its eventually enormous output as compared with that of the " hand " process, the coming of the railways, and the change to other types of power and raw materials—all tended in the long run to put the small and remotely situated manufacturer out of the trade. Several paper-makers in Devon and Cornwall showed enterprise in installing machinery at an early date and in other ways, and the mills which have survived have built up a considerable and often varied trade. Some mills were finally burnt out, but a number, even of those which possessed machines, had to close for other reasons. In some cases almost all traces of the paper-mills have disappeared, and their sites are barely distinguishable on the ground ; in others, the site has been converted out of all recognition. The Tuckenhay Mill, with its production of high-quality hand-made paper, is the only " vat " mill left in Devon ; all the other surviving mills are machine-equipped and, compared with several of the extinct mills, well-placed with regard to main railways and roads, supplies of raw materials and fuel.

The summary which follows is not an attempt to survey the history of the industry in the localities concerned, but deals only with the early phase in each case. Information about the early history of paper-making is particularly elusive and, as readers will see below, there are still some topographical puzzles which I have not solved. I should be glad to have any references to paper-mills or paper-makers before, or about the time of the dates given, which are the earliest I have for each locality or mill. Where possible, the specific name of the mill is given, if it is known to be different from that of the locality named. The figures before each place-name are the reference numbers of the mills shewn on my map[5] and have no other significance. Several of my early references are, of course, simply to parishes or districts, and not to the actual sites of the mills.

---

[4] e.g. an advertisement in Woolmer's *Exeter and Plymouth Gazette*, 23rd December, 1813, for the sale of the premises of a yarn factory which " may at a small expense be converted into a Paper Mill . . . for which they are well calculated, from their centrical position between Exeter and Plymouth, and as the stream, which flows by the side of the mill, is considered as peculiarly adapted for the manufacture of paper."

[5] On such a small-scale map it is impossible to show more than the approximate position of the mills. I have thought it best to include on the map the " unconfirmed " paper-mills mentioned in the text.

PAPER MILLS IN DEVON AND CORNWALL

CORNWALL.

(1) *Penzance, Castle Horneck.*[6] A paper-mill here appears in a list of Rate Assessments given in the Churchwardens' Account Book, Madron Parish,[7] 1817–18 and onwards.

(2) *Stithians, Kennall Vale.* An entry in the Stithians Parish Registers,[8] 1803, gives John Ochisten, paper man, but no locality. My earliest reference to the Kennall Vale Paper Mill occurs in *The Royal Cornwall Gazette,*[9] 4th March, 1809, in which an advertisement states that William Tucker had established a Manufactory there, for Writing Papers of a superior Quality.

(3) *and* (4) *Ponsanooth.* St. Gluvias P.R.[10] have an entry for 1813 : Martin Boswarthack, paper-maker, but no location. Stithians P.R. refer to William Taylor, Ponsanooth, paper-maker, in 1814, and in the same year the name of William Hetherington, Ponsanooth, paper-maker, appears in the Perranarworthal P.R. Drew's *History of Cornwall,* 1824,[11] mentions "a large paper manufactory " at Ponsanooth, and several newspapers in later years[12] advertise two paper-mills there, one for white paper and the other for brown.

(5) *Penryn.* Several of the early references to paper-making here seem to be to the district, which would include Ponsanooth and Stithians, rather than specifically to the town, but a work of 1817[13] states that Penryn had added paper-making to its activities. According to an advertisement in *The West Briton* for 25th May, 1821, the Tresooth, or Lower Mills, near the Town Quay, had been occupied as a paper-mill, and it is possible that the paper-maker concerned was Mr. William Tucker, who is described as " of Penryn, paper-maker " in an advertisement in *The Royal Cornwall Gazette,* 28th March, 1807.

(6) *Truro, Coosebean.* Thomas Martyn's Map of Cornwall, 1784, shows a paper-mill North-West of Truro, but much further from the city than Coosebean, which name does not appear. I think it probable, however, that the map really refers to Coosebean, as all my enquiries have failed to trace any other paper-making site in the locality, and an advertisement in *The Royal Cornwall Gazette* for 22nd September, 1804, refers to the " long-established " paper manufactory there. As it is just possible that Martyn's map refers to an earlier paper-mill, I have indicated this on the map as No. 6a.

6 I am grateful to Mr. W. H. Eva, of Penzance, for information on this site.
7 Consulted by kind permission of the Vicar, the Rev. H. M. W. Hocking.
8 Unless otherwise stated, my references to Parish Registers are to the transcripts and publications of the Devon and Cornwall Record Society. Grateful acknowledgement is made to the Society for permission to consult their collection.
9 The early files of this newspaper were searched by kind permission of Mr. P. A. Birch, Editor.
10 In the text hereafter, " P.R." is my abbreviation for " Parish Registers."
11 Vol. II, p. 621.
12 e.g. *The West Briton,* 11th May, 1827. The early files of this newspaper were studied by kind permission of Mr. Claude Berry, Editor.
13 C. S. Gilbert, *An Historical Survey of the County of Cornwall,* Vol. I, p. 338.

PAPER MILLS IN DEVON AND CORNWALL

(7) *Lanteglos by Fowey, Stoney or Straney Bridge.* The sale of this " new-erected paper-mill " is advertised in the 4th April, 1793, number of *The Exeter Flying Post.*[14]

(8) *Liskeard, Boduil.* This paper-mill is marked on the Ordnance Survey Map, dated 11th October, 1809, and electrotyped 1872 ("Mudge's Map ").

(9) *Treganhawke.* An early, possibly the original, lease of this paper-mill appears to have dated from 1727, according to information given on the " Plan of His Majesty's Brewhouse etc. called Southdown near Plymouth in the Parish of Maker, Cornwall ; surveyed by Cs. Moody in 1794 ".[15]

(10) *Calstock, Danescoombe.*[16] This paper-mill is advertised for sale in *E.F.P.*, 26th September, 1811.

(11) *Gunnislake.* Slater's *Royal National and Commercial Directory and Topography,* 1852-3,[17] refers to the " Tamar Millboard Co.," at " Gunnerslake." It is possible that paper was manufactured there, but I have no other reference.

DEVON.

(12) *and* (12a) *Paper-mills in or near Plymouth.* Mr. Rhys Jenkins[18] refers to the two paper-mills of the Frenchman, Dennis Manes, who had settled near Plymouth. The date would be shortly before 1684, and, in the absence of evidence as to the site of these mills, I regard them as possibly distinct from (13), (14) and (15) below.

(13) *Millbay.*[19] This was probably the paper-mill leased to R. Netherton in 1710 (Lease No. 539, in " Calendar of the Plymouth Municipal Records," ed. R. N. Worth, 1893, p. 284).

(14) *The Paper-mill near the Row of Trees in Plymouth.* *E.F.P.* of 15th October, 1795, contains a notice of a sale here.

(15) *The Paper-mill with one wheel in Stonehouse Lane,* for which Wm. Derby and Co. paid a rent of ten shillings in 1777-8, according to a Town Rental of that time.[20]

(16) *Horrabridge, the Phoenix or Furzehill Mill.* Journeymen Paper-makers were required for this mill in 1794 (advertisement in *E.F.P.*, 10th July).

(17) *Shaugh.* References to paper-makers here occur in the Marriages listed in the Shaugh Prior P.R. from 1756.[21] The first paper-maker named is William Perry.

---

[14] In the text hereafter the title of this newspaper is abbreviated to *E.F.P.*

[15] I discovered this information on a photograph of the Plan, kindly lent me by Miss C. V. F. Little of Venton, Millbrook, to whom I am also grateful for first drawing my attention to the tradition of a paper-mill at Treganhawke.

[16] I am indebted to Mr. T. Maunder for detailed information about this mill.

[17] Section on Cornwall, p. 9. In the section on Devonshire (p. 135), there is a reference to mill-board manufacturers at " Tammar Mill."

[18] " Paper-making in Devon," *Devon and Cornwall Notes and Queries,* VIII, 1914–15, pp. 119–121.

[19] I gratefully acknowledge the help given me by Mr. C. W. Bracken and Mr. Rhys Jenkins in my study of paper-making in the Plymouth area.

[20] In the Muniment Room, Plymouth.

[21] I am indebted to the Rev. T. F. Rider, Vicar of Shaugh Prior, for this information.

PAPER MILLS IN DEVON AND CORNWALL

(18) *Lee Mill Bridge.* Samuel Willis, of Lee Mill Bridge, paper-maker, appears in the Ermington P.R., 1833.

(19) *Yealm Bridge.* Yealmpton P.R. give James Miller, of Yealm Bridge Mills, paper-maker, in 1814, but paper-makers, without specific reference to the Mills, appear in these Registers as early as 1804.

(20) *and* (21) *Ivybridge ; Stowford Paper-mill and the Lower Paper-mill.* John Dunn, of Ivybridge, paper-maker, appears in the Ermington P.R., 1813. Burt's *Review of Mercantile . . . Interests of Plymouth*, 1816, states[22] that " Mr. Fincher has a white paper mill at Ivybridge." This was probably the Stowford Mill, which is still working. Two paper-mills are mentioned in W. White's *History, Gazetteer and Directory of Devon*, 1850 ed.[23] I have no record of the date of commencement of work at the Lower Mill, but some of the paper-makers given in the Ermington P.R. were probably employed there.

(22) *South Brent.* A notice with regard to a Runaway, apprenticed to William Westbrook, paper-maker, of Brent, is printed in *The Exeter Evening Post*, 17th October, 1766.

(23) *Buckfastleigh, Kilbury or Dart Paper-mill.* The Burials listed in the Buckfastleigh P.R. include Edward Ceryl, paper-maker, 1785.

(24) *Tuckenhay.* Cornworthy P.R.[24] record the name of Stephen Spry, paper maker, in 1830.

(25) *Dartmouth, Warfleet.* Dartmouth, St. Saviour's, P.R. give Robert Coombes, paper manufacturer, 1790.

(26) *Newton Abbot, Bradley Mill.* The paper-mill is mentioned in deeds relating to the water rights of the mill, about 1790.[25]

(27) *Aller.* Woolmer's *Exeter and Plymouth Gazette* for 12th October, 1816, advertises paper made here.

(28) *Moretonhampstead, Town Mills.* A paper-mill here was for sale in 1776, according to an advertisement in *E.F.P.*, 15th March. I am at present unable to identify the site of the " Town Mills."

(29) *and* (30) *Countess Wear.* Topsham P.R. refer to William Bond, drowned at " ye Paper Mills " in 1704. Two paper-mills, called the Upper and Lower Wear Mills, were to let in 1778 (*E.F.P.*, 29th May).

(31) *Exeter, Trew's Weir.* This mill was converted from a cotton factory to a paper-mill, and is so described in Robson's *Commercial Directory of London and the Western Counties*, 1834.[26]

(32) *Exeter, Head Weir.* An account of the proceedings at the opening of this paper-mill appears in *E.F.P.*, 12th July, 1798.

(33) *Exwick.* *E.F.P.*, 20th February, 1806, records the marriage of T. B. Pim, paper-maker, whose extensive paper-mills at Exwick were later destroyed by fire (same paper, 7th December, 1809), and afterwards rebuilt.

(34) *Newton St. Cyres, Marsh Mills.* Newton St. Cyres P.R. mention William Matthews, paper man, in 1758.

---

[22] p. 196.   [23] p. 541.

[24] Consulted by kind permission of the Churchwardens.
[25] I am indebted to Mr. C. L. Vicary for this information.
[26] Section on Devonshire, p. 39.

PAPER MILLS IN DEVON AND CORNWALL

(35) *Stoke Canon.* *E.F.P.*, 20th March, 1806, reports an accident to Mr. Craig, paper-maker, of Stoke.

(36) *and* (37) *Huxham.* A fire at the paper-mills here is recorded in *E.F.P.*, 4th February, 1771. The Upper and Lower Mills are so named in W. White's *History, Directory and Gazetteer of the County of Devon*, 1850.[27]

(38) *Upexe.* A paper-mill in Upexe, parish of Rewe, is advertised to let in *E.F.P.*, 4th October, 1771. This mill is possibly distinct from :

(39) *Rewe.* The earliest entries of paper-makers in the Rewe P.R. appear in 1813, but it is possible that some of these people worked at Upexe and/or Huxham. *The Devonshire Chronicle and Exeter News*, 15th April, 1837, however, reports a fire at " the paper-mill at Rew "; that there was a mill at Rewe is confirmed by many old maps, including the Tithe Map,[28] but none of those I have seen mentions it as a paper-mill.

(40) *Silverton Paper-mill* (*Etherleigh, Elleris, etc., Bridge Mill*). Broadclyst P.R. record John Radford, paper-maker, in 1787, and John Matthews, of Etherleigh Mills, paper-maker, in 1813.

(41), (42) *and* (43) *Bradninch; Hele and Kensham Paper-mills.* Bradninch P.R.[29] include the name of John Warren, paper-maker, married in 1762, and Colyton P.R. give under Marriages for the same year Thomas Warren, of Bradninch, paper-maker. Paper-mills near Bradninch were for sale in 1767 (*The Exeter Evening Post*, 20th November) ; the Hele Mill at least is as old as this, but the Kensham Paper-mills must also have been at work about this time.[30]

(44), (45) *and* (47) *Cullompton.* Cullompton P.R.[31] mention Simon Mills, paper-maker, in 1757. H. B. Mills, paper-maker, King's Mill, appears in W. White's *History . . . etc.*, 1850.[32] S. Lewis, *Topographical Dictionary of England*,1842,[33] refers to " a paper-mill on a stream between the river and the town "; this would certainly be different from King's Mill. I have found no confirmation of this mill.

In *E.F.P.* for 5th August, 1813, there appears a notice with reference to a Runaway (Apprentice) from Mr. John Smith, of " Langsford " Paper Mills, Cullompton.

(46) *Kentisbeare.* The P.R. give George West, paper-maker, in 1813, and " the Paper-mills " are listed in the Parish Rate Book, 1825.[34]

(48) *Honiton.* The P.R. record Richard Martyn, paper-maker, 1813, and in Pigot's *Directory of Devonshire*, 1830,[35] appear the names of Veysey and Newbery, paper-makers, " Dowlas la."

(49) *and* (50) *Colyton ; Umborne Mill, Coles's Mill.* In the Colyton P.R. the second marriage of the daughter of John Warren, paper-maker, is recorded in 1768. If this John Warren was the same as he who appears under the Burials for 1722, Colyton could almost certainly be numbered among the earliest paper-making centres in Devon. *The Western Luminary*,

27 pp. 196–7.   28 Consulted by kind permission of the Rector, the Rev. B. A. Parsons.
29 Searched by kind permission of the Vicar, the Rev. R. A. L. Fell.
30 C. Croslegh, *History of Bradninch*, 1911, p. 305 onwards.
31 Searched by kind permission of the Vicar, the Rev. J. G. Downward.
32 p. 290.   33 Vol. I, p. 729.
34 The Kentisbeare Parish Registers and other Records were consulted by kind permission of the Rector, the Rev. R. A. Abigail.
35 p. 216. I have confirmed that the paper-mill was in Dowell's Lane.

14th February, 1832, advertises the Umborne Paper-mill for sale, and Coles's Mill is similarly advertised as a paper-mill in *The Exeter Independent*, 27th September, 1831.

(51) *Playford*. *The Directory of Paper Makers of the United Kingdom*, 1885 ed., lists Abbott and Co., Playford Mill, Pilton, Barnstaple. Paper-makers appear much earlier, however, in the records of Pilton Parish.[36] The P.R. contain the name of Edward Hastings, paper-maker, 1819, and "Pim's Paper Mill" appears in the Churchwardens' Account Book, 1825.

(52) *Blakewell*. I have no documentary evidence as to the use of this mill for the manufacture of paper, but according to local information collected by Mr. A. H. Slee it was as such that it was burned down in 1867.[37]

(53) *Blatchford*. M. Billing's *Directory and Gazetteer of the County of Devon*, 1857,[38] gives William List and Sons, paper-makers, Blatchford Mills.

(54) *Barnstaple*. " Here is a good Paper-Mill," according to T. Read in 1746.[39] Unfortunately this writer, like many who refer to paper-mills in the Barnstaple area in the nineteenth century, does not give the exact location, and it is possible that this very early paper-mill is quite distinct from those given under (51), (52) and (53) above.

ACKNOWLEDGEMENTS.—In addition to acknowledgements already made in this article and in my contributions to this magazine and *Geography* in 1938, I should like to express my thanks to all those who have kindly assisted me in this study, and especially to the staff of Exeter City Library, to the many owners, managers and occupiers of mills and other property which I have been allowed to visit and explore, and to the Council of the University College of the South West, Exeter, for a grant in aid of travelling expenses.

[36] Searched by kind permission of the Vicar, the Rev. L. H. Dukesell.
[37] A. H. Slee, " Some Dead Industries of North Devon," *Trans. Devonshire Ass.*, LXX, 1938, p. 219.
[38] p. 361.　　　　[39] *The English Traveller* . . . , Vol. I, p. 288.

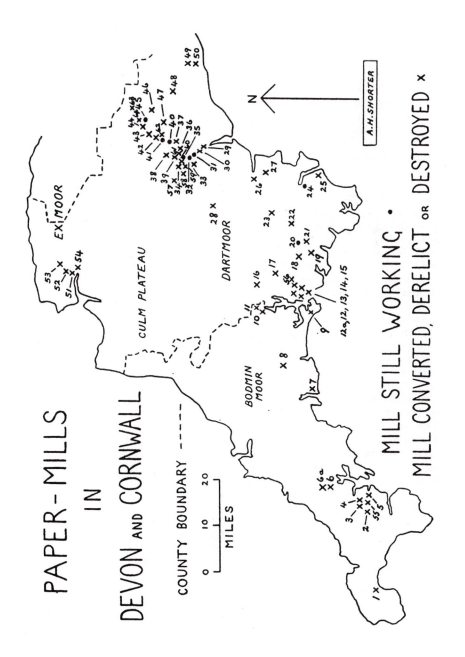

PAPER-MILLS

IN

DEVON AND CORNWALL

COUNTY BOUNDARY ----

0   10   20
MILES

EXMOOR

CULM PLATEAU

DARTMOOR

BODMIN
MOOR

N

A.H.SHORTER

MILL STILL WORKING •
MILL CONVERTED, DERELICT OR DESTROYED ×

XIV

Paper-Mills in Devon and Cornwall : Further Evidence.—
The list and map of paper-mills which were given in an earlier contribution
to this Volume (pp. 97 to 103) may now be supplemented by material
recently acquired from various sources. The writer is indebted to the
many people who have supplied new information with regard to the
" unconfirmed " mills and the sites which have since been discovered.

Among the most important of the new sources are the volumes of
" General Letters " or " General Orders ", some in manuscript and
others in printed form, which are in the Library of H.M. Customs and
Excise, City Gate House, London. These were searched by kind
permission of the Librarian, to whom I am grateful for many suggestions
and sanction to quote from the volumes concerned. A brief statement
of the connection between the Excise and paper-mills is necessary to
an understanding of these sources. For many years, Excise Duties were
levied on paper made in this country, the first Duty after the Restoration
managed by the Excise commencing in 1712. The collection of the
Duties was part of the work of the Excise Officers, and, for Excise
purposes, the country was divided into areas known as " Collections ",
with further sub-divisions called " Districts ", " Divisions " and " Rides ".

As far as Devon and Cornwall are concerned, paper-mills appear
in the Excise Records under the following Collections :—Barnstaple,
Cornwall, Exeter, Plymouth and Wellington (Somerset). The areas
covered by these Collections were adjusted from time to time, so that
certain paper-mills appear in different Collections at different times.
The paper-mills were distinguished by numbers, and the names of the
paper-makers and the localities or names of the mills were listed opposite
their numbers. The numbering of all premises subject to Excise Duties
was made statutory by 58 Geo. 3 c. 65 (1818), but the Excise Commissioners had already published an official list of paper-mills, paper-
makers and numbers in a General Letter dated 8th October, 1816.[1]
This is apparently the first list, and it may be of special interest to
Devonians and paper-makers in the county to know that the first five
mills given in the " Country Establishment " of the Excise, i.e. the areas
outside London, were all in Devon and in the Barnstaple Collection,
that being at the head of the list of Collections alphabetically. These
mills, paper-makers and localities were :—

Mill No. 1	John Waycott	Moretonhampstead
„ 2	Wm. Drake	Four Mills (near Crediton Town)
„ 3	— Godfrey	Marsh Mill (parish of Newton St. Cyres)
„ 4	Kingwell & Hayes	Oakford (parish of Upton Pyne)
„ 5	Philip Rock	Playford Mill (near Barnstaple)

(The notes in brackets are the present writer's own.)

None of these five mills has survived as a paper manufactory and, in
due course, their original numbers given above were allotted to other
paper-mills. Of the paper-mills which survive in Devon, the following
are still known by the numbers which they bore in the list of 1816 :—

---

[1] Chester Collection, Ellesmere District, Ellesmere Division, General Letter Book
No. 4, fol. 22–37.

Head Weir, Exeter (No. 94), Higher King's, Cullompton (No. 450), Silverton (No. 456) and Stoke Canon (No. 457).

The local Supervisors of Excise were required to inform the Head Excise Office in London of the establishment of new paper-mills, cessation of work, changes in the paper-makers concerned and so on. The Head Office allotted numbers to new mills and from time to time issued General Letters or General Orders to the Supervisors and Excise Officers, giving details of these and other amendments. From a study of all such Letters which are available, it is possible, first, to confirm certain of the mills about which some doubt existed when the previous article in this Volume was written and, second, to identify additional paper-mills in Devon and Cornwall. Readers may wish to insert these newly-discovered mills on the map which was published in the previous paper, and to refer to the position of the mills now finally confirmed. The figures in brackets before the names of the following mills are the writer's own, for the purpose of reference to the map, and should not be confused with the Excise Numbers, which are given separately in each case.

Paper-mills now confirmed by the Excise Records.

(11) *Gunnislake, Tamar Mill.* A General Letter dated 20th May, 1851[1] lists Mill No. 269, Plymouth Collection, Callington Ride, Tamar Mill, manufacturing millboard, paper and pasteboard, and occupied by George Samuel Lee. The Excise Number of this mill seems to have been transferred from Bircham Mill, which left off work in 1846[2].

(39) *Rewe.* The General Letter dated 8th October, 1816, already cited gives, in the Wellington Collection, Mill No. 459, Alexander Caryl, paper-maker, Rew Mill. This mill appears in several later General Letters, including that of 2nd May, 1827[3], which gives the following paper-makers there: John, Robert and Gilbert Ware. John and Gilbert Ware are named in the Tithe Apportionment of Rewe Parish, dated 1837, as the occupiers of Little Heazille, and mills are shewn at that place on the Tithe Map, dated 1840 (consulted, together with the Apportionment, by kind permission of the Rector, the Rev. B. A. Parsons). This is the site now occupied by Heazille Barton, where a mill-wheel is still worked by the River Culm, and parts of old walls exist next to the modern buildings. This was, doubtless, the site of the paper-mill at Rewe, and was quite distinct from the older paper-making site at Upexe, in the same parish.

(44) *Cullompton.* Two paper-mills at Cullompton appear in the General Letter dated 8th October, 1816, already quoted. The details are: Wellington Collection, Mill No. 449, occupied by John Mills, paper-maker, Cullompton, and Mill No. 450, Elizabeth Dart, paper-maker, Longmoor. The name of the latter mill was later changed to Higher King's, as it is known to-day. The former was probably the mill referred to by Lewis (*Topographical Dictionary of England*, 1842, Vol. I, p. 729) as being on a stream between the river and the town. Pigot's *Directory*

---

1 In " Excise General Orders ", Vol. V (printed), 1844–53.
2 General Letter dated 23rd February, 1846, also in " Excise General Orders ", Vol. V (printed).
3 Tarporley 1st Ride, General Letters Book No. 13, fol. 122.

112

of Devonshire for 1830, p. 192, gives John Mills, paper-maker, end of Fore Street.

Additional Paper-mills given in the Excise Records.

The figures given in brackets before the names of the localities or mills carry on the system adopted in my previous paper, and readers may wish to insert these additional numbers on the map given therein.

(55) *Penryn.* It is now clear that there were two paper-mills here. The General Letter of 8th October, 1816, includes, in the Cornwall Collection, Mill No. 53, Richard Rowe, paper-maker, Penryn, and Mill No. 54, Wm. Tucker, paper-maker, also in Penryn. Richard Rowe is mentioned in the St. Gluvias Parish Register as the father of a child baptized in 1819. His mill should be inserted on my map next to the mill numbered 5 thereon.

(56) *Bircham.* The same General Letter lists, in the Plymouth Collection, Mill No. 269, John Weetman, paper-maker, Bircham. This mill was in the parish of Egg Buckland, and should be placed on the map immediately to the north-east of the group of mills at Plymouth, numbered 12a to 15. The name of John Weetman, paper-maker, appears among the Banns of Marriage given in the Shaugh Prior Parish Register for 1807 (consulted by kind permission of the Vicar, the Rev. T. F. Rider). With the assistance and kind permission of the Vicar of Egg Buckland, the Rev. G. S. Lodge, the writer obtained abundant confirmation of the site from the various Parish Records. " Bircham Mill ", occupied by John Weetman, and " Paper Mill Orchard " close by, appear in the Tithe Map and Apportionment dated 1839. Several paper-makers are recorded in the Parish Registers, and three apprentices to John Weetman, paper-maker, are given in the Book of Parish Apprentices (numbers 57, 160 and 235). The Parish Rate Book gives the rate value of the Paper Mills, occupied by John Weetman, as twenty shillings in 1831.

(57) *Crediton, Four Mills.* The General Letter of 8th October, 1816, lists this as Mill No. 2. The site of Four Mills is shewn on Donn's Map of Devon (1765) and on Greenwood's Map (1827), and is immediately north of Crediton Railway Station. A deed dated 1st November, 1821, for a sight of which I am indebted to Mr. Wallace Harding, the Manor Offices, Crediton, confirms that the paper-mill was on this site ; this deed was between Hele Webber Payne, of the Borough of Tavistock, on the one hand, and William Drake, of Crediton, on the other, and stated that the latter was " seised of the fee simple of a room or grist mill commonly called or known as Lords Four Mills and of a room of paper mills or paper manufactory situate or lying at Four Mills ". The Vat House of the paper-mill appears on a plan of the buildings incorporated in this deed. Relevant entries in the Crediton Parish Registers suggest that the paper-mill worked for only a short time, but indicate that paper-makers came into the parish from near and far. The earliest reference is under Marriages for 1813—Richard Hutton, of Upton Pyne, but there is also mention of Edward Hastings, of the parish of Cossey in Norfolk (under Baptisms for 1815), and of John Daulton, of Wells (Marriages for 1815). This mill should be placed immediately to the west of that numbered 34 on the map.

(58) *Marsh Mills*. My previous paper listed a paper-mill here, but it is now apparent that this was only one of the paper-mills in the parish of Newton St. Cyres. The General Letter of 8th October, 1816, already cited gives, in the Barnstaple Collection, Mill No. 3, —. Godfrey, paper-maker, Marsh Mill, and a General Letter of 1833[1] includes, in the Exeter Collection, Mill No. 3, Marsh Mill, with John Hayes as the paper-maker. Two other General Letters,[2] however, give another paper-mill at Marsh Mill, No. 535, with John Hodge as the paper-maker in 1823, and William Henry Pim in 1825. This mill was in the Barnstaple Collection in 1823, and in the Wellington Collection in 1825. It is probable that one of these mills was on the site of the present Marsh Mills and that the other was at Lower Marsh, where the leat has been filled in, but which is shewn as a paper-mill on the Tithe Map and Apportionment of Newton St.Cyres parish, dated 1842 (consulted in the Diocesan Registry, Exeter).

(59) *Rape Mill*. A General Letter dated 31st August, 1819,[3] gives, under the Barnstaple Collection, Mill No. 511, William Henry Pim, paper-maker, Rape Mill. This mill may also be placed in Newton St. Cyres parish, from a clue given in an advertisement in " Alfred " for 24th February, 1824 ; this included in a list of lands to let a field called " Rape Mill Marsh ", part of Marsh Barton, parish of Newton St. Cyres. This mill, together with No. 58 above, should be inserted on the map next to No. 34.

(60) *Oakford*. The General Letter of 8th October, 1816, lists, in the Barnstaple Collection, Mill No. 4, Messrs. Kingwell and Hayes, paper-makers, Oakford. References to families of these names occur in the Upton Pyne Parish Registers, without mention of occupation, 1817–20, and the Register Book of Parish Apprentices (consulted by kind permission of the Rector, the Rev. D. S. Northcote) contains the following entry for 25th August, 1826 : John Perkins, aged 9, of Upton Pyne, apprenticed to James Hayes, Oakford Mills, Farmer and Paper-maker. This mill should be placed between those numbered 34 and 35 on the map.

(61) *Stoke Mill*. The General Letter dated 8th October, 1816, gives, under the Wellington Collection, Mill No. 457, Daniel Crags, paper-maker, Stoke, and Mill No. 460, Richard Sharland, paper-maker, Stoke Mill. The paper-mills working to-day at Stoke Canon bear the number 457, but no reference has been found to the industry on a different site in the same parish. Richard Sharland's name appears in the Stoke Canon Parish Registers, Marriages in 1806. It is probable that he had a mill of his own on the same site as the Stoke Canon Paper Works, and so was given a separate Excise Number. The deeds of the Works, for a sight of which I am indebted to Sir Arthur C. Reed, refer to the place as " Stoke Mills ", which is the title of Sharland's site. This mill should be inserted next to that numbered 35 on the map.

1 Canterbury Collection, Tenterden District, Tenterden Ride, General Letter Book No. 12. General Letter dated 28th November, 1832, corrected agreeable to the General Letter of 1st July, 1833.
2 The first, of 19th February, 1823, is in " Excise General Orders " (printed), Vol. I, 1819–23, fol. 517. The second, dated 2nd April, 1825, is in Tarporley 1st Ride, General Letters Book No. 13, fol. 38.
3 Northwich Collection, Frodsham District, Tarporley 1st Ride, General Letter Book No. 11, fol. 13.

(62) *Bradninch.* A General Letter dated 1st September, 1821,[1] gives, under the Wellington Collection, Mill No. 240, William Holding, paper-maker, Bradninch. Included in the Bradninch Parish Registers, Baptisms for 1819 and 1821, are references to William Holdin, paper-maker ; for this information, I am grateful to the Vicar, the Rev. R. A. L. Fell. This mill must have been distinct from the sites at Hele and Kensham, the Excise Numbers of which were quite different. It probably lasted only a short time, as in a General Letter dated 27th December, 1821,[2] the number 240 is allotted to a mill in the Newcastle upon Tyne Collection. This mill should be placed next to Numbers 41 and 42 on my map.

A Scaleboard Mill.

A General Letter dated 26th June, 1819,[3] lists Mill No. 510 under the Barnstaple Collection, Geo. and Charles Harrison or Hearson, Scaleboard Makers, Pilton. There is no evidence that paper, or board other than Scaleboard, was produced at this mill, and I mention it simply as a matter of related interest.

Additional Paper-mills from other sources.

(63) *Uffculme.* Mr. C. K. Croft Andrew has kindly drawn my attention to the following reference in a book sent to him by Mr. J. Were Clarke, of Bridwell, near Uffculme : ".10 Oct. (1713) was a very great floud. Mr. John Wood paperman of Ufculm & his family narrowly escaped being drowned, yᵉ house & mill being almost destroyed ". This occurs on p. 152 of a manuscript called " Samuel Short's Book ".

Wood's Paper Mills are listed several times in the 1740's in the Uffculme Churchwardens' Book, for a sight of which I am indebted to Mr. E. J. Baker, of Beech House, Uffculme. The earliest reference to the industry in Uffculme Parish appears in the Parish Registers for 1707, when the Burials included the child of Tom Norton, paperman, of Cold-harbour. Messrs. Fox Bros., the present owners of the Factory at Coldharbour, are unable to say whether the paper-mill was on their site, but two facts suggest that it was—the paperman mentioned above, and an advertisement in Trewman's *Exeter Flying Post* for 4th December, 1788, when there were to let, grist mills at Coldharbourmills, Uffculm, lately built entirely new, with a very large head of water. It is known that Wood's Paper Mills were in the " Town Quarter " of Uffculme, from a " New Survey of the Poor Rate, Uffculme Parish, 1745 " (consulted by kind permission of Mr. J. Were Clarke), and if, as suggested below, they were damaged by the flood of 1753, they would need to be " built entirely new ".

(64) *Selgar's Mills (Halberton Parish).* In the Uffculme Churchwardens' Book, there is mention of the great flood of 12th October, 1753, when there fell part of the Paper-mill House (evidently Wood's Paper Mills) and the House, Barn and Stables belonging to the Paper Mills at " Silgis Mills ". That there were such mills at Selgar's Mills is confirmed by a series of indentures in the possession of Mr. J. Were Clarke, who kindly permitted me to search them.

---

[1] In " Excise General Orders " (printed), Vol. I, 1819–23, fol. 275.
[2] Also in Vol. I of " Excise General Orders " (printed), fol. 329.
[3] Tarporley 1st Ride, General Letters Book No. 10, fol. 52.

In a tripartite indenture of 6th January, 1692, Selgar's Mills are described as grist mills and fulling mills, but in another tripartite indenture of 1st April, 1703, between Richard Eveleigh of Halberton, Elizabeth his wife, and Richard Clarke of Halberton, grist mills and paper mills are recorded at the place. It seems that the flood of 1753 did permanent damage to the paper-mills as, by an indenture of 10th October, 1754, James Parkhouse undertook to repair " the said Paper Mills, fifteen hammers and all other utensils thereto belonging " ; but in an addition to this indenture, and written on the reverse, it is stated that the Paper Mills were " quite Rund down and become quite Ruinous and perfectly decayed and not worth repairing "—this is dated 22nd October, 1781.

Mills numbered 63 and 64 above should be placed on the map immediately to the north-east of those numbered 44 and 45.

Summary.

If all the additional mills given in this article are inserted on my map, it will be seen that the effect is to emphasize the concentrations of mills in certain areas, principally the valleys of the Rivers Culm and Creedy, to the north-east and north-west of Exeter respectively, thus supporting my tentative suggestions as to the factors concerned in the distribution of the industry.

A survey of all the material so far accumulated shews that there are documentary references to twelve paper-mills having existed in Cornwall and fifty-two in Devon, plus two doubtful cases—No. 6a on the map, north-west of Truro, and No. 52, Blakewell, near Barnstaple. It is not unlikely that even more paper-mills existed at one time or another.

References to Parish Registers in this article are, unless otherwise stated, to the transcripts and publications of the Devon and Cornwall Record Society. Grateful acknowledgment is made to the Society for permission to consult their collection.

XV

The Paper-making Industry
in Cornwall

PAPER-MAKING is one of the manufacturing industries which have not survived in Cornwall, yet in the eighteenth and nineteenth centuries it was carried on in widely separated localities in the county. The numbers employed were probably always small ; the Census Returns for 1871 gave 44 persons in the industry in Cornwall, and for 1891 only 21. This survey deals with the twelve paper-mills which worked in the county at one time or another.

During the general expansion of the industry in this country in the eighteenth century, many mills were established in South-West England for the manufacture of common papers for local use. Proximity to towns which could supply at least part of the raw materials and could absorb the finished product, was an important factor in the localization of the mills. A prime requirement of the early paper-makers, both for power and the "hand" or "vat" manufacturing process, was an abundant and constant supply of water, which had to be as clean and pure as possible. With their powerful streams, Devon and Cornwall offered many possible sites for paper-mills, several of which were converted to this industry from the declining woollen manufacture, or from corn-milling. Another advantage, especially in the southern areas of South-West England, was the number of ports, into which linen and other rags could be brought from Western Europe, the Mediterranean ports, the Channel Islands, or by coastwise trade, and which themselves supplied old junk in the form of rags, discarded sailcloth, nets and old rope, all of which were used as raw materials for paper-making.

As in many other regions of the British Isles, the number of paper-making establishments in Cornwall reached a maximum in the first quarter of the nineteenth century. After that time, the effects of the invention of the paper-making machine, with its greatly increased output of paper, became very widely and strongly felt by small manufacturers who found it difficult to compete, particularly those in the counties more remote from metropolitan and industrial England. About 1810, some coarse woollen, several paper, and a carpet manufactory, made up the principal manufactures in Cornwall, but the total was "few and inconsiderable."[1] Two paper-mills persisted at Penryn and Kennall Vale, significantly situated in the "demographic heart" of Cornwall, until the end of last century ; proximity to an area of relatively high density of population as well as to sea navigation was important in keeping the industry active there. These, the last paper-mills to work in the county, left off within living memory, and some of the former employees are still alive.

As will be seen, many of the early references in this article are to local sources of information, but during most of the first half of the nineteenth century evidence as to the location of paper-mills, and the paper-makers concerned, is recorded in the archives of the Commissioners of Customs and Excise. The writer is indebted to the Commissioners for permission to search and to quote from the relevant records in their Library at City Gate House, London, and to the Librarian for his kind assistance. The first duty on paper managed by the Excise after the Restoration began in 1712, but there is apparently no official list of paper-makers in this country until 1816, when the authorities issued a "General Letter" containing the numbers allotted to the various paper-mills, and the names of the paper-makers and localities concerned. This was followed by other lists and amendments until 1851, and many of them are bound in manuscript and printed volumes in the Customs and Excise Library. The Excise Collections under which the Cornish paper-mills appear are named in the relevant sections below, where a

---

1. G. B. Worgan, "General View of the Agriculture of Cornwall," 1811, p.165.

118

summary is given of the principal items of information on each mill.

Treganhawke

About a quarter of a mile from Millbrook, on the road to Whitesand Bay, stands a ruined building, supplied with water in former days by a well and a small stream, and known to-day as "the Paper-Mills," a name which is confirmed by the Tithe Apportionment of St. John Parish, 1840.[1] An advertisement in the newspaper "Alfred" for 7th September, 1824, dealing with the sale of the Southdown Brewery, mentions the water from the paper-mills near Treganhawke, but paper-making had long ceased there. In fact, contention over the water-supply was the reason for the closure of this mill. On the "Plan of His Majesty's Brewhouse etc. called Southdown nr. Plymouth,"[2] surveyed by C. Moody in 1794, are notes giving the history of the paper manufactory. The lease of the paper-mill was granted for three lives in 1727 but, as a result of complaints by officers of the Royal Navy that rags and filth from the paper manufactory were frequently received into the pipes supplying the Southdown Brewery, James Parkin (who appears to have possessed the lease and to have been the Master Brewer at Southdown) closed the mill in 1736 ; by 1757 the buildings were already in ruins.

Coosebean

T. Martyn's Map of Cornwall, editions of 1748 and 1784, shews a paper-mill to the North-West of Truro, but further from the city than the present site of Coosebean. No reference has been found, however, to a paper-mill other than Coosebean in this locality. An advertisement in "The Royal Cornwall Gazette"[3] for 22nd September, 1804, deals with the

---

1. All Tithe Records quoted in this paper were consulted at the Diocesan Registry, Truro.
2. The writer is indebted to Miss C. V. F. Little, of Millbrook, for the loan of a photograph of this Plan.
3. The files of this newspaper were searched by kind permission of the Editor, Mr. P. A. Birch.

"long-established" Coosebean Paper Manufactory which, from that date, was to be carried on by Messrs. Harry, Rouse, John and Vice. For several years up to that time, the manufactory had been in the possession of William Allen, who had "a larger demand for paper than he could supply."[1] "The West Briton"[2] for 3rd May, 1811, advertises the sale of the paper-mill, in the occupation of Messrs. Harry, Rouse & Co., who, according to the first Excise List,[3] were still at work there in 1816. Until it was recorded as "left off" in 1848,[4] this mill was known to the Excise authorities as No. 51, and was in the Cornwall Collection of Excise. The paper-makers at Coosebean are given as follows in the Excise Letters[5]:—1818, Reuben Magor, Edmund Turner, Jun., and Wm. Traer ; 1820, Wm. Traer ; 1822, Edmund Turner, Reuben Magor and Anthony Plummer ; 1828, Joseph Ferris ; 1826 and 1829, Anthony Plummer and Joseph Ferris ; 1831, Anthony Plummer. According to "Alfred" for 9th November, 1830, the partnership between Plummer and Ferris was dissolved in that year.

The Baptisms listed in the Kenwyn Parish Registers[6] between 1823 and 1835 give the names of the following paper-

---

1. "The Royal Cornwall Gazette," 14th July, 1804.
2. The writer is grateful to Mr. Claude Berry, Editor, for kind permission to search the files of this newspaper.
3. Chester Collection, Ellesmere District. Ellesmere Division, General Letter Book No. 4, General Letter dated 8th October, 1816, hereafter referred to as the Excise List of 1816.
4. Northwich Collection, Runcorn District, Tarporley First Ride. General Letters Book No. 19, General Letter dated 29th June, 1848.
5. Tarporley First Ride, General Letters Book No. 10, General Letter dated 31st December, 1818. Northwich Collection, Frodsham District. Tarporley First Ride, General Letter Book No. 11, General Letter dated 3rd March, 1820. Excise General Orders (Printed) Vols. I, II and III. General Orders dated 9th October, 1822, 17th February, 1829, and 17th September, 1831. Tarporley First Ride General Letters Book No. 13, General Letters dated 15th May, 1826, and 20th March, 1828. Northwich Collection, Frodsham District, Tarporley First Ride. General Letter Book No. 15, General Letter dated 28th November, 1832.
6. Unless otherwise stated, all references in this article to Parish Registers are to the collection of the Devon and Cornwall Record Society. Grateful acknowledgement is made to the Society for permission to consult and to quote from these sources.

makers, mostly of Coosebean :—Wm. Bennett, John Warren, Benjamin MacBean, John Wroath, Wm. Atkinson, John Trestrail, John Sealey, John Waycott. The Baptisms in the Truro Parish Registers include the names of other paper-makers :—Thomas Geo. Atkinson (1821) and Josephus Ferris (seven entries between 1822 and 1833).

About forty persons who worked at Coosebean, described as "one of the largest paper manufactories in the West of England," were thrown out of employment by a fire which totally destroyed the mill,[1] an extensive store of paper and rags, and very valuable machinery. The estimate of ten tons of paper manufactured weekly at Coosebean[2] suggests that a paper-making machine had been installed by the 1830's. The materials used in the manufacture here are indicated by the advertisement of the Coosebean Paper Manufactory for "any quantities of Ship or Mine Junk, white or coloured rags, canvas or bagging."[3] According to Robson's "Commercial Directory of London and the Western Counties,"[4] some paper was exported from Truro.

Penryn

By 1791[5] a paper-mill was at work in Penryn, the occupant probably being William Tucker, who is shewn in tho Excise List of 1816 as the paper-maker at Mill No. 54, while Richard Rowe was at Mill No. 53 ; both mills thus numbered were in Penryn and in the Cornwall Collection of Excise. The latter mill was discontinued in 1819[6] and the former in 1828.[7] Both these mills were probably on the site then known as the Tresooth or Lower Mills, which were for

1.   "Alfred," 6th March, 1827.
2.   W. Penaluna, "An Historical Survey of the County of Cornwall," 1838 ed., II, p.256.
3.   "The West Briton," 25th May, 1827.
4.   1834-38, Cornwall, p.73.
5.   "The Universal British Directory of Trade," 4, p.258.
6.   Northwich Collection, Frodsham District, Tarporley First Ride, General Letter Book No. 11, General Letter dated 2nd December, 1819.
7.   Tarporley First Ride, General Letter Book No. 13, General Letter dated 20th March, 1828.

sale in 1821[1] and again in 1826[2]. In the advertisement of 1821, it is stated that they "were fitted up for the purpose of an oil and mustard-mill, but originally built as a flour-mill, and have been also occupied as a paper-mill." James Mead, in conjunction with his brothers Joseph and John, here established a flour and a paper-mill, and introduced steam in place of water-power in the Penryn Mills in 1844.[3] According to a work of 1868,[4] the steam mills were for the manufacture of straw paper, large quantities of which were almost weekly sent to London. The material used was oat straw, and it was stated that the fabric was "complete and perfect."

This mill was given the number 2, and persisted in the hands of the Mead family, manufacturing the following types of paper in 1885[5]:—news, printings, cartridges, middles and small hands ; in 1890[6] the products were :—printings, cartridges, middles, butter papers, caps and small hands. The mill was demolished in 1938, under a County Council road-widening scheme.

Lanteglos by Fowey

Trewman's "Exeter Flying Post" for 4th April, 1793, contains an advertisement of the new-erected paper-mill situated in the parish of Lanteglos, about one mile from Fowey. It is stated that the mill was calculated for two engines ; it had two vat houses, comprising a water-wheel 14 ft. by 3 ft. 6 ins., engine, vat-chest and iron press ; it was well supplied with a constant stream of water, and was a quarter of a mile from water carriage.

---

1. "The West Briton," 25th May, 1821.
2. ibid, 23rd June, 1826.
3. C. H. J. Mead, "A Record of the Mead and West families in County Cornwall, 1751-1941," 1941, pp. 10 and 13.
4. Lake's "Parochial History of the County of Cornwall," II, p.89.
5. "Directory of Paper-makers of the United Kingdom," p.21.
6. ibid, 1890 ed., pp. 21-3.

In 1791[1] the paper-maker was Samuel Asty, and in 1808[2] the mill was occupied by William Hawkins. The site of the paper-mill was at Gragon, immediately upstream from Stoney Bridge, by which name the mill, number 50 and in the Cornwall Collection, was known to the Excise authorities. According to the 1816 list it was occupied by William Jones, and in later General Letters[3] it appears with the following occupiers :—1818, William Jones and William Dook ; 1819, Wm. Jones ; 1820, George Bedford Pim ; 1829, Samuel Jackson. It was to let in 1828,[4] when it was stated to be in full work, equipped with two vats and capable of working four. The mill had ample room for a machine ; it was claimed that at a trifling expense it might be converted into a "white" mill, thus confirming that up to that time only common papers were made. Despite its advantages of being "eligibly situated for obtaining rags, materials and labour at very low prices," the mill seems to have left off work by 1832, as the General Letter of 28th November, 1832, has no entry against its number.

Between 1815 and 1828, the names of the following paper-makers appear in the Lanteglos Parish Registers[5] (Baptisms) :—1815, William Groves of Lower Gragon ; 1823, William Chedley of Carnehill ; 1825, William Squire of Carn ; 1827, George Bazeley and John Warren of the Paper Mill ; John Bond of Lanteglos.

Kennall Vale

According to "The Royal Cornwall Gazette" of 4th March, 1809, William Tucker had here established a manufactory for writing papers of a superior quality. He offered "most money for rags of every description," and advertised

---

1. "The Universal British Directory of Trade," 3, p.129.
2. "The Royal Cornwall Gazette," 26th November, 1808.
3. Tarporley First Ride, General Letter Book No. 9, General Letter dated 6th March, 1818. Northwich Collection, Frodsham District, Tarporley First Ride, General Letter Book No. 11, General Letter dated 2nd December, 1819. ibid, General Letter dated 26th September, 1820. Excise General Orders (Printed), II, General Order dated 17th February, 1829.
4. "Alfred," 10th June, 1828.
5. Searched by kind permission of the Churchwardens.

the following kinds of paper :—thick and thin post, plain, black and gilt edge ; foolscap and pot ; copy and large post ; blotting, blue and cartridge, whited brown and brown of all sizes. The establishment of a manufactory of white paper was probably welcome in West Cornwall, for as late as 1795 it was stated that through the whole of Cornwall there was not one mill for this purpose[1]; even so, assignments of writing paper continued to arrive in Truro from Somerset, London and Kent.[2]

This mill, known to the Excise Commissioners as No. 55, in the Cornwall Collection, worked until the end of the nineteenth century. By 1851,[3] it had passed to W. S. Williams and W. S. Powning, and was producing paper and millboard. In 1885[4] it was equipped with one paper-making machine fifty-four inches wide, and the types of paper manufactured were fine double small hands, double small caps, white grocery papers, royals, etc. Among the materials used for paper-making here towards the end of the mill's existence were old calico and hessian flour-bags sent from mills at Plymouth. Women were employed in sorting the materials.[5]

It is possible that the Kennall Vale Paper-mill began earlier than 1809, as "paper-men" Richard Ochisten and John Taylor are named in the Stithians Parish Registers (Baptisms) in 1803 and 1805 respectively. These men may, however, have worked at Ponsanooth, where the date of commencement of the paper-mills is not known to the writer. The name of William Falkner, paper-maker, of Ponsanooth, occurs in these Registers in 1814. Thereafter, there are many names of paper-makers given in the Registers of the parishes of Stithians, St. Gluvias and Perranarworthal. In the second of these, the paper-makers may have worked at either Ponsanooth or Penryn. In the lists below, the first appearance only of the name is given. Many appear several times.

---

1. Trewman's "Exeter Flying Post," 29th October, 1795.
2. "The West Briton," 14th June and 27th December, 1816.
3. Excise General Orders, (Printed), V, General Order dated 20th May, 1851.
4. "Directory of Paper-makers of the United Kingdom," 1885, p.33.
5. For this information, the writer is indebted to Mr. John Rosewarne, of Truro.

Stithians (Baptisms) :—1815, William Hoskin, of Kennal ; 1816, William Day, of Tregose, and Joseph Mellions, of Kennal ; 1818, James Macartney, of Kennal ; 1819, George Saunders, of Kennal Vale ; 1820, Alexander Henna, of Kennal ; 1822, Angus Ross, of Ponsanooth ; 1824, John Forsight, of Trewinher ; 1827, William Saunders, of Kennall Vale ; 1832, James Snow, of Ponsanooth ; 1834, Joel Richards, of Gribbis ; 1834 (Burial), Thomas Oley or Oliver.

St. Gluvias (Baptisms) :—1813, Martin Boswarthack ; 1817, George Rundell, John Kidd, of Budock ; 1818, Thomas Bishop, Daniel Collet and William Cock ; 1819, George Laving, Richard Rowe and John Thomas ; 1820, Angus Ross ; 1821, James Macherty ; 1823, John Swann ; 1826, Joseph Slack ; 1827, John Wheeler ; 1828, William Day ; 1830, John Knuckey.

Perranarworthal (Baptisms):—1814, William Hetherington, of Ponsanooth ; 1824, James Michael, of Cosawes Wood ; 1825, William Day, of Ponsanooth.

Ponsanooth Paper-mills

Some of the above entries suggest that these mills may have been at work before 1816, in which year the Excise List gave Mill No. 56, John Dunstan & Co., paper-makers, Ponsanooth, in the Cornwall Collection. Several newspaper advertisements referred to two paper-mills here :—"The West Briton," 11th May, 1827, and 25th June, 1830 ; "The Royal Cornwall Gazette," 12th May, 1827 ; "Alfred," 29th June, 1830, and 12th April, 1831. The gist of these is that the two mills were in the occupation of Dunstan and Jenkins, one mill being for white paper and the other for brown. These advertisements do not seem to have attracted new manufacturers to the Ponsanooth mills, for in the Excise General Letter of 1832, Mill No. 56 has no entry against it.

Boduil

For some years the Boduil Paper-mill worked on the
Looe stream between Moorswater and Looe Mills. It is
marked on Mudge's Map of Devon/Cornwall, 1809 ed., and
was advertised in Trewman's "Exeter Flying Post" dated
30th May, 1811, the owner then being William Dyer, of
Stonehouse. Among the advantages of the situation of the
mill were that the district was notorious for a great collection
of rags and for a stream of water excellent for bleaching, and
that the mill was only ten miles from sea freight. The Excise
List of 1816 gives this mill as No. 267, in the Plymouth
Collection of Excise, the paper-makers being William
Radford and Thomas Hix. The mill appears again in a
General Letter dated 14th June, 1817,[1] but is absent from
the list of 1832. Lake's "Parochial History of the County of
Cornwall" (1872, III, p.156) states that the paper manufactory was in existence in 1824, and was afterwards converted
to a grist mill. From the Tithe Map of Liskeard (1842), it
appears that the paper-mill was on the site of the Iron
Foundry West of Liskeard.

Castle Horneck, near Penzance

This mill is named in the Excise List of 1816. It bore
the number 52 and was occupied by John Major & Co.,
paper-makers, in the Cornwall Collection. It is unlikely that
the mill began much earlier than that year, as the first reference to it in the Rate Assessments of Madron Parish[2] occurs
in 1817-18. Between then and 1829, it was occupied in turn
by the following paper-makers :—James Vivian and Hugh
Mason Moyle, Henry Cock and Richard Nicholas ; it was
unoccupied 1829-30, then revived by John Warren, followed
by John Boase and Henry Lugall ; again unoccupied
1836-37, it was taken over by Benjamin Downing in 1838. A
work of 1839[3] reports that the district did not contain any

1. Tarporley First Ride, General Letter Book No. 9.
2. The Records of Madron Parish were searched by kind permission
   of the Vicar, the Rev. H. M. W. Hocking.
3. "A Statistical Account of the Parish of Madron . . . " by
   Richard Edmonds, Junior, 1839.

factory, "with the exception of a small paper manufactory, recently recommenced, in which only six individuals are occasionally employed." The present writer's last reference to it is in the Excise General Order dated 1st December, 1842,[1] when the paper-maker was William Lugg. In the Rate Assessment for 1842-3, it was shown as unoccupied, and it does not appear in the Rate Lists after 1844. The only paper-maker's name which can be added to those given above appears in the Baptisms in the Madron Parish Registers for 1827, Mark Phillips Rowe.

Danescoombe, near Calstock

This paper-mill is advertised for sale in Trewman's "Exeter Flying Post" of 26th September, 1811. Occupied by John Warren, it was equipped with one large vat and was used for the manufacture of brown paper. Coarse paper was being made here in 1825,[2] when the manufacturer was Peter Hill.

In the following Excise Letters,[3] the paper-makers at this mill, No. 266, in the Plymouth Collection, were :— William Nightingale, 1816 ; William Chudley, 1818 (this paper-maker died in 1832, according to "The Devonshire Chronicle" of 8th July of that year) ; John Vincent, 1827 and 1832 ; by 1841 the mill had left off work, and the Calstock Tithe Map (1839) shows the landowners, John Michael and William Williams, as the occupiers. It appears to have been revived by George Samuel Lee and Edward Cox, under whose names it appears in Excise Letters of 1847 and 1848, manufacturing paper, millboard and pasteboard.

Only one entry of a paper-maker here appears in the Calstock Parish Registers[4]:—James Haines, of Danescoombe,

---

1. Excise General Orders, (Printed), IV.
2. "Alfred." 19th April, 1825.
3. Tarporley First Ride, General Letter Book No. 9, General Letter dated 16th June. 1818 ; ibid, No. 13, 2nd May, 1827 ; ibid, No. 15, 28th November, 1832 ; ibid, No. 17. 30th November, 1841 ; ibid. No. 19. 13th May, 1847 and 29th June, 1848.
4. Searched by kind permission of the Vicar, the Rev. A. H. W. Harlow.

in the Baptisms for 1849. In 1851, another entry concerning the same man refers to Netstakes, which is in another part of the parish, and suggests that he was then employed at Gunnislake.

Tamar Mill, Gunnislake

Mill No. 269 appears as a "new entry" in the Excise List of 1851.[1] This was Tamar Mill, in the Plymouth Collection, manufacturing millboard, paper and pasteboard, with George Samuel Lee in occupation. Slater's "Royal National and Commercial Directory and Topography" for 1852-3 refers to the Tamar Millboard Co. (section on Cornwall, p.9) and to G. S. Lee & Co., Millboard Manufacturers, Tamar Mill (section on Devonshire, p.135). These are the writer's last references, and the mill appears to have been short-lived.

---

1. Excise General Orders, (Printed), V, **General Order dated 20th May**, 1851.

XVI

THE HISTORICAL GEOGRAPHY OF THE PAPER-MAKING INDUSTRY IN DEVON, 1684—1950

ALMOST two hundred years separate the earliest references to a paper-mill in England (at Hertford in 1495) from those concerning the first of the fifty-three which have existed in Devon at one time or another. During that period paper-mills had been established at various places in England, including Bemerton in Wiltshire and Wookey Hole in Somerset. It is unlikely that even small quantities of paper reached Devon by land from these, the nearest paper-mills; until the industry was firmly established in the county the main supply must have come from continental countries, especially France,[1] and by coastwise vessels, e.g. from Southampton.[2]

Among the paper-mills which by the early eighteenth century were already scattered over England from Kent to Cumberland and from Durham to Devon were a few which had been established or taken over by French paper-makers who had sought refuge in Britain. French Protestants were arriving in Plymouth by 1681[3] and the earliest reference yet found to paper-mills in Devon concerns two set up by 1684 in or near Plymouth by and in the possession of Dennis Manes[4] who had been forced to leave France "because of his religion." The exact sites of his mills are not known and no link has yet been established between them and those paper-mills which were at work in the Plymouth area in the eighteenth century, although such is possible. In any case, Manes's activities here must have been short-lived as in the 1690's his name appears in documents relating to the Scots White Writing Paper Company at mills near Edinburgh.[5]

Knowledge of the craft of paper-making may have spread from Plymouth (where the Millbay paper-mill had been established by 1710) to other parts of the South-West, for

---

[1] Examples of imports via Plymouth are recorded in *Cal. S. P. Dom. Ch. II*, cLxxix, 165, and cci, 51.

[2] E.g. shipments 1697—1700 (*Customs Correspondence, London and Exeter*, 1698/9—1701/2).

[3] *London Gazette*, 8th September, 1681.

[4] Rhys Jenkins, *Paper Making in Devon, Devon and Cornwall Notes and Queries*, VIII, 1914—15, pp. 119—121.

[5] Robert Waterston, *Early Papermaking near Edinburgh, Book of the Old Edinburgh Club*, XXV, 1946.

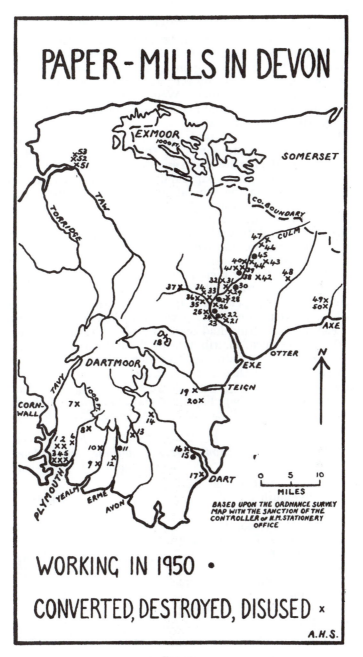

FIG. I.

there was a paper-mill at Treganhawke near Millbrook in Cornwall as early as 1727.[1] It is also possible that paper-making in the Exeter region had already started in the seventeenth century, for by 1703 and 1704 paper-mills existed at Uffculme and Countess Weir respectively. By 1710, therefore, some paper could be supplied locally to at least the two greatest towns in Devon.

A paper-mill at Barnstaple is recorded in 1746 and paper-makers at Colyton are named in the parish registers of the 1760's. Thus the northwestern and eastern parts of the county had at least one early paper-mill each. The chief areas in Devon to share in the general expansion of the industry in the second half of the eighteenth century were, however, Plymouth (two more mills in the town and one each near Horrabridge and Shaugh Prior), the southern and eastern fringes of Dartmoor and parts of South Devon (South Brent, Buckfastleigh, Dartmouth, Newton Abbot and Moretonhampstead) and the Exeter region ; within the area from Countess Weir to Cullompton and from Broadclyst to Newton St. Cyres, twelve paper-mills appeared during this period. Although seven out of all those which worked in Devon during the eighteenth century had ceased by 1800, the broad pattern of the geographical distribution of the industry in the nineteenth century had already been determined. Twenty-four new paper-mills in Devon appear in local and national records between 1800 and 1835 and all were in the regions already mentioned (see the map, Fig. 1). As is seen from the following list, no new paper-mill has been added since 1834.

No. of Mill on Map	Location	M if paper-making machine was installed	First and last known dates as paper-mills
1. Manes's Mill in or near Plymouth		—	c. 1684
2. Ditto.		—	do.
3. Millbay, Plymouth		—	1710—1811
4. Stonehouse Lane, Plymouth		—	1777—1791
5. Row of Trees, Plymouth..		—	1791—1795
6. Bircham		—	1814—1846
7. Phoenix Mill near Horrabridge		—	1794—1795
8. Paper-mill near Shaugh Prior		—	1756—1832
9. Yealm Bridge		—	1804—1835

[1] Details of the earliest known references concerning almost all the paper-mills in the two counties are given by A. H. Shorter, *Paper-mills in Devon and Cornwall* (two articles), *Devon and Cornwall Notes and Queries*, XXIII, 1948.

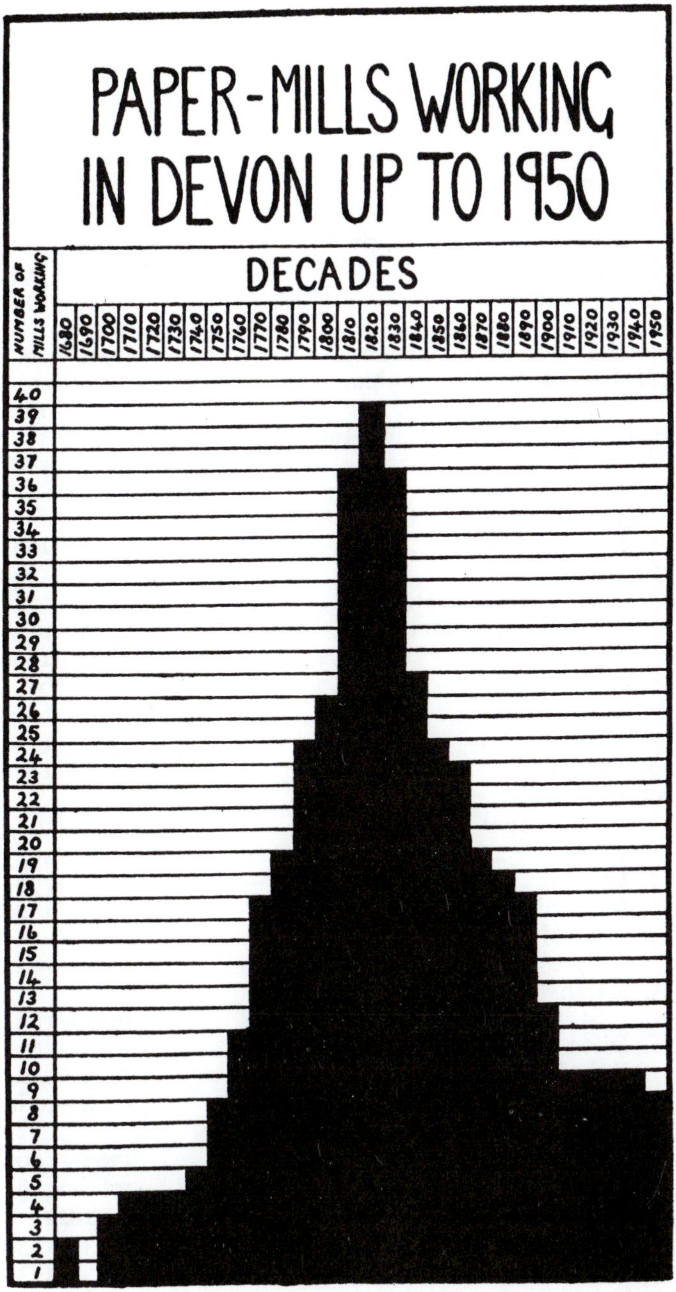

FIG. 2.

No. of Mill on Map	Location	M if paper-making machine was installed	First and last known dates as paper-mills
10. Lee Mill Bridge		M	1833—1908
11. Stowford Mill, Ivybridge		M	1808—today
12. Lower Mill, Ivybridge		M	1816—1906
13. South Brent		—	1766—1832
14. Kilbury or Dart Mill, Buckfastleigh		M	1785—1940
15. Tuckenhay		—	1829—today
16. Tuckenhay		—	1832—1860
17. Warfleet, near Dartmouth		—	1790—1830
18. Town Mills, Moretonhampstead		—	1776—1826
19. Bradley Mill, near Newton Abbot		—	1790—1848
20. Aller Mill, near Abbotskerswell		—	1809—1866
21. Countess Weir		M	1704—1884
22. Countess Weir		—	1778—1829
23. Trew's Weir, Exeter		M	1834—today
24. Head Weir, Exeter		M	1798—today
25. Exwick		M	1806—1860
26. Stoke Canon		—	1816
27. Stoke Canon		M	1806—today
28. Huxham		—	1770—1860
29. Huxham		M	1774—1890
30. Etherleigh Bridge Mill (Silverton)		M	1783—today
31. Rewe		—	1790—1837
32. Upexe		—	1771—1784
33. Oakford		—	1816—1826
34. Rape Mill, near Newton St. Cyres		—	1819—1821
35. Marsh Mills, near Newton St. Cyres		—	1758—1834
36. Ditto		—	1823—1832
37. Four Mills, Crediton		—	1813—1821
38. Hele		M	1762—today
39. Kensham Mill, near Bradninch		M	1767—1890
40. Ditto.		M	1767—1891
41. Ditto.		—	1821
42. Langford		—	1813—1852
43. Kentisbeare		—	1813—1831
44. Cullompton		—	1816—1860
45. Longmoor or Higher King's Mill, Cullompton		M	1757—today

No. of Mill on Map	Location	M if paper-making machine was installed	First and last known dates as paper-mills
46. Selgar's Mill near Uffculme		—	1703—1754
47. Wood's Mill, Uffculme	..	—	1707—1753
48. Honiton	.. .. ..	—	1813—1836
49. Umborne Mill, Colyton	..	M	1768—1890
50. Coles Mill near Colyton	..	—	1828—1841
51. Barnstaple	.. ..	—	1746—1790
52. Playford Mill near Barnstaple	.. .. ..	M	1816—1906
53. Blatchford Mill near Barnstaple	.. .. ..	M	1823—1897

FACTORS INFLUENCING THE EARLY INDUSTRY

The factors affecting the rise and geographical distribution of the paper industry in Devon up to about the 1830's must now be examined. It must be borne in mind that there was a very general expansion of paper-making in England during the period under review ; this expansion was due to various causes which included the greatly increased demand for paper arising from the development of printing, trade and industry, and the cessation or interruption of supplies of paper during the wars with France, hitherto the great source of many kinds of paper, particularly white sorts.

Firstly, there was a relatively large population in Devon, especially in the Exeter and Plymouth areas and in east and south Devon, attractive to paper-makers as a source of the requisite raw materials which in those days were mainly linen and cotton rags, old sailcloth, canvas, bagging, rope and other hempen materials. A well-populated region with many harbours and a flourishing trade could offer good supplies of all these. Lists of shipping arrivals given in the Exeter newspapers between 1789 and 1819 and occasionally thereafter show that there were frequent imports via Exmouth of linen and other rags, old junk, hemp and " paper-stuff "; cargoes came from overseas, including Hamburg, Morlaix, Leghorn and Guernsey, and coastwise from Plymouth, Dartmouth, Weymouth, Poole and Portsmouth. Occasional imports of fine white or linen rags into Dartmouth, Plymouth and Barnstaple appear in lists of the same period. The *Exeter Flying Post* between 1782 and 1812 also contains many notices of periodical sales of old stores at the Hamoaze Dockyard and elsewhere in Plymouth ; these included paper-stuff, rags, rope, hammocks and canvas, all of which would be of use to paper-makers.

Secondly, there was the market for paper offered by the large population, its industries and trade. Some of the Devon mills, e.g. Countess Weir, Stowford and Hele Mills, produced white writing and printing papers in the eighteenth and/or early nineteenth century, but probably the majority made mainly common or shop papers for local sale, including wrapping papers and boards for the woollen trade. In 1776, the Moretonhampstead mill was equipped with ten hammers to make pasteboard, which was in demand for packing bales of serge (two pasteboards to every " long ell "). In reverse, the woollen trade would be able to supply felts needed by the paper-makers.

Information about the export trade in paper from Devon is less plentiful, but as the industry developed this trade must have been a third favourable factor. The newspapers already mentioned contain references to shipments of paper from Exmouth to London ; as late as 1834 paper was regarded as one of Exeter's principal exports.

Fourthly, an essential requirement of the paper-makers—abundant and reliable supplies of clean water (especially spring water) for the process of manufacture and of river water for power—was fulfilled in Devon ; on this account alone one writer in 1811[1] expected to find more paper-mills in the county. The absence of paper-mills from the north and west of Devon (except Barnstaple) suggests the possibility that water from the clay soils of the Culm Measures, which occupy so much of that area, was considered by the paper-makers as inferior to that from the Culm and lower Exe valleys and the powerful streams draining south off Dartmoor. In general, however, it appears that the early start of the paper-making centres in east and south Devon and the overall advantages of those regions for industry and trade (including comparative accessibility) were factors at least as strong as any great superiority in quality or quantity of water as compared with other parts of the county. When we examine the detailed location of certain paper-mills within these two areas, we may partly explain their situation in rather remote valleys[2] or *outside* towns and villages by the paper-makers' search for pure water. Spring water was used for making the paper at Countess Weir, where the mills were situated close to tidal river water. Sometimes the paper-makers found that there was too much water, as at Uffculme in 1753, when both paper-mills were severely damaged by floods.

[1] " Paper mills are to be found occasionally in Devon, though not so generally as might be expected from the purity of the water, which is so grand a requisite in this elegant manufacture."—*Remarks on the Present State of the County of Devon, Introductory to the New Edition of Risdon's Survey*, 1811.

[2] E.g. Shaugh mill, " on a constant stream of beautiful clear spring water, that is never flooded, and at the distance only of one mile from the spring head."—*Reading Mercury and Oxford Gazette*, 31st January, 1791.

At least two other factors may reasonably be added to the above. One was (fifthly) the availability (during the period of the geographical expansion of the paper-making industry) of water-driven fulling- or tucking-mills which were going out of work with the decline of the Devon woollen industry towards the end of the eighteenth and in the early nineteenth century. Kensham, Rewe and Head Weir Mills are examples of such conversion. In the early nineteenth century advertisements were still (unsuccessfully) attempting to attract paper-makers to sites until lately used either as woollen factories, e.g. Ashburton, and Taviton Mills, Tavistock, or as grist mills, e.g. Earle's Mill, Ridgeway.

There is little direct evidence as to the sixth factor—relatively cheap labour—but as late as 1837 the journeymen paper-makers in Devon complained that they were paid much less than paper-makers up country (a point disputed by the mill-owners). Local unskilled labour was probably plentiful, but many of the operators of the paper-mills must have introduced skilled workmen from other parts of England and/or have trained members of their families and parish apprentices. Thus in the eighteenth century paper-makers from centres of the industry in Lancashire and Hertfordshire are named in the parish registers of Newton St. Cyres. In the early nineteenth century appear paper-makers from Berkshire (Yealmpton Parish Registers), Norfolk and Somerset (Crediton). Parish apprentices were trained, e.g. at Oakford mill, from the age of nine. As the industry spread through the Westcountry, members of paper-making families originally centred on one mill went off to others. For example, members of the Bedford Pim family of paper-makers who seem to have first taken up the craft in the Exeter area towards the end of the eighteenth century were by 1830 operating or employed in paper-mills in north and south Devon, Cornwall, Dorset and Guernsey.

Among other considerations sometimes advanced as to the development and distribution of the paper-making industry, we must not take too seriously the alleged advantage of the early Devon paper-makers in being able easily to evade the Excise Duty: "in the county of Devon if anywhere the duty is evaded, it is from the facilities they have of disposing of their paper into the neighbourhood, they send it into Cornwall and the different parts of the country round."[1]

On turning to the later story of the industry in Devon, it must be remembered that many of the early mills with which we have been dealing so far were quite small, being worked by one or two paper-makers with perhaps their families, parish

[1] *House of Commons Papers*, 1824, XI, Appendix 36, fol. 145. It should be noted that the evidence quoted is that of a paper-maker in Ireland !

apprentices and labourers. Sometimes, as at Oakford and Kentisbeare, the occupier was a part-time paper-maker, devoting the rest of his work to farming or corn-milling. Almost all the Devon paper-mills started as " hand " or " vat " mills with a small number of vats each. In 1778 one of the Countess Weir mills had two vats, the other one ; in 1793, 1808 and 1827 the Shaugh, Lower Kensham and Marsh Mills had two, three and two vats respectively. One of the largest mills of that time was Head Weir, Exeter, which in 1814 was said to be capable of working eight vats.

THE GEOGRAPHICAL CONTRACTION OF THE INDUSTRY

As is shewn in the diagram[1] (Fig. 2) the peak figure of 39 paper-mills working in the 1820's quickly fell in the 1830's and 1840's. Much of this was due to the effective competition of mills equipped with paper-making machines and the process of consolidation of production into fewer and bigger units. The machine, whereby paper is made in continuous lengths as opposed to the single sheets produced by the hand method, was invented at the beginning of the nineteenth century. Because of their cost and the time taken in their construction, machines at first came but slowly into use, so that in many parts of England up to about 1826 two major developments in the industry were proceeding at the same time : (a) a great but temporary increase in the number of paper-mills, (b) a gradual increase in the use of paper-making machinery.[2]

Between 1840 and 1890 at least five major factors were working against the survival of paper-mills in many predominantly rural areas in this country and their effects can be clearly seen in the case of Devon : (a) the spread of railways which, while benefiting some mills close to main lines, for long had a generally adverse effect upon the more remote or poorly-equipped mills ; (b) changes in the sources and nature of the raw materials used in the paper industry ; (c) changes in the type of power used, from waterpower to steam and,

[1] Certain reservations should be borne in mind when studying this diagram. One is that it has proved possible to record the paper-mills only by the decades in which there is evidence concerning them or the paper-makers who worked them ; another (which also applies to the list of paper-mills given above) is that there must have been periods *within* these decades when some mills were idle ;, and a third is that for the period before the Excise Letters begin (i.e. up to 1816) much of the evidence is " secondary," e.g. paper-makers named in the Parish Records, newspaper references to the mills or paper-makers.

[2] Among the first Devon mills to install machines were Head Weir (which had a 48-in. machine by 1829), Exwick (by 1829) and Ivybridge (a 48-in. machine in 1837). Devon never became very important in the engineering branches of the paper trade, but for some years last century an Exeter firm made paper " engines and machines."

later, electricity ; (d) the general change in the regional balance of industry in this country ; (e) foreign as well as home competition. The effect of (a) was obvious in the case of mills far from main railway lines, many of which could no longer hope to compete ; ·it can be seen even in the case of the Countess Weir Mills—after their closure about 1884 it was stated in 1889 that the great cost of cartage was the serious drawback in meeting competition. Had the original proposal of 1825 been carried through, whereby an Exeter—Exmouth railway would have passed close by, these mills might have survived. Under (b) must be noted the relative decline of local rag materials with the great increase in the use of esparto grass from the 1860's onwards and wood pulps from the 1880's. Of the new materials which were being used, the South-West could offer only china clay which, although of great importance to the paper industry, is not a primary material in the same sense as is a fibrous plant, pulp or rag. From the commercial point of view, the Westcountry was not so well placed as the great industrial regions for the importation of grasses and pulps, although for some Devon and Somerset mills Watchet is important in this connection.

Under (c) the improvements effected by the introduction of steam power meant that mills with easy access to coal could compete on better terms than many in Devon and Cornwall, far from coalfields. Under (d) we may contrast the story of the closure of many mills, both hand and machine, in Devon and several other counties, with the increased importance of Lancashire and Kent in the paper industry. As regards (e), a contemporary view of the relative decline in Devon was that " Paper mills have been closed and hundreds of hands thrown out of work because the manufacturers have been beaten out of the market by unfair competition " (home and foreign).[1]

Depressing as these trends must have been to the papermakers, the fact is that the expansion of some of the surviving mills partly compensated, in terms of numbers employed in the industry in the county as a whole, for the disappearance of so many. The Census Returns show that in the nineteenth century the total numbers employed in paper-making in Devon increased from 334 in 1841 to a peak of 815 in 1861 ; from then until 1901 the figure varied between about 750 and 790. In 1931 the total was 617. Part of the drop as between the 1890's and 1930's was due to the disappearance of more paper-mills from the active list, indicated on the diagram (Fig. 2) by the steep fall in the early part of that period. Fire put an end to some, e.g. Kensham and Lee Mills, but most of

[1] *Exeter Flying Post*, 31st December, 1884, and *The Exeter Evening Post*, 7th January, 1888.

these casualties were small or medium-sized mills, producing sugar, grocery or brown papers on a machine of the order of 50 or 60 inches in width ; these could not compete with better placed mills making cheap brown and other wrapping papers from imported pulps or waste paper in bulk. The last paper-mill to close was that at Buckfastleigh (1940), which was relatively isolated, being situated on a branch railway in south Devon. Very probably other mills in Devon would have closed but for the enterprise shown by firms who were determined to carry on through economic storms and by those who came into the region and gave new life to the industry.

Of the eight survivors today only one (Tuckenhay) is a vat mill, working eight vats. The other mills range from one machine, as at Trew's Weir, to four (Silverton). A remarkable feature is the wide variety of papers produced, not only in total, but in individual mills. The paper trade is to be congratulated not only on its success in keeping these mills going but also on the way in which it has adapted them to changing circumstances.

Principal Sources on Which This Article is Based

Excise General Letters and Orders, Manuscript and Printed, 1816—1852.

Parish Records : Registers, Rate Assessments, Church-wardens' Accounts, Registers and Indentures of Parish Apprentices, Tithe Surveys.

House of Commons Papers.

British Museum, Add. MSS, 15054 (1786).

Paper Mills Directory, 1860, 1866, 1876.

Directory of Paper Makers, from 1885.

The World's Paper Trade Review.

The Paper Maker.

A. Dykes Spicer, *The Paper Trade*, 1907.

The Exeter Evening Post (later *Trewman's Exeter Flying Post*), from 1765.

Woolmer's Exeter and Plymouth Gazette, from 1813.

Alfred, Exeter Independent, and *Western Luminary*, 1823—1832.

The Devonshire Chronicle and Exeter News, from 1831.

London Gazette, from 1665.

Gentleman's Magazine, from 1731.

Census of England and Wales, from 1801.

Universal British Directory of Trade and Commerce, 1791.

Pigot's (later Slater's), Robson's, White's, Billing's and Harrod's *Directories*, from 1822.

Post Office Directories, from 1856.

S. Lewis, *A Topographical Dictionary of England*, 1840.

216

C. E. de Rance, *The Water Supply of England and Wales*, 1882.
W. A. Churchill, *Watermarks in Paper in the Seventeenth and Eighteenth Centuries*, 1935.

ACKNOWLEDGMENTS

The writer wishes to express his best thanks to all who have so kindly helped him in this study, particularly the following : The Devon and Cornwall Record Society for granting him access to their collection of Parish Records, printed and manuscript ; the incumbents of many Devon parishes ; the staffs of public reference libraries in the West country ; the owners or occupiers of past and present paper-mills ; Sir Arthur C. Reed, Mr. C. W. Bracken, Mr. W. A. Gay, Mr. Rhys Jenkins and Mr. John Pitts. He is also specially indebted to the Board of Commissioners of H.M. Customs and Excise for permission to read in their Library and to make full extracts from their records, and to the Council of the University College of the South West of England, Exeter, for a grant in aid of the research.

XVII

Paper-Mills in Devon and Cornwall.—Certain information concerning some of the early paper-mills in the two counties has been gathered since the printing of the writer's previous papers on this subject (*D. & C. N. & Q.*, XXIII; *Report of the Royal Cornwall Polytechnic Society*, 1948; and *Trans. Devon. Assoc.*, LXXXII).

CORNWALL.

Paper-making was being carried on at PONSANOOTH by 1815. In that year (*London Gazette*, 21st January) the partnership between Richard Rowe, John Dunstan and James Jenkins, paper manufacturers at Ponsanooth and Penryn under the name of Rowe and Company, was dissolved.

That there were already two paper-mills at PENRYN by 1805–7 is suggested by references to two paper-makers there, Thomas Pearce and William Tucker, in *Holden's Triennial Directory*, 2, p. 247.

The suggestion that there were two paper-mills near Truro in the eighteenth century is supported by the mention of COOK'S MILL and COOSBEAN MILL (the former unidentified, but both apparently in the parish of Kenwyn) where paper-making was carried on by the firm of Odgers and Wills; the partnership of William Allen, Richard Odgers and Edmund Wills, paper-makers there, was dissolved in 1791 (*London Gazette*, 16th July).

DEVON

ALLER paper-mills were already at work by 1797 (*London Gazette*, 28th February) when the partnership there between Joseph Turner and Francis Fincher, paper-makers, was dissolved. In 1816, Francis Fincher was the occupier of one of the Ivybridge paper-mills.

Paper-making had started at either CREDITON or NEWTON ST. CYRES by 1750, for in that year Thomas Dewdney was apprenticed to John Godfrey of Crediton, paper-maker (*The Apprentices of Great Britain, 1710–1762*, typescript; extracted from the Inland Revenue Books at the Public Record Office for the Society of Genealogists, 1921–28, Book 51, Fol. 24). Thomas Dewdney of Newton St. Cyres, paper-maker, and Ann Godfrey of the same, widow, were married in 1761 (*Exeter Marriage Licences*, Pt. II, Devon and Cornwall Record Society).

UPEXE paper-mill must have been working in the first half of the eighteenth century. In 1744, Chris(topher ?) Browne was apprenticed to Charles Warren of "Epex", Devon, paper-maker (*The Apprentices of Great Britain . . .*, Book 50, Fol. 235).

An important and interesting item concerns one of the HUXHAM paper-mills. An advertisement in *The Post Man*, 16th May, 1706, states that "a compleat new White Paper Mill" was to be sold. As this is the earliest newspaper reference to a Devonshire paper-mill yet found, and as the description is so detailed as to give not only a clear idea of the equipment of a one-vat paper-mill of that time, but also the claims of the owner as to the advantages of the situation for the paper-making industry, it may be of interest if a summary is given here. Joseph Anthony, Merchant in Exeter, after his apprenticeship with a Merchant, had lived eleven years in Holland as a Factor and now intended to return to Amsterdam where he was to reside again "for the better bringing up his two sons to business and settling them in it". He had therefore resolved to sell his most profitable white paper-mill (built for him about 2½ years earlier by the old Mr. G. Knight) now that it was brought to perfection. The equipment included 1 vat, 2 presses, 1 furnace, 1 large cistern, 3 chests, 48 trebles with lines, 1 great water-wheel, 1 cog-wheel, 1 5-hammer mortar, 4 4-hammer mortars, 1 pit mortar, 9 pairs of moulds with 2 deckels each, 7 pairs with 3 different deckels ; also felts, basins and strainers. The paper-mill was situated in the village of Huxham, four miles north of Exeter "betwixt the great Roads of Tiverton and Taunton". There was stated to be "no other White Paper Mill within 100 miles of the same".

Mr. Anthony had "had a constant cheap supply of Linnen Rags, most proper for his occasion, more than enough, and quick Vent at good prices ready money" for all the paper he could make. He was prepared, if desired, to "give the Purchaser the best Information, Insight and Assistance in all things relating to that Mystery".

Information concerning the paper-mill near HONITON in the eighteenth century has also been found. An advertisement in *Felix Farley's Bristol Journal*, 3rd December, 1774, states that "a large Room of Water-Grist Mills, and another large Room of Paper Mills" were to be sold, for the remainder of a term of 99 years. The mills were well situated for employment and trade, being within a mile of the town of Honiton.

Paper-making appears to have started at CULLOMPTON (probably at Higher King's Mill) by 1729, for in that year the name of Edward Carill of Cullompton, paper-maker, is recorded in *Marriage Allegations for Devon and Cornwall*.

XVIII

THE PROVENANCE OF WRITING PAPER USED IN DEVON IN THE LATE EIGHTEENTH CENTURY

One of the many aspects of the history of paper-making by hand in England which offers an interesting field for local study is the question as to how far writing-papers made in any given region of this country were in fact used within that region. It appears that this aspect of the subject has not yet been treated systematically; for example, very little has hitherto been known about the extent to which locally-made paper was used in Devon in the eighteenth century. A recent trial investigation has thrown a little light on the matter, as is shown in the map accompanying this article. No doubt more intensive research along similar lines and using a variety of source materials could be profitably carried out in many other parts of England.

As a fair sample of a mass of writing-papers which must have been used locally, the sheets on which the Land Tax Assessments for Devonshire parishes were written from 1780 on were studied; a great number of these are in the Devon County Record Office at Exeter. Not all the parishes are represented in the collection of papers for any given year, and not all the available sheets are watermarked. But in a great many cases it proved possible to identify the mills where the papers were made by a study of the water-marks and countermarks in the sheets. A study of the papers used for the Assessments for the year 1780, for example, yielded the following results: the papers used in 72 parishes were made at the Countess Weir Mills near Exeter and those in 81 parishes at Aller Mill near Newton Abbot, South Devon. Papers produced at Wookey Hole Mill near Wells, Somerset, were used in 77 Devonshire parishes, those from Post-

THE PROVENANCE OF WRITING PAPER USED IN DEVON

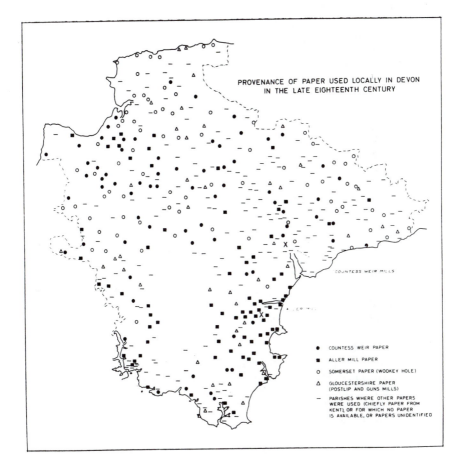

PROVENANCE OF PAPER USED LOCALLY IN DEVON
IN THE LATE EIGHTEENTH CENTURY

COUNTESS WEIR MILLS

● COUNTESS WEIR PAPER

■ ALLER MILL PAPER

O SOMERSET PAPER (WOOKEY HOLE)

Δ GLOUCESTERSHIRE PAPER
(POSTLIP AND GUNS MILLS)

— PARISHES WHERE OTHER PAPERS
WERE USED (CHIEFLY PAPER FROM
KENT), OR FOR WHICH NO PAPER
IS AVAILABLE, OR PAPERS UNIDENTIFIED

lip Mills, Winchcombe, Gloucestershire, in 23 parishes, and those from Guns Mills in the Forest of Dean, Gloucestershire, in 19. Papers made in Kentish mills were found in 22 cases. The sheets for 99 parishes could not be identified; in many cases either the names or initials of the paper makers do not appear on the sheets or parts of sheets which were used, or only a countermark or part of a mark appears.

In the following list, the name of the paper maker is given in respect of whom watermarks or counter-marks in papers made at the West-Country mills have been identified in the Assessment sheets. Also given are items of documentary evidence by means of which the identification of the papers and mills is proved or supported. Examples of the watermarks and counter-marks as well as a summary of the evidence from documents are given in A.H. Shorter, *Paper Mills and Paper Makers in England*, 1495-1800, published by The Paper Publications Society, Hilversum, 1957.

Countess Weir Mills
Paper maker identified in watermarks or countermarks: T. BOND

In 1771 Thomas Bond, paper maker, insured the Higher and Lower Mills at Countess Weir, in his tenure. (*Sun Fire Insurance Policy* 301839, Sept. 17, 1771). In 1781 two paper mills at Countess Weir in the possession of Thomas Bond were for sale. (*Trewman's Exeter Flying Post*, Jan. 12, 1781).

Aller Mill
Paper makers: FINCHER & TURNER

In 1779 Francis Fincher, paper maker, insured the utensils and stock at Aller Mill. (*Sun Fire Insurance Policy* 420188, Oct. 27, 1779). In 1797 the partner-ship between Francis Fincher and Joseph Turner, paper makers at Aller Mill, was dissolved. (*London Gazette*, Feb. 28, 1797).

Wookey Hole Mill
Paper makers: BAND & SON (Edward & John Band)

In 1743 Edward Band, paper maker, insured the millhouse at Wookey Hole Mill. (*Sun Fire Insurance Policy* 93109, Nov. 8, 1743). In 1795 John Band, paper maker, insured the millhouse. (*Sun Fire Insurance Policy* 640959, May 15, 1795).

THE PROVENANCE OF WRITING PAPER USED IN DEVON

Postlip Mills
Paper makers: DURHAM & CO.
In 1771 William Durham, paper maker, insured the Upper, Middle and Lower paper mills at Postlip. (*Sun Fire Insurance Policy* 293639, Jan. 23, 1771). In 1795 William Durham, junior, paper manufacturer, insured the mills. (*Sun Fire Insurance Policy* 649640, Dec. 30, 1795).

Guns Mills
Paper maker: JOSEPH LLOYD
In 1766 an apprentice eloped from Joseph Lloyd, paper maker at Guns Mills. (*Gloucester Journal*, Sept. 1, 1766). In 1803 Joseph Lloyd was the proprietor of Guns Paper Mills. (*Notes at Springfield Mill*, Kent, 1803.)

On the accompanying map symbols representing papers made at the West-Country mills mentioned above have been placed within the Devonshire parishes (one symbol for each parish). The map shows that such papers were widely used in Devon for the purpose of recording the assessments in 1780. Countess Weir paper was well distributed (presumably from Exeter) as far as the west of Devon. Aller Mill paper had a quite different distribution, for it was used predominantly in south Devon, especially in parishes near the actual source of the paper. (The mill was at Abbotskerswell, between Newton Abbot and Torquay.) Wookey Hole paper was well represented in north Devon and in east Devon, and was probably distributed within those areas from Barnstaple and Taunton respectively. The use of Gloucestershire papers appears to have been more dispersed; the explanation may be that as these papers came from a greater distance they were probably part of several small consignments taken by sea from Bristol or a harbour near the River Severn to various ports in north and south Devon, and were distributed from there.

XIX

PAPER-MAKING IN SOUTH-WEST ENGLAND

At various times during the 17th and 18th centuries the papermaking industry in England was stimulated by the cutting off of supplies of paper from Continental countries as a result of wartime conditions. The Excise duties imposed during the 18th century, though burdensome enough for the English papermakers, were not as heavy on the home product as on imported paper. Until the use of the papermaking machine began to spread in the early 19th century, the English industry responded to the increase in demand mainly by a multiplication of the number of vat mills, which were still almost entirely water-driven.

Devon's first mill

Devon's first paper mill was established at Countess Wear about the year 1638, and 30 years later another mill was at work at Exwick. Both these mills were near Exeter, the county town and the great centre of the woollen trade at that time. French Protestant refugees were arriving in Plymouth by 1681, and two paper mills had been set up there by 1684. They were in the possession of Dennis Manes, who appears to have made good-quality white paper. The exact sites of his mills are not known, and no link has yet been established between them and any other paper mill in south-west England. Manes's activities at Plymouth were probably very short-lived, for in the 1690s his name appears in documents relating to the Scots White Writing Paper Company at mills near Edinburgh.

By 1710 four more mills were started in Devon — one at Plymouth, and three in the Culm valley. But it was not until 1716 that papermaking began in Cornwall, at a mill just outside Truro. By 1727 the county had another mill, this time in the south-east corner, at Treganhawke, near Plymouth. Throughout the 18th century, and especially in the second half, there was a great overall increase in the number of paper mills in south-west England. Almost without exception, the mills that dropped out during this period did so from purely local causes. Two mills at Uffculme were so severely damaged by floods that they were not re-started as paper mills. The Treganhawke mill in Cornwall had to close following complaints by officers of the Royal Navy that rags and filth got into the water-pipes connected with His Majesty's Brewhouse, which was situated near the mill.

The peak in the number of paper mills at work in south-west England was reached in the 1820s, and almost all the mills which had been active up to that time are known to have been converted from the grinding of corn or the fulling of cloth. Although some, particularly in the Exeter district, produced good-quality writing and printing paper over a long period, and although there were considerable shipments of paper out of the region, especially from Exeter, it is probable that until the later part of the 19th century much of the output consisted of common wrapping or shop papers for local sale. While the woollen industry and trade was still of importance in Devon — down to the early 19th century — some mills specialised in the production of glazed paper for use in the hot-pressing of cloth ; and others were equipped with hammers to make pasteboard, which was in demand for packing bales of serge.

No new mills after 1830

Except for a steam-driven factory at Penryn (1844–1898) and a board mill near Calstock (1851–1876), no paper mill was founded in south-west England after the 1830s. Of the 52 mills that have existed at any time in Devon, and the 15 in Cornwall, all but the two near Barnstaple have been situated south of a NE-SW axial line through the region. The marked concentration of paper mills in the trading focus of the lower Exe valley and its tributaries, especially the Culm, contrasts with the complete absence of papermaking from the remote and thinly peopled tracts of mid and west Devon, and north Cornwall. The southern areas of both Devon and Cornwall were attractive to papermakers because they were comparatively well populated, and they had numerous streams of regular flow which could be harnessed for power. Save in the mining and china-clay quarrying districts of Cornwall, there were abundant supplies of clean water for use in the preparation of materials and the manufacture of paper. It is possible

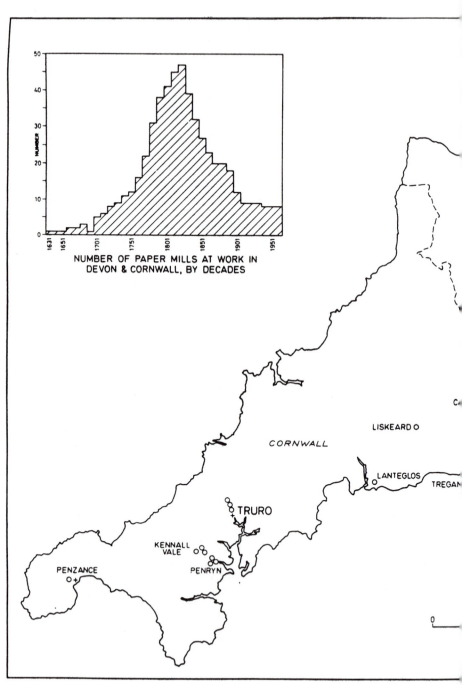

NUMBER OF PAPER MILLS AT WORK IN
DEVON & CORNWALL, BY DECADES

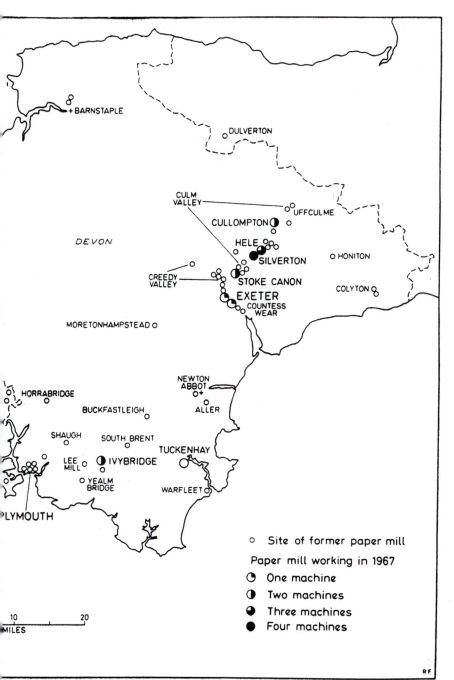

that one reason for the absence of paper mills from a large tract of mid and west Devon is that the clay subsoils of the Culm Measures which occupy much of the area were regarded as inferior by the papermakers. These clays tend to get waterlogged in wet weather, yet they dry out quickly under sunny, windy conditions; consequently the water supply is not so reliable as that of east and south Devon.

Undoubtedly, however, the southern half of Devon and Cornwall was much more attractive for reasons of trade. With a few exceptions such as Barnstaple in north Devon, the southern areas had the important towns and ports, and they were the principal sources of the papermakers' raw materials — linen and cotton rags for good-quality papers, and disused sacking, canvas, netting and ropes for the poorer sorts. Quantities of material were also brought in. notably via the port of Exeter. Lists of cargoes during the second half of the 18th century and the early part of the 19th show that already there were frequent shipments of rags, ropes and canvas. The imports came chiefly from Brittany and northern France, Italy and west Germany; and there was an appreciable coastwise trade from southern ports in England.

It is sometimes stated that the cost of labour in south-west England was comparatively low, but there is little direct evidence to prove this. As late as 1837, however, the journeyman papermakers in Devon were complaining that they were paid much less than the papermakers up country. This point was always disputed by the mill owners. Local unskilled labour was probably plentiful, but the skilled workmen were either imported into the region or trained as apprentices to the master papermakers. From time to time during the 18th and early 19th centuries — and this point can be proved from entries in the Parish Registers — papermakers came in from other counties where the industry was well established: Lancashire. Hertfordshire, Berkshire, Norfolk and Somerset.

From the 1830s onwards the number of paper mills in the south-west was inexorably reduced, and the geographical contraction of the industry in this region has gone on at varying speeds right down to the present time. Similar trends have occurred in many other English counties, but in some regions — notably north Kent and Lancashire — they have been offset in modern times by the establishment of entirely new, large mills. In Cornwall the industry gradually thinned out until the last mill left in the county — at Kennall Vale, near Penryn — ceased work in 1900. In Devon, however, the papermaking industry has continued and the number of closures in the 20th century has been much less than in the 19th. Since a mill at Buckfastleigh closed in 1940, there have been no other casualties until July of this year, when one of the Exeter mills — Head Weir — ceased work.

The principal causes of the reduction in the number of mills and of the severe contraction of the industry in the 19th century may now be summarised. A primary cause was the increasingly effective competition of mills equipped with papermaking machines and steam engines, and with this went the process of consolidation of production into fewer and bigger units. Because of their cost and the time taken in their construction, machines at first came but slowly into use, so that in many parts of England down to about the late 1820s there was still a considerable increase in the number of paper mills equipped with vats and/or machines, in response to the ever-growing demand for paper. About this time, the first machines were installed in the south-western mills, and at one time or another four of the Cornish mills had one machine each and 18 mills in Devon installed one or more machines.

Between 1840 and 1890 at least five other factors were working against the survival of paper mills in predominantly rural areas such as the south-west: (a) the spread of railways which, while benefiting some mills close to main lines, for long had a generally adverse effect upon the more remote, small and poorly-equipped mills; (b) changes in the sources and nature of the materials used in the paper industry; (c) changes in the type of power used, from water power to steam and, later, electricity; (d) the general change in the regional balance of industry in this country; and (e) foreign as well as home competition. These factors, some of which continued to operate in the 20th century, were instrumental, firstly in almost completing the elimination of the vat mills, and eventually in deleting the remote machine mills.

Devon is fortunate in having seven paper mills at work now, for they give employment to about 1,150 people. Trew's Weir mill at Exeter is the smallest, with one machine; and Tuckenhay, where papermaking by hand was carried on until quite recent years, is now concerned

PAPERMAKING IN SOUTH-WEST ENGLAND

with the production of pulp for other mills. Three mills in the Culm valley — Cullompton (two machines), Silverton (four machines) and Stoke Canon (two) — are owned and worked by a firm which is based in this area, but has other mills in Somerset and Buckinghamshire. Hele (also in the Culm valley) has three machines, and Ivybridge (in south Devon) has two. These mills are owned by firms based outside Devon. There can be little doubt that the survival of papermaking in the county, and its increased importance in recent years, owes much to the enterprise and determination of all these firms.

The foregoing paper was read at the International Paper Historians Congress held at Oxford in September, 1967.

XX

PAPER-MILLS IN DORSET During the last three and a half centuries, the paper-making industry has been tried in many localities in the South-West of England. The number of paper-mills which have worked at one time or another in Dorset, however, does not approach the totals for the neighbouring counties, among which Devon and Somerset have had particularly large numbers ; the former has had fifty-two paper-mills, of which eight are working today. The sole survivor of the Dorset paper-mills is that at Witchampton, and the writer has found references to only three others, which were situated at Wimborne, West Mills and Carey Farm, the last two being near Wareham.

The eighteenth century saw a large increase in the number of paper-mills at work in Britain, and the West Country played a noteworthy part in this expansion. Most of these early mills were quite small, consisting of one or two vats for the production of hand-made paper, and often manned by two or three paper-makers, sometimes with members of their families and parish apprentices. Linen and cotton rags, discarded sailcloth and ropes were among the chief materials used ; where possible, therefore, many paper-makers tried to establish their mills near towns of considerable regional importance which would yield these materials and also provide a market for their papers, many of which were coarse or common types, shop or wrapping papers. Local information as to early materials used in the Dorset mills would be welcomed, but at least it can be said that the Wareham and Wimborne districts, where the paper-mills were set up, would be good centres in this respect, and that the advantage of proximity to Poole and to coastal trade would be considerable.

Abundant and permanent supplies of water were essential to the paper-makers for both power and the manufacturing process. Although the chemical qualities of the water were probably not an over-riding factor in the localization of the industry, cleanliness and purity were very important and, to ensure this as far as possible, many paper-mills were placed outside towns and upstream so as to be above other manufactories ; some were established in rather remote valleys.

At least one of the Dorset paper-mills was set up by paper-makers from South Wiltshire, the nearest of the early paper-making areas to the towns of East Dorset ; westwards, the nearest paper-mill was at Colyton, in East Devon. In Devon and Cornwall, the number of paper-mills at work seems to have increased to a remarkable peak in the eighteen-twenties, but in Dorset all four mills were already at work in the eighteenth

154

century. The disappearance of a large proportion of the West Country paper-mills after the 'twenties, including three in Dorset, was part of a process which occurred in many predominantly rural counties where the industry had been established. An important factor was the advent of the paper-making machine, with which many small manufacturers, especially those in the more remote parts of the country, found it difficult to compete.

The Excise Records contain valuable evidence regarding paper-mills in the first half of the nineteenth century. The writer is indebted to the Board of Commissioners, H. M. Customs and Excise, City Gate House, London, for permission to consult these sources. For many years, paper was subject to Excise duties, and the numbering of all premises where paper was made became statutory by 58 Geo. 3 c.65 (1818). The Excise Commissioners, however, had already published an official list of paper-mills, their numbers and the paper-makers who occupied the mills, in a " General Letter " of 1816. Subsequent General Letters and General Orders contain details of new paper-mills, changes in the paper-makers in occupation of the mills, types of product and so on. These lists are arranged under the Collections, Districts, Divisions and Rides into which the country was divided for the purpose of the Excise Collectors. The Dorset paper-mills are listed under the Dorset Collection.

Carey Mill

This is the only paper-mill in the county for which the writer is at present able to give the approximate year of establishment. Hutchins[1] states that a paper-mill, belonging to South Carey Farm (situated about one and a half miles West of Wareham, on the River Piddle), was erected about 1747, and a lease dated 24th August 1752 refers to the " new-erected paper-mill." This is one of a series of indentures in the possession of the present owner, Mr. Alan Sturdy, to whom the writer is grateful for kind permission to search and to quote from the relevant documents. Leases dated 6th July 1697, 24th August 1752 and 9th April 1811 show that there were two ancient mills, at various times grist, tucking and malt mills, which were worked as one paper-mill from the middle of the eighteenth century. Deeds dated 24th August 1752 and 20th January 1756 refer to the lease of the paper-mill by Nathaniel Bond to Samuel Snelgar and Anthony Berryman of Downton, Wilts., (where paper-mills worked for many years). In 1752 the

---

1. *"The History and Antiquities of the County of Dorset,"* 1774, Vol. I, p.28.

former is described as a paper-maker and the latter as a butcher, but the deed of 1756 refers to both as paper-makers.

A deed of 10th September 1810 refers to the lease of the paper-mill to Joseph Mould, paper-maker, of Bulford, another paper-making place in Wiltshire. From 1801 to 1810 the lease of Carey Mill was held by John Snelgar, paper-maker, who surrendered it by a document dated 18th January 1810 ; this gives the equipment of the mill, including one water-wheel, one engine, two presses, one vat and one chest.

Carey Mill does not appear in the Excise List of 1816,[2] and may have been temporarily out of work. The writer's last reference to it occurs in a list of 13th May 1817,[3] with the following details :—Mill No. 494, George Rossiter, Carey. This man may have come from a famous centre of the industry in Devon, for a paper-maker of the same name at Bradninch is given in *"The Universal British Directory of Trade,"*[4] 1791 ; if so, his occupation of Carey Mill could not have lasted long, for Woolmer's *"Exeter and Plymouth Gazette"* for 18th October 1817 mentions "the late George Rossiter, paper-maker, of Bradninch."

WEST MILLS, WAREHAM

Hutchins[5] states that West Mills (which lie about half a mile West of Wareham, on the River Piddle) belonged to Humphrey Sturt, Esq., and that there was both a paper and a corn mill there when he wrote. For many years, the paper-maker concerned seems to have been Robert Bacon, whose name appears in the Churchwardens' Rate Book of the Parish of Lady St. Mary, Wareham ;[6] in 1753 he was the occupier of West Mills which were rated at 4/6. The Register of Holy Trinity Parish, Wareham, contains the following entry under Marriages for 1761 : Robert Bacon, Parish of St. Mary's, paper-maker. This man is also named in a list of paper-makers of 1786,[7] and in *"The Dorset Poll Book"* for 1807.[8] Other paper-makers appear in the Wareham Parish Registers as follows :—

St. Martin's, Marriages, 1762. Francis Musclewhite.
St. Martin's, Banns, 1772, Ventris Hollaway.
St. Mary's, Banns, 1772, James Twyne.

2. Chester Collection, Ellesmere District, Ellesmere Division, General Letter Book No. 4, General Letter dated 8th October 1816.
3. ibid, General Letter dated 13th May 1817.
4. Vol. 2, p. 353.
5. op. cit., Vol. I, p. 31.
6. The Parish Records of Wareham were searched by kind permission of the Rector, the Rev. D. R. Maddock.
7. British Museum, Additional MSS, 15054, fol. 9.
8. May 1807, p. 15.

By 1816[9] the paper-mill, numbered 73 by the Excise authorities, had passed to Henry Bacon. In 1820[10] it was occupied by John Snelgar, with Henry Bacon remaining the proprietor.[11]. It seems probable that John Snelgar transferred his paper-making from Carey to West Mills nearby. Between 1816 and 1821, references to paper-makers named William Shepherd and William Whitland occur in the Baptisms given in the St. Martin's, Wareham, Parish Registers. The writer's last references to paper-makers at West Mills are in the Exeter newspaper "*Alfred*" of 8th June 1830, where there is mention of George Unwin, paper manufacturer of Wareham ; and the Wareham Churchwardens' Rate Book for 1831, when the mills were rated at 15/–, the occupier being " late Unwin." Some of the paper-makers mentioned in the Wareham Registers may, of course, have worked at Carey or West Mills.

WIMBORNE

I. Taylor's *Map of Dorsetshire*, 1765, shows a paper-mill near Wimborne Minster, just above the confluence of the Rivers Allen and Stour. "*The Universal British Directory of Trade*,"[12] 1791, lists Stephen Burt, paper-maker, Wimborne, whose name also appears in connection with the Witchampton mill in the list of 1786.[13] In 1806, "*The Dorset Poll Book*"[14] states that Stephen Burt had a residence at Witchampton and a freehold in Wimborne.

The Excise General Letters show that this mill, number 71, changed hands as follows between 1816 and 1829, the date of the writer's last reference :—

> 8th October 1816, Joseph Mould (who seems to have transferred from Carey Mill, see above)
> 16th June 1818[15], William Burt and William Potter
> 14th April 1819[16], William Burt
> 11th July 1822[17], Edmund White and John Toop
> 4th November 1825[18], Richard Hubberd
> 13th September 1826, John Bedford Pim
> 20th March 1828, Jeremiah Rose

---

9. Excise General Letter of 8th October 1816 already cited.
10. Northwich Collection, Frodsham District, Tarporley First Ride, General Letter Book No. 11, General Letter of 4th July 1820.
11. Wareham Parish Churchwardens' Rate Book, 1821.
12. Vol. 4, p. 766.
13. Add. MSS., loc. cit.
14. November 1806, p. 60.
15. Tarporley First Ride, General Letters Book No. 9.
16. Tarporley First Ride, General Letters Book, No. 10.
17. Excise General Orders, Printed, Vol. I.
18. Tarporley First Ride, General Letters Book No. 13.

17th February 1829[19], Richard Kingwell.

The last-named may have been the Richard Kingwell who was partner with James Hayes in the paper-mill at Oakford near Exeter between 1816 and 1820, and John Bedford Pim was probably one of the Pim family whose members worked in many paper-mills in Devon and Cornwall between 1790 and 1840.

Pigot's *"Commercial Directory of the Southern Counties"*[20] gives White and Teap, paper manufacturers, at Wimborne.

WITCHAMPTON

Certain details of the Witchampton Paper Mills are given in *"The Times"* for 28th April 1947, wherein it is stated that the business has been for some six generations in the same family. During the latter part of the eighteenth century, Stephen Burt was the paper-maker here, followed by William Burt, whose name appears ·in the Excise General Letters of 8th October 1816 and 28th November 1832[21] as at Mill No. 72, Witchampton. Other paper-makers are named in the Witchampton Parish Registers[22] between 1815 and 1837 :— John Pickford, Joseph Rabetts or Frampton, George Carter, Joseph Drew and Peter Graham.

About 1840[23] this mill afforded employment to twenty persons, and Slater's Directory[24] describes it as " an extensive paper-mill." The number of people now employed is about seventy. Whereas air-dried browns and grocery papers were made in 1885,[25] the Company now manufacture paper and board specialities, including wall papers, box paper, photographic papers and boards, cover paper and boards, blotting paper and similar products.

ACKNOWLEDGMENTS

In addition to acknowledgments in the text above, the writer's thanks are due to Lt. Col. C. D. Drew, D.S.O., O.B.E., F.S.A. (Curator of the Dorset County Museum), the Secretary of Witchampton Paper Mills Ltd., and Miss Ruth Legg of Wimborne, for their kind help.

19. Excise General Orders, Printed, Vol. II.
20. 1823-4, p. 281
21. Northwich Collection, Frodsham District, Tarporley, First Ride, General Letter Book No. 15.
22. Searched by kind permission of the Rector, the Rev. E. M. Cox.
23. S. Lewis, "*A Topographical Dictionary of England*," 1840, Vol. IV., p. 562.
24. "*Royal National and Commercial Directory and Topography*," 1852-3, section on Dorset, p. 44.
25. "*Directory of Paper-makers of the United Kingdom*," 1885, p. 7.

XXI

PAPER AND BOARD MILLS IN SOMERSET   In their pioneer article on *Papermaking in Somerset (Geography,* XV, 1929–30), Professor W. W. Jervis and Mr. S. J. Jones showed that in addition to the paper-mills then working, several others had existed in various parts of the county at one time or another.   The present writer has accumulated evidence about these and other paper-mills, largely from sources similar to those mentioned in his article *Paper-mills in Dorset* in Vol. XXV of this magazine, wherein are sketched the broad trends and factors at work in the history of the paper industry in the West Country.

Papermaking is still, of course, an important industry in Somerset.   The number of mills at work is much smaller than in the first half of the nineteenth century, but the expansion of the survivors from that time until now, and the establishment of a few new mills within the last hundred years have prevented such a large drop in the numbers employed as has occurred in some other western counties.

Nos. employed in papermaking in Somerset (Census Returns)

Year	Males	Females
1841	116	15
1851	130	184
1861	145	151
1871	272	280
1881	376	477
1891	428	356
1901	403	224
1931	339	159

The accompanying map[1] shows a remarkable geographical distribution of paper-mills past and present, with two regions particularly well represented : the flanks and foot of the Mendips, and the valley and tributaries of the Avon. Many of these mills had the great advantage of very clear and pure spring-water and, as is demonstrated by many watermarks, produced writing or letter paper of good or fine quality. The absence of early paper-mills from the Somerset Plain is to be expected, as in general there was neither the natural fall of water nor the purity of water required by the paper-makers. It is less easy to account for the total absence of the industry from Southeast and East Somerset.

The following account is simply a summary of the present writer's information about each mill ; further details of the early phases of the industry in Somerset, particularly from the early seventeenth to the late eighteenth century, would be very welcome.

I am indebted to the Board of Commissioners, H.M. Customs and Excise, City Gate House, London, for permission to consult and to quote from their records. During the period when the Excise duty on paper was in force, the paper-mills at work in North Somerset were in the Bath or Bristol Collections of Excise ; those at Stoke Lane and in the Wookey—Wells district were in the Somerset Collection ; and those in South-West Somerset were in the Wellington or Barnstaple Collections. From time to time the limits of the Collections were adjusted so that any given mill might be found in different Collections in different years. The reason why several mills in North Somerset were given such low Excise Numbers e.g. No. 7, Compton, is simply that in what is apparently the first of the Excise Lists of Paper-mills,[2] they came in the Bath Collection, which was second to Barnstaple alphabetically in the " Country Establishment " (i.e. outside London) of Excise.

1. St. Decuman's, Watchet

Paper-making here seems to have commenced about the middle of the eighteenth century. W. Symonds, *Early Methodism in West Somerset*, c. 1870, states that William Wood was born at the St. Decuman's Paper-mills in 1768, and succeeded his father there in 1804. William Wood, paper-maker, Watchet, is listed in the *Universal British Directory of Trade and Commerce*, 1791, 3, p. 924, and at St. Decuman's Mill (Excise Number 462) in the Excise Letter of 1816.

The mill passed from the Wood family to Messrs. Wansbrough, Peach and Date about 1835. For many years the firm maintained offices in Bristol and Bridgwater in

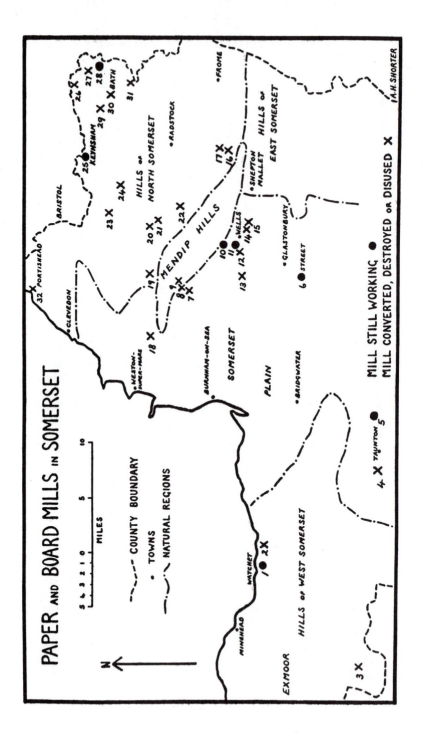

PAPER and BOARD MILLS in SOMERSET

MILES
5 4 3 2 1 0   5   10

– · – · COUNTY BOUNDARY
• TOWNS
– · – · NATURAL REGIONS

MILL STILL WORKING ●
MILL CONVERTED, DESTROYED or DISUSED ✗

I.A.H.SHORTER

N

EXMOOR

HILLS OF WEST SOMERSET

3 ✗

MINEHEAD

WATCHET
1 ● 2 ✗

4 ✗ TAUNTON
5 ●

BURNHAM-ON-SEA

WESTON-
SUPER-MARE

SOMERSET

PLAIN

BRIDGWATER

CLEVEDON

PORTISHEAD
32 ✗

18 ✗

19 ✗
9 ✗
8 ✗✗
7 ✗

BRISTOL

KEYNSHAM
25 ●
29 ✗
30 ✗ BATH
31 ✗
24 ✗ 27 ✗ 28 ●

HILLS OF
NORTH SOMERSET

23 ✗
26 ✗
20 ✗
21 ✗
22 ✗

RADSTOCK

MENDIP HILLS

10 ●
11 ●
13 ✗ 12 ✗
WELLS
14 ✗✗
15

GLASTONBURY

STREET
6 ●

SHEPTON
MALLET
17 ✗
16 ✗

FROME

HILLS OF
EAST SOMERSET

connection with this mill. By 1860[3] the firm had changed to Wansbrough and Strange, and by 1890 to Wansbrough and Worrall. By 1900 it was in the hands of the Wansbrough Paper Co., Ltd., its present owners. It is now a four-machine mill which has been extensively remodelled and re-equipped since the war. *Dir. P.M.* 1948 lists its products as follows :— Industrial and Technical Papers, Base Papers for Plastics, Insulating Papers, M.G. Colours, M.G. and Unglazed Krafts, M.G. Wallpapers and Envelope Papers, and Glazed Casings.

For much detailed information about the Watchet paper-mills I am indebted to the Rev. H. Saxby, Vicar of Williton, the Rev. A. Symon, Vicar of Watchet, Mr. A. L. Wedlake, and the firm of Reed and Smith Ltd.

Watchet Harbour serves as an importing point for fuel from South Wales and for certain raw materials for some of the paper-mills in Somerset and Devon. In 1946, the first shipment of 1,200 tons of Swedish wood pulp to arrive in this country since 1939 was unloaded at Watchet, and from there distributed in the West Country.

2. EGROVE

The Excise Letter of 1816 records that William Wood was also the paper-maker in charge of No. 461, Egrove Mill (Williton). By 1830 (*Pigot's Directory*), this mill was in the hands of Robert Pole who in 1841[4] was making paper and pasteboard. His name appears in *Pigot* for 1844, but his mill had ceased work by 1847[5] ; according to a report in the *West Somerset Free Press* of 7th June 1902, paper-making ceased when the proprietor was drowned in the River Parrett on returning from a trade journey to Wales.

3. DULVERTON

The only available evidence of a paper-mill at Dulverton has kindly been supplied by Mr. H. W. Kille (to whom I am also indebted for information about the Watchet mills) and Mr. L. G. Sloman. There are two cottages in Lady Street, formerly known as " Paper Mill Cottages " and now as " Birdcage," which stand beside a channel which takes off from the River Barle. This property may well be connected with that described as " Paper Mill House " in a sale list, 1818, given in the *History of the Sydenham Family*, p. 370. The Rev. N. Owen, Vicar of Dulverton, kindly searched the Dulverton Parish Registers for relevant evidence, but the result was negative, as was also my search of the Tithe Map and Apportionment.

4. FIDEOAK

Mill No. 463 at Fideoak, with John Wood as the paper-maker, appears in the Excise Letter of 1816. The fact that a

162

list of property for sale at Fideoak in 1810[6] does not mention the paper-mill may mean that it was established between then and 1816, but the paper-mill may have been much older. No connection has been proved between the Wood family of paper-makers here and either the Woods at Egrove and Watchet or at Wood's Paper-mill which worked at Uffculme in Devon in the first half of the eighteenth century,[7] although it is interesting that these paper-mills were the nearest to Fideoak in the directions of northwest and southwest respectively. This paper-mill, near Bishop's Hull, west of Taunton, is shewn on Greenwood's Map of Somersetshire, 1822. My last reference to it occurs in *Pigot's Directory* for 1830, when Martha Wood was the paper-maker.

My thanks are due to Mr. H. J. Wickenden for identifying and describing this site.

5. CREECH ST. MICHAEL

This paper-mill, a distinctive feature to the east of the railway running north from Taunton, is owned by R. Sommerville & Co. Ltd., and bears the number 1875, not from the Excise, but from the date of its establishment, since when it has worked continuously. According to *Dir. P.M.* for 1876, it was then equipped with one machine 100-in. wide, producing Engine-sized Writings and Fine Printings. It has always manufactured Fine Papers, Writings, Drawing Cartridges, Printings and the like. The Director informs me that the two principal factors affecting the choice of the site were the abundant supply of excellent water and the close proximity to the main G.W.R. *Dir. P.M.* for 1948 states that it has one machine of 86-in., and makes E. S. Writings, Drawing and Offset Cartridge, Duplicator and Envelope Papers, Varnish Resisting Lithos, S.C. and M.F. Fine Printings.

6. STREET

" Avalon Leather Board " has been made at Bowlingreen Mill, Street since the opening of the factory in 1870. I am grateful to the present firm for details of their history. The firm does not produce paper, but manufactures fibre boards for the boot and shoe industry on plant (six machines) which is similar to the wet end of a paper making machine. The quality of the water does not affect board making, and the localizing factor in this case was proximity to the shoe factory at Street.

7, 8 and 9. CHEDDAR

The Rev. John Collinson, *The History and Antiquities of the County of Somerset*, 1791, III, p. 572, states that there was " a very considerable manufacture of paper " at Cheddar, and (p. 573) mentions the source and quality of the water there:—"nine small springs, pure as crystal, burst from the foot of the cliffs, all within the space of about thirty feet, and joining together within forty yards of their source, form a broad rapid river of the clearest and finest water in the world. This river....a few years ago turned thirteen mills within half a mile of its source. The number is now reduced to seven, three of which are paper-mills, the other grist-mills." It is probable that two of the paper-makers here at this time were Grove and Pountney who had offices in Bristol[8]; a Joseph Pountney, paper-maker of Cheddar, went bankrupt in 1809.[9]

According to the Excise Letter of 1816, there was then only one paper-mill at Cheddar, which was No. 9, worked by John Gilling and Co. An Excise Letter of 28th November 1832[10] records this mill as occupied by John Gilling and Robert Alford; this and another Letter of 16th March 1833[11] refer to this mill as "Cheddar Four Mills." In the latter year there also appears Mill No. 7 at Cheddar, occupied by A. T. Tanner, whose name again occurs as the occupier of Mill No. 59, Cheddar, on its first appearance in the Excise Letters in 1835.[11]

The Census Report for 1851 stated that a decrease in the population of Cheddar could be partly ascribed to the closing of the paper-mills, which caused several persons to emigrate. The *Dir. P.M.* for 1860, however, still lists Mills 9 and 59, both operated by William, Samuel and Arthur Tanner and both producing writing papers, hand-made only at No. 59, and both hand and machine-made at No. 9.

In other *Dirs. P.M.* the following details of Mill No. 59 only appear:— 1876, Tanner and Budgett, with one machine producing News and Printings; 1890, Wansbrough and Worrall, with two machines (52" and 74") making Manillas, Cartridge, Tea-lapping, Best, Common and Glazed Browns, Caps, Skips, and Royal Hands; 1900, the Wansbrough Paper Co., Ltd., with four machines. This mill does not appear in the *Directory* for 1905.

10, 11, 12, 13, 14 and 15, WOOKEY–WELLS area.

10. The oldest record of a paper-mill yet found in Somerset is a Deed of Sale of 1610, in the possession of Mr. Guy A. Hodgkinson, Governing Director of W. S. Hodgkinson and Co., Ltd., Wookey Hole Paper Mill, to whom I am indebted for details. The Deed refers to "all those two turking mills under one roove whereof one is now converted to a paper mill." This mill, one of the very few still producing hand-made paper in this country, appears in the Excise Letter of 1816 as No. 366, Wookey Hole, worked by Golding and Snelgrove, the firm whose name as a watermark in 1798 is noted by W. A. Churchill (*Watermarks in Paper in the Seventeenth and Eighteenth*

Centuries, 1935). The *Dir. P.M.* for 1876 states that this mill was then owned by William Sampson Hodgkinson & Co., with ten vats, making Hand-made Writing, Drawing, Loan and Bank Note Papers. It is now equipped with thirteen vats and produces (1948 *Dir. P.M.*) Hand-made Account Book, Writing, Drawing, Loan, Bank Note and Printing Papers and Parchment Substitute, also Deckle-edged Note Paper and Envelopes.

11. Mr. Rhys Jenkins kindly informs me that the name of Joseph Coles, of Wookey Hole, paper-maker in 1788, is mentioned in the *Report of the Hist. MSS. Com.* in the MSS of the Dean and Chapter of Wells. A paper-maker of this name is listed in the Excise Letter of 1816, as at Mill No. 364, Lower Wookey. The mill of this number has been named in turn Lower Wookey, the Mendip Mills and the St. Cuthbert's Paper Works, as is shewn in the following details from *Dir. P.M.* —in 1860, Burgess and Ward were producing Straw Printings and News at Lower Wookey Mill ; in 1876, Burgess and Co. had two machines (60″ and 105″) at Mendip Mills, the products then being Printings and News ; in 1890, Dixon, Horsburgh and Co. Ltd. had two machines (65″ and 98″) at the St. Cuthbert Works, manufacturing T.S. and E.S. Writings and Fine Printings ; in 1948, two machines were making the following papers :—Tub-sized, Air-dried, Rag Writings, Ledgers, Loans, Drawing Cartridge, Type-writing Papers, Engine-sized Esparto Writings, Envelope Papers, White and Tinted Bonds, Cartridge and Cover Papers, Printings, Duplicating Paper, Pulp Boards and Photographic Base Paper. Linen Finished and Fancy Finished Papers are a speciality.

My thanks are due to the Manager of the St. Cuthbert's Works for information about the present mill.

12. In the Excise Letter of 1816, Mill 365 was recorded as occupied by James K. Coles, at Lower Wookey. Later entries make it clear that this number referred to the Henley Paper-mill. My last reference to it occurs in the *Dir. P.M.* for 1860, wherein Henry Coles is entered as the paper-maker.

13. There is some doubt as to whether the Excise Number 486 was in 1816 applied to a mill at Wookey or at Bleadney. There are two entries in the Excise Letter, the first giving Golding and Snelgrove, Wookey, and the second (deleted) referring this number to Bleadney. If the first is correct, it might refer to Glencot Mill, mentioned by Professor Jervis and Mr. Jones (*op. cit.*), but against this is the fact that there is no reference at all to Glencot in the Excise Letters.

Pigot's Directory for 1822–3 lists Clarke and Horsington, paper-manufacturers, Bleadney, and this is confirmed by the

Excise Letter of 28th November 1832, already quoted, which records Richard Clark and William Horsington at Mill No. 486, Bleadney.

Mr. C. Horsington, grandson of William, has kindly furnished me with many particulars from the mill's account books, from which it is shewn that the chief buyers of Bleadney paper were in Bristol, Bath and London. The last local record of the Bleadney paper-mill dates from 1849 ; according to the Excise Records it had ceased by 1850.[13]

My thanks are due to the Rev. A. B. Roberts, Vicar of Wookey, for obtaining local information about this mill.

14 and 15. Two mills at Dulcot are recorded in the Excise Letter of 1816 :—No. 367, occupied by John Snelgrove, and No. 368, by Charles Gumm. In 1833 (Excise Letter of 16th March, already quoted) these mills were occupied by Mary Snelgrove and Charles Gumm respectively ; in 1838,[14] however, No. 368 is recorded as " left off." The *Dir. P.M.* for 1876 describes Mill 367 as " Dulcote Mills," in the name of James Black, making Air dried Browns, Middles and Millboards on one machine of 36″ and one vat. Similar details appear in the *Dir. P.M.* for 1885 (my last reference), with the addition of a second machine, of 48″.

16 and 17.   STOKE BOTTOM

Collinson (*op. cit*, III, p. 484) notes a logwood and paper-mill in the hamlet of Stoke Bottom. The Rev. P. A. Northam, Vicar of Stoke St. Michael, has kindly provided me with much local information about these mills. The Baptisms in the Parish Registers for 1815 record the names of James North and Walton Fussell, paper-makers, and certain of the Parish Records are on paper watermarked " Fussell 1822."

The Excise Letter of 1816 lists Henry Fussell at Mills No. 363 and 485, Stoke Bottom (in the Somerset Collection, later in the Bath Collection of Excise). In 1826[15] Jacob Fussell, paper-maker of Stoke-lane, was declared a bankrupt. The Parish Rate Books shew that he was followed at the mill by Thomas Gilling up to 1832, after which year the Excise Letters record Henry Coles here. My last reference—the 1860 *Dir. P.M.*—gives Mill No. 485, Stoke Bottom, worked by Henry Coles and producing Hand-made Writing Papers. Mill No. 363 had ceased in 1839.[16]

18.   BANWELL

I am grateful to Mr. N. Ruscombe-Emery for details from his family history which show that in 1710 Thomas Emery bought the Banwell Mills and carried on the business of a paper-manufacturer, miller, tanner and brewer up to his death in 1747. In the Excise Letter of 1816, the mill is listed as No. 10, worked by George Emery. It appears to have ceased work as No. 10 in 1841[17] and to have been revived for a short time as No. 12 in 1847[18] by George Bedford Pim.

19. RICKFORD

My thanks are due to Preb. E. Marriott, Rector of Blagdon, for his research into the Parish Records on my behalf. The name of James Carpenter, paper-maker, appears in the Registers for 1813, and there are several references to the family of Hall, paper-makers, up to the 1850's. Further entries of paper-makers occur as late as 1895.

The Excise Letter of 1816 records Mill No. 11, with Giles Hall, paper-maker at Rickford. According to the *Western Luminary* of 29th May 1832, his paper-mill was broken into and fifteen reams of writing paper stolen. My last definite reference to the Rickford Mill (the 1860 *Dir. P.M.*) shows that it had acquired a different number (368). It is described as Rickford Mill, Burrington nr. Bristol, and as being worked by John Blatchford, producing Superfine Handmade Book Papers.

20. COMPTON MARTIN

This paper-mill appears in the Excise List of 1816 as No. 7, Compton, in the hands of James Bryant ; by 1822[19] it had been taken over by Thomas Holder and John King. Confirmatory details have been kindly furnished by the Rev. T. R. Narrilow, Rector of Compton Martin, who finds references to Thomas Holder, paper-maker, in the Parish Registers for the 1820's, and to " paper-makers in distress " in the Churchwardens' Accounts for 1821. This mill does not appear in the Excise List of 1832 and no further reference to it has been found.

21. HERRIOTTS

This mill is recorded as No. 8 in the Excise Letter of 1816, when Charles Gumm was the paper-maker in charge. It was situated near Herriotts Bridge in the parish of West Harptree, to whose Vicar, the Rev. G. Shipman Fox, I render my thanks for his kind searches of the Parish Records which yielded many confirmatory details. This paper-mill ceased work in or about 1828.[20]

22. SHERBORNE

Sherborne Mill, in the Chewton 2 Ride of the Bath Collection, appears in the Excise Records in the 1820's and 1830's. It is listed in Excise Letters as follows :—19th. Feb. 1823[21], occupied by John King ; 2nd April, 1825,[22] by Thomas Gilling ; and 16th March, 1833[23], by Walton Fussell. I think this mill was almost certainly the old Sherborne Mill in the parish of Litton, but the Rev. W. Ross Urquhart tells me that there is nothing to confirm this in the Parish Records or the local memory. The Chief Engineer of the Bristol Waterworks Company, who purchased the Sherborne spring for their reservoir, has also found no confirmatory evidence.

23. NORTH WICK

The *Universal British Directory of Trade and Commerce,* 1791, 2, p. 196, notes a paper-mill on the rivulet between Chew Magna and Windford ; although this is not exactly the same locality, the statement apparently refers to the paper-mill shewn at North Wick on Greenwood's Map of Somersetshire, 1822. This was Mill No. 12 in the Excise Letter of 1816, Thomas Kendall then being the paper-maker. Apparently it worked sporadically, as in 1848[14] North Wick appears under a different number (463), and this is my last reference.

The Rev. M. Luxmoore-Ball, Vicar of Chew Magna, kindly searched local records, and made enquiries for me, but found that little information was available.

24. PENSFORD

My only reference to Bye Mills, Pensford, appears in the *Dir. P.M.* for 1876. It was a post-Excise mill and thus bore no Excise Number. The firm of John Mardon produced Browns, Middles, Blue and White Royal Hands, Small Hands and Mill Wrappers on two machines of 60". The mill does not appear in the *Dir. P.M.* for 1860 or 1885.

25. KEYNSHAM

According to the 1933 *Annual of the House of Robinson,* the Keynsham Paper Mills[15] were founded in that year on the site of the old brass mills. Favorable factors influencing the location of the paper-mills were that the site was close to the main railway, and within easy reach of the Bristol docks, the Somerset coalfield and potential markets, as well as being near the firm's Malago bag factory. Water is pumped from the river and softened and filtered for use. The mill has a 162" machine, manufacturing high grade M.G. sulphite papers, primarily for use in the bags made by the firm, and also Krafts.

26. CATHARINE MILL

The Excise Letter of 1816 records Mill No. 21, in the hands of Thomas Bevan, Catharine Mill. On Greenwood's Map, 1822, this paper-mill is shewn at the head of St. Catharines' Valley, almost on the county border. My last reference to it occurs in the *Dir. P.M.* for 1860, which lists Mill No. 21, Thomas Cross, St. Katharine's Vale, producing Brown Papers, Cartridges, Small Hands, Millboards, Box Boards and Engine Boards.

The Census Report for 1871 attributes an increase in population in the parish of St. Catharine to the re-opening of a paper-mill, possibly this one.

27. BATHEASTON

The *Dir. P.M.* for 1860 provides my only reference to Mill No. 406 worked by T. Dewdney, " Bathesdon " Mill, Bath, making Grocery Papers and Double Small Hands. This mill must have been the lower of the two paper-mills in the St. Catharine's Valley to the north of Bath. I am indebted to Mr. G. Strutt for local information which implies that the ruins of one and " Paper-mill Cottages " of the other remain today.

28. BATHFORD

The present Director of the Bathford Paper Mills Co., Ltd., informs me that watermarks from this mill dated 1809 have been observed. The Mill still bears the number (18) by which it was known to the Excise Commissioners in 1816, when it was worked by George Yeeles and John Midhurst. It has sometimes been described as the Trevarno Paper Mill e.g. in the *Dir. P.M.* for 1876, when it was owned by Reed Brothers, making News, Printings and Cartridges, on one machine of 54". The *Dir. P.M.* for 1948 states that the machine is now 84" wide, and the products are White and Tinted M.F. Printings, Opaque, Book Papers, E.S. Writings and Banks, in Reams or Reels and packed for export.

29. WESTON

Two Directories[16] list James Henry Bryant, Weston Mills, under paper-makers, Bath, in 1834–8 and 1844. I have no reference to this mill outside this period.

30. BATH

The Excise Letter of 28th November 1832, already quoted, contains my only reference to the working of a Scaleboard Mill, No. 550, in James Street, Bath. The occupier was William Fear. This number appears in an Excise Letter of 1834[17] as " left off."

31. MONKTON COOMBE

Mudge's Map of Somerset (1817) shows a paper-mill at Monkton Combe, which was apparently the de Montairt or de Montalt Mill, from which W. A. Churchill (*op. cit.*) notes a watermark dated 1811. This must have been one of the mills which produced the Bath writing paper which was widely used in the West Country early last century.[18] It appears in the Excise Letter of 1816 as No. 20, with three paper-makers named John Bally, William Allen and George Steart ; *Pigot's Directory* for 1822–3 gives John Bally and Co., paper manufacturers, Bath. It may be that, as Mr. F. Buckley suggests, the names of this mill and of some of the paper-makers are due to French (Huguenot ?) origin, but no evidence has been found to support this.

In 1832[19] the Excise authorities called this the Coombe Down Mill. My last reference to it occurs in S. Lewis's *Topographical Dictionary of England*, 1840, which notes a large paper manufactory at Monkton Combe.

32. PORTISHEAD

The *Dir. P.M.* for 1925 records that the mills of Severn Kraft Mills Ltd. (incorporating Jonathan Bracken and Sons, Ltd. and Trent Paper Mills Ltd.) were in course of erection at Portishead. In 1930 they were "nearing completion," and last appear in the *Dir. P.M.* for 1937. Jervis and Jones (*op. cit.*) state that chemical wood pulp was imported from Finland and Sweden for the manufacture described in the *Directories* as genuine M.G. Krafts (strong brown paper).

ACKNOWLEDGMENTS

I am indebted to many who have helped me in this study and who could not be named in connection with any particular item in the text. My special thanks are due to Preb. G. W. Saunders, who also collated notes kindly supplied him by Mr. F. Buckley, but I ask all others also to accept this acknowledgement.

1. The numbers marked next to each mill on the map refer to those given before each mill in the text of this article.
2. This is a General Letter of 8th October 1816, in General Letter Book No. 4 of the Ellesmere Division of the Chester Collection. In the text hereafter, this letter is referred to as the Excise Letter of 1816.
3. *Paper Mills Directory* (1860 and 1876) and later the *Directory of Paper Makers*. In the text hereafter, this is abbreviated to *Dir. P.M.*, accompanied by the year of issue.
4. Excise Letter of 30th Nov. 1841, in General Letter Book No. 17 of the Tarporley 1st Ride, Northwich Collection.
5. Excise Letter of 30th April 1847, in General Letter·Book No. 19 of ditto.
6. *Sherborne and Yeovil Mercury*, 22nd Jan. 1810.
7. A. H. Shorter, *Paper-mills in Devon and Cornwall: Further Evidence, Devon and Cornwall Notes and Queries*, XXIII, 1948, p. 197.
8. *Universal British Directory of Trade and Commerce*, 1791, 2, p. 149.
9. *Trewman's Exeter Flying Post*, 9th November 1809.
10. In General Letter Book No. 15 of the Tarporley 1st Ride, Northwich Collection.
11. In Vol. III of Excise General Orders (Printed).
12. 20th July 1835, in General Letter Book No. 16 of Tarporley 1st Ride, Northwich Collection.
13. Excise Letter of 16th May 1850, in Excise General Orders, Vol. V. (Printed).
14. Excise Letter of 15th September 1838, in General Letter Book No. 16 of Tarporley 1st Ride, Northwich Collection.
15. *Alfred*, 26th December 1826.
16. Excise Letter of 10th September 1839, in General Letter Book No. 17 of Tarporley 1st Ride, Northwich Collection.
17. Excise Letter of 30th Nov. 1841, already quoted.

170

18. Excise Letter of 30th April 1847, already quoted.
19. Excise Letter of 11th July 1822, in Excise General Orders, Vol. I.
     (Printed).
20. Excise Letter of 20th March 1828, in General Letters Book No. 13
     of Tarporley 1st Ride.
21. Excise General Orders, Vol. I. (Printed).
22. In General Letters Book No. 13 of Tarporley 1st Ride.
23. already quoted.
24. Excise Letter of 29th June 1848, in General Letter Book No. 19 of
     Tarporley 1st Ride, Northwich Collection.
25. The information on this mill has kindly been supplied by the firm.
26. *Robsons Commercial Directory of London and the Western Counties*
     and *Pigot's Royal National and Commercial Directory and Topo-
     graphy.*
27. 17th January, in General Letter Book No. 15, Tarporley 1st Ride,
     Northwich Collection.
28. *The West Briton* for 14th June and 27th December, 1816, advertises
     (among others) Bath writing paper for sale in Truro.
29. Excise Letter of 28th November, already quoted.

XXII

PAPER-MILLS IN SOMERSET AND DORSET : FURTHER
EVIDENCE   (XXV. 245)

BEAMINSTER (DORSET)

Lists of prisoners in the Fleet Prison given in the *London
Gazette* contain the name of William Northam, late of
Beaminster, in Dorsetshire, paper-maker.   The date is 31st
May 1729, and this suggests (by comparison with the dates
given in my original paper on Dorset) that the paper-mill at
Beaminster was working earlier than any of the others in the
county.   Miss M. Trotman, of Beaminster, has most generously
given me all the information about the mill which she has been
able to obtain.   Mr. Hine (*History of Beaminster*, 1914) states
that there was a paper-mill in East Street 1767–1809 or earlier ;
if this was the case (documentary evidence is lacking at the
moment) there must have been two in Beaminster, for Miss
Trotman quotes several deeds to show that there was a paper-
mill at Whatley Farm.   An Admittance Deed of Walter Henry
Cox, Butcher, dated 1st July 1884, refers to the " Paper Mill
now called Whatley Farm."   The Paper Mill and Whatley
Coat (nearby) are the property mentioned in several Title
Deeds from 1742 to 1814 ;   none of these contains evidence
that the Paper-mill was working as such during that period,
but they prove the site.   By the first deed, 22nd March 1742,
John Gifford of Shanks in the Parish of Cucklington, Somerset,
Esq., surrendered the Paper Mill and Whatley Coat, formerly
in the tenure of Mary Gudge, deceased, and late in the possession of John Gifford, to William Canterbury of Langdon,
Yeoman, and Catherine his wife, on mortgage.   Among the
other deeds are those dated 9th July 1767—Elizabeth Smetham
of Beaminster, Spinster, lent William and Catherine Canterbury
£100 mortgage, secured on the Paper Mill and Whatley Coat ;
29th September 1784—The Paper Mill and Whatley Coat were
surrendered to John Banger Russell ; 2nd January 1786—
the Paper Mill and Whatley Coat were sold to John Davy of
Horn Park, Yeoman : 3rd October 1814—Clement Davy of
Netherbury, Yeoman, borrowed £300 of John Davy of Broad-
windsor, maltster, and Thomas Pearce of Meerhay, Linman,
on security of the Paper Mill and Whatley Coat.

LONG ASHTON (SOMERSET).

My only reference to a paper-mill here occurs in a recently-
discovered news item in *The Daily Post* of 23rd December 1740.
Under " News from Bristol " it is stated that a fire had broken
out in the Drying Room of the Paper-Mill at Long Ashton
" about two miles from this City," and that before it was
extinguished the damage amounted to £150.   The newspaper

172

report ends " It seems that it was designedly set on Fire by the Owner's Apprentice."

The following additional information about certain paper-mills already recorded in the two counties is of importance in relation to the early history of the industry.

WIMBORNE (DORSET)

In the *Kent County Herald* of 5th January 1809, there is an advertisement stating that in Dorset (apply C.L.T., Wimborn Post Office) there was for sale a very compact Freehold Paper Mill, where there was every requisite for working two Vats which were then " in full trade." The position given (four miles from the sea and six from a large seaport town) establishes that this advertisement referred to the Wimborne Paper-Mill. *The National Register* for 15th February 1813 records as bankrupt, P. Graham of Wimborne-Minster, paper-maker.

CAREY MILL (DORSET)

An advertisement ln the *Sherborne and Yeovil Mercury* of 6th August 1810 says that there was to let, at Carey near Wareham, a Paper Mill with one Vat and capable of receiving another ; the premises were situated so as wholly to command " a copious and powerful stream."

WOOKEY HOLE (SOMERSET).

In W. Tunnicliff's *Topographical Survey* (of Somerset etc.), 1789, p. 30, appears the name of John Band, Esq., paper-maker, Wookey-Hole. W. A. Churchill, *Watermarks in Paper in the Seventeenth and Eighteenth Centuries*, 1935, notes a watermark, Band & Son, of 1783.

WESTON MILLS (SOMERSET).

Two advertisements in the *London Gazette* of 6th March 1738 and 17th November 1739 suggest that Weston Mills worked as paper-mills in the early eighteenth century. Perhaps there was then a long gap in paper-making until the first half of the nineteenth century. The first advertisement concerns the estate late of Thomas Banks, of Weston, in the County of Somerset, Paper Maker, deceased, consisting of certain Paper Mills, Messuages, Lands and Tenements in Weston, Bath Easton and Katharine, in the said County. The second advertises " to be peremptorily sold," certain Paper Mills and several Messuages or Tenements in Weston near Bath ; part of the estate late of Thomas Banks, of Weston, paper-maker.

XXIII

PAPER-MILLS IN SOMERSET   Since the publication of my previous contributions on this subject [Vol. XXV] a few further important references have been found.

Paper-making at SALTFORD is referred to in two notices in *Felix Farley's Bristol Journal* (3rd September, 1757, and 20th April, 1765).   The first concerns the sale of Two Thirds of the Paper Mills.... situate at " Safford " in the County of Somerset.... in the possession of Mr. Francis Hunt.   The second notice states that an apprentice to Francis Hunt, paper-maker, of " Salford " near Bath, had eloped.

Paper-making seems to have been carried on at CHEWTON KEYNSHAM up to 1749.   *The Worcester Journal*, 13th April, 1749, contains a report that the fire at " the Paper Mill near Keynsham " had destroyed the dwelling-house, the mill and all the utensils belonging to the business, a great quantity of paper, the stable, outhouses and a great part of the household furniture.   The total damage amounted to about £500.

The will of Thomas Weare, paper-maker, of WOOKEY HOLE, was proved in 1656[1].   *Farley's Bristol News Paper*, 19th October, 1728, contains an advertisement that there were for sale at Wookey Hole two overshot mills, a paper-mill and a corn-mill, which even in the driest summer never wanted water to drive them.   They were then in the possession of John Sherborne.   Two apprentice indentures[2] suggest that by the 1760's there were two paper-mills at Wookey Hole. In 1761 and 1762, John Riddle and James Snelgrove were apprenticed to James Coles and Edward Band respectively, both of Wookey Hole, paper-makers.

---

1. *Index of Wills proved in the Prerogative Court of Canterbury*, VII, 1653–56, ed. T. M. Blagg and J. S. Moir, The Index Library, Vol. 54, British Record Soc., 1925. 1656, Fol. 48.

2. *The Apprentices of Great Britain* .... Book 54, Fols. 96 and 171.

XXIV

PAPER MILLS IN THE WYE VALLEY, BUCKINGHAMSHIRE

Paper mills must have been at work in the Wye Valley very early in the seventeenth century, for there are references to paper makers in the parish of High Wycombe in the 1630's and in Wooburn parish in the 1620's. By 1690 there were eight paper mills in the parish of High Wycombe, and West Wycombe and Wooburn had at least one each[1]. In the late seventeenth and early eighteenth centuries there are numerous references to paper makers and paper mills at West Wycombe, High Wycombe, Loudwater and Wooburn, but in many cases the mills are not specified by name, so that it is not always easy to assign the references to the correct sites. During the nineteenth century many of the records are much more specific, and it is possible to identify most of the mills which were then working. Altogether, some 33 paper and board mills have certainly been at work at one time or another (there may have been three others) within a total distance of between seven and eight miles along the River Wye. The map shows the approximate positions of the mills.

There is a considerable amount of information about the products of the mills in the nineteenth and twentieth centuries, but much less about the papers and boards which were made in earlier times. In 1690 it was claimed that the eight mills in the parish of High Wycombe employed fifty families in making white paper and that the paper makers made good printing paper. In view of the large number of mills at work here in the eighteenth century, we might expect to have many examples of watermarks used by the Wye Valley makers during that period; but so far only two mills (Wycombe Marsh and Beech Mills[2]) are known to have produced watermarked

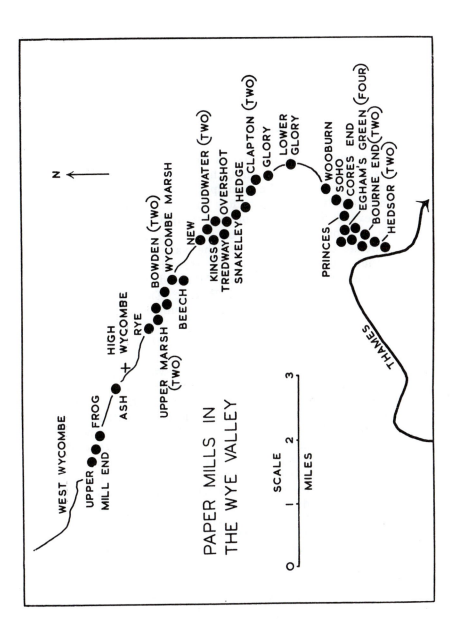

N

WEST WYCOMBE
UPPER
MILL END
FROG
ASH
HIGH
WYCOMBE
RYE
UPPER MARSH
(TWO)
BEECH
BOWDEN (TWO)
WYCOMBE MARSH
NEW
KINGS
TREDWAY
LOUDWATER (TWO)
OVERSHOT
SNAKELEY
HEDGE
CLAPTON (TWO)
GLORY
LOWER
GLORY
WOOBURN
SOHO
PRINCES
CORES END
EGHAM'S GREEN (FOUR)
BOURNE END(TWO)
HEDSOR (TWO)

THAMES

PAPER MILLS IN
THE WYE VALLEY

SCALE
0   1   2   3
MILES

paper before the year 1800. However, we also know
that early in the eighteenth century the paper mills
near Wycombe and Marlow were making great quantities of printing paper "very good of its kind, and
cheap, such as generally is made use of in printing
our newspapers, journals, etc., and smaller pamphlets; but not much fine, or large, for bound books,
or writing[3]." Now it is an interesting fact that much
of the paper on which English eighteenth century
newspapers were printed is not watermarked, and I
am inclined to think that the Wye Valley mills may
have been one of the principal sources of that paper,
particularly for the London market. It appears that
in several mills from Loudwater upstream the empha-
sis was on the making of white paper[4], but in the
mills at the lower end of the valley it was on the
manufacture of boards. A brown board mill at
Bourne End is recorded in 1719, and by 1800 several
mills at Egham's Green, Bourne End and Hedsor
were engaged in the making of millboard or pasteboard.

In 1830 the High Wycombe district was the scene
of anti-machine riots. In an attempt on the paper
mill of Messrs. Lane[5], the rioters were repulsed by
a troop of the Buckinghamshire Yeomanry and
retired vowing vengeance. Armed parties occupied
all the paper mills[6], but the rioters eventually did
damage estimated at £12,000, and it was reported
that the machinery in the mills had been "generally
destroyed[7]." Most of the leaders in this affair were
transported[8]. During the nineteenth and early
twentieth centuries, and as happened in many other
papermaking districts, the number of mills was much
reduced, but with the modern expansion and variety
of production on the surviving sites this area remains
one of the important centres of English paper and
board manufacture.

The following list gives the names of the mills in
order from West Wycombe downstream to Hedsor
Mills, their Excise Numbers (in the case of the mills
which were at work in or after 1816, when these
Numbers were first recorded), and the first and last
known dates of the working of each mill, with the

PAPER MILLS IN THE WYE VALLEY

relevant sources of information where necessary. As the dates and references earlier than about 1800 have already been mustered and published[9], the sources of information need be given only after that year; acknowledgments are the same.

West Wycombe, Francis Mill, Upper Mill, No. 423. 1684-1832. Alfred Lane appears to have been the last master paper maker. He is recorded as the paper maker in 1832[10] and as the occupier in 1847[11], but it is not known whether the mill was still making paper in the latter year.

West Wycombe, Fryer's Mill, Mill End Mill, No. 422. 1725-1844. Michael Fryer, paper maker, is recorded in 1844[12]. He was the occupier in 1847[13], but the mill may have ceased work by then.

West Wycombe, Ball's Mill, Frog Mill, No. 421. 1717-1828. John Crofton was the master maker in 1828, when this mill was discontinued[14].

Ash Mill, Lane's Mill, No. 420. 1726-1844. The last known reference is to John and Joseph Lane, paper manufacturers at Ash Mill, in 1844[15].

Rye Mill, No. 411. 1788-1931. The last proprietors, T. H. Saunders & Co. Ltd., made writing, drawing and account book papers[16].

Upper Marsh Mill, No. 419. 1760-1828. This mill was discontinued in 1828, when it was in the tenure of George Lane[17].

Upper Marsh Mill, No. 412. 1750-1844. Alfred Lane and Joseph Edmonds were probably the last to work this mill. In 1844 they were described as paper manufacturers at the Marsh[18].

Bowden(s) Mill, No. 415. 1748-1827. The last known reference to paper makers here is to Alfred Lane and Joseph Edmonds[19].

Bowden(s) Mill, No. 416. 1760-1866. Abraham Turner, a maker of fine small hands, etc., appears to have been the last proprietor. He was recorded at this mill in 1866[20].

Lower Marsh Mill, Wycombe Marsh Mill, No. 414. 1724 onward. This mill is still working, under the firm of Wycombe Marsh Paper Mills Ltd.

Lower Marsh Mill, Beech Mill, No. 413. 1740-1900. The last proprietors, H. M. Greville & Son Ltd., were working four vats here up to 1900[21].

New Mills. 1725-33. It is possible that this mill continued under another name. New Mill is named on T. Jefferys' *Map of Buckinghamshire*, 1770, and on other maps about that time, but not as a paper mill.

King's Mill, Bryant's Mill, Loudwater, No. 417, 1779 onwards. This mill was incorporated by Wycombe Marsh Paper Mills Ltd.

Loudwater Mill, No. 431. 1762-1816. Richard Plaistowe was the occupier in 1816, the date of the last known reference[22].

Loudwater Mill, No. 430. 1638 onwards. The statement that Loudwater Mill was "partly built in 1814-15"[23] seems to fit in well with the fact that in 1814[24] Richard Plaistowe insured his "new paper mill" at Loudwater, but this mill may have been built on the site of an older mill. In 1816[25] Richard Plaistowe held Mills Nos. 431 and 430, and one of these was probably on the site now occupied by Loudwater Paper Mills Ltd.

Tredway Mill, Loudwater. 1682-1762. As with New Mills (above), this may have been the site of one of the other mills recorded at Loudwater in later years.

Overshot(s) Mill, Loudwater, No. 418 (later 429). 1766-1894. This mill was eventually taken over by Henry Wheeler & Co., Wycombe Marsh Mill.[26]

Snakeley Mill, Loudwater, No. 428. 1763 onwards. The mill is still working under the firm of T. B. Ford Ltd.

Hedge Mill, No. 427. 1690 onwards. This mill is still at work in the hands of G. H. Hedley Ltd.

Clapton(s) Mill, Red Cap Mill, No. 429. 1764-1832. Peter John Fromow was the last known master paper maker. He was at this mill in 1832[27].

Clapton(s) Mill, No. 509. 1819-93. In 1819 George Venables and Peter John Fromow were the master makers[28]. The mill was last used (for half-stuff) by Thomas Burch Ford[29].

Glory Mill, No. 426. 1627 onwards. Glory Mill is now worked by Wiggins, Teape & Co. Ltd.

Lower Glory Mill, Wooburn, No. 425. 1803-1919. This paper mill was probably first worked by James Pegg, junior, who was a master paper maker in 1803[30]. James Pegg was the occupier in 1816[31]. The last proprietors were Impervex Ltd., who made boards and waterproof paper[32].

Wooburn Mill, No. 628. 1827-47. [33] Samuel Newel Wright was the paper manufacturer. The mill left off work in 1847[34].

Soho Mill, Wooburn, No. 424. 1759 onwards. Thomas & Green Ltd. are the present proprietors.

Fuller's Mill, Core's End, No. 289. 1777-1835. The last known occupier was Thomas Lunnon, a maker of millboards in 1835[35].

Prince's Mill, Core's End, No. 288. 1785-1896. Mill No. 288 was incorporated by Thomas & Green, Soho Mill[36].

Egham's Green Mill, No. 287. 1781 onwards. This mill appears to have been the one which late in the nineteenth century became known as Jackson's Upper Mill, used for the making of boards.

Egham's Green Mill. 1807. In that year Harry Pegg had a paper mill and a pasteboard mill at Egham's Green[37]. In 1816[38] he held only Mill No. 287 (above), so his second mill may have existed for only a short time.

Egham's Green Mill, Gunpowder Mill, No. 286. 1763 onwards. This was probably the mill which late in the nineteenth century became known as Jackson's Lower Mill; it is still worked by Jackson's Millboard & Fibre Co. Ltd.

Egham's Green Mill. 1778. In that year Henry Revell had a paper mill and a millboard mill at Egham's Green. One was probably Mill No. 286 (above), the other was a separate and possibly a short-lived mill.

Bourne End Mill. 1775-1807. The Wildman family held a paper mill and a board mill here, and both mills are recorded in this period. One appears to have continued as Mill No. 284 (below).

PAPER MILLS IN THE WYE VALLEY

Bourne End Mill, Lower Mill, No. 284. 1719-1890's. The last proprietors were the Buckinghamshire Millboard Co.[39].

Hedsor Mill. 1724-1812. There were two paper mills at Hedsor from 1724 to 1812[40].

Hedsor Mill, No. 285. 1724 onwards. This mill became Jackson's Hedsor Mill in 1920, continuing with the manufacture of boards.

REFERENCES

1. Authorities for the dates and occupiers of paper mills before about A.D. 1800 are given in A. H. Shorter. *Paper Mills and Paper Makers in England, 1495-1800*. The Paper Publications Society, Hilversum, Holland. 1957, especially pp. 132-144.
2. *Ibid.*, pp. 277 and 310. In 1787 John Bates of Wycombe Marsh was awarded a gold medal by the Society of Arts for his manufacture of high-quality plate papers. *Ibid.*, p. 60.
3. D. Defoe, *Tour Thro' the Whole Island of Great Britain*, II, 1725, pp. 70-1.
4. In addition to Wycombe Marsh and Beech Mills, white paper was probably also made at West Wycombe and Loudwater, where there were "sizing houses." A. H. Shorter, *op. cit.*, p. 390.
5. Probably Ash Mill, held by John and Joseph Lane in 1832.
6. *Trewman's Exeter Flying Post*, 2nd December, 1830.
7. *Ibid*, 9th December, 1830. Fuller accounts are probably given in the London, Reading and Oxford papers.
8. H. Kingston, *History of Wycombe*, 1848, p. 86.
9. A. H. Shorter, *op. cit.*, pp. 132-144 and elsewhere.
10. *Excise General Letter*, 28th November, 1832.
11. *West Wycombe Tithe Map*, 1847.
12 *Pigot's Directory*, 1844.
13. *West Wycombe Tithe Map*, 1847.
14. *Excise General Letter*, 20th March, 1828.
15. *Pigot's Directory*, 1844.
16. *Directory of Paper Makers*.
17. *Excise General Letter*, 20th March, 1828.
18. *Pigot's Directory*, 1844.
19. *Excise General Letter*, 2nd May. 1827.
20. *Paper Mills Directory*, 1866.
21. *Directory of Paper Makers*.
22. *Excise General Letter*, 8th October. 1816.
23. A. D. Spicer, *The Paper Trade*. 1907, p. 193.
24. *Sun Fire Insurance Policy*, No. 900839, 5th December, 1814.
25. *Excise General Letter*, 8th October, 1816.
26. *Directory of Paper Makers*.

27. *Excise General Letter,* 28th November, 1832.
28. *Ibid.,* 14th April, 1819.
29. *Directory of Paper Makers.*
30. General Meeting of Master Paper Makers, 13th June, 1803. *Papers from Springfield Mill,* Kent.
31. *Excise General Letter,* 8th October, 1816.
32. *Directory of Paper Makers.*
33. *Excise General Letters,* 2nd May, 1827, and 28th November, 1832. He was bankrupt in 1841. *Devonshire Chronicle and Exeter News,* 10th August, 1841.
34. *Excise General Letter,* 13th May, 1847.
35. *Ibid.,* 1st January, 1835.
36. *Directory of Paper Makers.*
37. *Wooburn Rate Book,* 1807.
38. *Excise General Letter,* 8th October, 1816.
39. *Directory of Paper Makers.*
40. In 1812 Richard and William Lunnon, paper makers of Hedsor, insured their first and second paper mills. *Sun Fire Insurance Policy,* No. 870526, 5th May, 1812. Boards must have been made at one or both of these mills about that time, for a similar policy in 1806 referred to a rolling house for millboards. *Ibid.,* No. 788660, 27th March, 1806.

XXV

PAPER MILLS IN GLOUCESTERSHIRE

THE possibility that some of the old mills in Gloucestershire may have been among the really early establishments in the paper-making industry in England led me to inquire first into the origins of those mills still working. The resultant research has shown that many more mills formerly existed and that during the geographical expansion of the paper-making industry in England in the 18th and 19th centuries some 29 mills were at work at one time or another, and were characteristically scattered about the county. There may have been more paper mills, of which no record has yet been found. There must certainly have been one at or near Stanway, where the name Paper Mill Farm still survives. I have found no information about paper making there, however.

In the early days of the industry, paper makers sought mill-sites where there was an ample supply of water for power and of pure, clear water for the paper-making process. As many of the early mills were very small as compared with paper mills to-day, we find that quite small streams sometimes sufficed, whereas a very big and rather muddy river might not be suitable for such mills, both on account of the danger of flooding and the absence of clean water. Thus in Gloucestershire no attempt seems to have been made to site a paper mill actually on the River Severn; at Gloucester in 1915, when 'The Gloucester Paper Mills Ltd.' proposed to erect a two-machine mill for the manufacture of greaseproof paper, the site offered was on the Gloucester and Sharpness Canal.[1]

Three parts of Gloucestershire were particularly well represented in the geographical distribution of the industry:—the Forest of Dean, the Cotswolds, and the Bristol area. When

[1] *Gloucester Journal*, 11 September 1915.

considering these we should add that two localities in Monmouthshire (Whitebrook and the Mounton Brook) formerly had several paper mills each, that there were others in the vicinity of Burford (West Oxfordshire), and that although on the Gloucestershire side there appear to have been only one or two early paper mills near Bristol, there were in fact several others on the Somersetshire side (near Bristol, around the Mendips and along the Avon valley), also along the By Brook in north-west Wiltshire. There can be little doubt that in the Forest of Dean and the Cotswolds several mills were converted to paper making from iron- and fulling-mills respectively, and the availability of such mills may have been an added attraction to paper makers seeking new sites in those areas.

Gloucestershire is still represented in the paper-making industry by the Postlip, Bristol and Golden Valley Mills, and in the board industry by Bristol, Cam and Nailsworth. There were formerly several board mills in and around Bristol, two in the Forest of Dean (Clanna and Soudley Mills) and one at Stonehouse (Meadow Mills). The board industry is outside our purview but as with the paper-making industry the general tendency since the 1830's has been a great reduction in the number of mills at work. Many of the small West of England paper mills, operating one or two vats or small machines, have gone out of existence in the last 120 years or so. Monmouthshire, Herefordshire, Shropshire and Cornwall have lost all their paper mills; in Gloucestershire and all the other neighbouring counties there has been a great decrease in the number of paper mills at work. The elimination of many of the small mills was almost inevitable in the face of effective competition from bigger and better-situated mills, the coming of the paper-making machine, the duties on paper, changes in transport and in the types and sources of raw materials.

Significant facts concerning early English paper mills can be discovered only by a search of many local, regional and general sources. In 1816 the Excise authorities,[1] who had

---

[1] I am indebted to the Commissioners of Customs and Excise for permission to read in their library and to quote from their records.

managed the duty on paper since 1712, issued the first of a series of General Letters or Orders which gave lists, and additions and amendments to lists, of paper mills and paper makers in the United Kingdom. The relevant details are the names and Excise numbers of the mills, the names of the paper makers in occupation and the Collection of Excise in which the mills were situated. The letters ceased in 1852, but from that time onwards various county and trade directories give a general guide to the course of the industry.

Having regard to the facts that the story of paper making in Gloucestershire certainly extends over the last 225 years or so, and that the paper mills were formerly so widely scattered about the county, it seems of interest to put on record my information concerning each mill, without giving all the same details as those already provided in *V.C.H. Gloucestershire*[1] and Miss Eleanor Adlard's recent work on the Postlip Mills.[2]

1, 2, 3, 4 AND 5, BRISTOL

A Bristol newspaper of 1756[3] reports an accident to a labouring man at the paper mills. The earliest reference I have found to paper makers in Bristol, however, occurs in 1739,[4] when Henry Cotten, parish of St. Nicholas, and John Rayner, junior, parish of St. Thomas, are recorded. The former may well have been the same Henry Cotton who was apprenticed to Ben Davis, paper maker of Overbury, Worcestershire, in 1729.[5] It seems probable that he had a paper mill in Bristol; he certainly had a paper business at the Golden Lion on Bristol Bridge from about 1740 to 1761.[6] After his death, his son opened a paper and stationery warehouse in Wine Street

[1] II, 1907, pp. 208–9.
[2] *A Short History of the Postlip Mill, Winchcombe*, 1949.
[3] *Felix Farley's Bristol Journal*, 6 November 1756.
[4] *The Bristol Poll Book*, 1739.
[5] *The Apprentices of Great Britain*, 1710–62 (typescript); extracted from the Inland Revenue Books at the Public Record Office for the Society of Genealogists, 1921–8, book 49, fol. 86.
[6] *Felix Farley's Bristol Journal*, 25 July 1761.

in 1773[1] and also traded in rags and paper stuff. On the other hand, Cotton may have dealt in Bristol only with paper made at mills elsewhere in Gloucestershire or Somerset. An advertisement by John Stock in 1744[2] states that *he* kept the original Paper Warehouse, next door to the Back Hall in Baldwin Street and that he 'maketh all Sorts of Writing, Printing and Shop Paper, and sells at the lowest Prices. Merchants may be supplied with any quantity for Exportation, and *as there is no other Maker in this City*, consequently can sell on the best Terms.' Another advertisement[3] states that Stock had removed from Baldwin Street to the late Alderman Taylor's warehouse, opposite to the Bridgwater Slip on the Back 'where he continues to make and sell all Sorts of Writing, Printing and Shop Papers.'

In 1749[4] there appeared an advertisement of many types of paper for sale at Thomas Houlding's Paper Warehouse at the Sign of the Cardiff-Boat, on the Back, Bristol. In 1756[5] a dwelling house in Tucker Street, then occupied by James Marchant, paper man, was to let, also three large warehouses lately occupied by Henry Cotton, paper maker. Kingsmill Grove (late apprentice to Henry Cotton) opened a Paper House opposite Dolphin lane in Wine Street in 1767,[6] and by 1771[7] Thomas Mullett had succeeded to the trade of the late John Stock. All these entries suggest the localization of the paper trade in one main area of Bristol.

Further Bristol Poll Books of the 18th century, however, contain the names of the following paper makers:—1754, Henry Cotton, St. Thomas; John Browning, Bedminster; 1774, Charles Montague, St. John; John Colmer, Henry Cotton and Kingsmill Grove, St. Thomas; 1781, the same, with the omission of Henry Cotton; 1784, Kingsmill Grove omitted, and Hugh

[1] *Felix Farley's Bristol Journal*, 28 August 1773.
[2] *The Bristol Oracle and Country Advertiser*, 1 December 1744. *My italics.*
[3] *Bath Journal*, 10 February 1745–6.
[4] *The Bristol Oracle*, 5 August 1749.
[5] *Felix Farley's Bristol Journal*, 3 July 1756.
[6] Ibid., 8 August 1767.
[7] Ibid., 23 February 1771.

Foskett Evans (St. Nicholas) and James Ablart (St. Philip Out Parish) added.

In 1792[1] the partnership was dissolved between Hugh Foskett Evans, Sam. Allen and Fra. Harris, paper makers and stationers, Bristol, under the firm of Evans, Allen and Co. Other partnerships were dissolved as follows:—1796,[2] Kingsmill Grove, John Pountney and Henry Ford Richardson of Bristol, paper makers and stationers; 1803,[3] William Cowley and John Richardson, Bristol, paper makers and stationers; 1808,[4] Joseph Pountney and John Smith Pountney, paper makers, bookbinders and stationers, Bristol.

It is more than probable that several of these paper makers were connected with mills outside Bristol. Kingsmill Grove, for example, was one owner of the Whitebrook Paper Mills in Monmouthshire,[5] which certainly existed by the 1780's, and Joseph Pountney was a paper maker at Cheddar in Somerset up to 1809.[6] It would be dangerous, therefore, to assume the existence in Bristol of more than one paper mill in the 18th century, especially as only one reference actually to the paper mill has been found.

No Bristol paper mill appears in the Excise Letter of 1816.[7] In later Excise Letters, however, the following paper mills are listed, in addition to several scaleboard and pasteboard mills in various parts of Bristol:—1839, Mill No. 56, Thomas Wescott, St. Philip's Marsh; 1841, Mill No. 26, Eliz. Manley, Castle Green; 1847, Mill No. 50, Robert Mullet and Samuel Rogers, Tower Hill. Wescott is described as a paper manufacturer of Marsh Mills, St. Philip's Marsh, in 1834–8[8]; together with J. P. Austin, he was bankrupt in 1840.[9]

[1] *London Gazette*, 11 September 1792.
[2] Ibid., 21 May 1796.
[3] Ibid., 8 January 1803.
[4] Ibid., 2 August 1808.
[5] *Torrington Diaries*, I, 1787, p. 270.
[6] His bankruptcy is recorded in *London Gazette*, 31 October 1809.
[7] General Letter of 8 October 1816, in General Letter Book No. 4 of the Ellesmere Division, Chester Collection.
[8] Robson's *Directory*.
[9] *The Devonshire Chronicle and Exeter News*, 23 June 1840.

150

Bristol is not represented in a return of all paper mills in the United Kingdom ordered by the House of Commons in 1851.[1] It thus appears that the three paper mills mentioned above were quite short-lived during the period 1834–47. Our next definite reference to the industry in Bristol occurs in 1876,[2] when John Sellick, at Avonside Paper Mills, St. Philip's, was making Browns and Skips on one machine 60 inches in width. He was followed by the firm of John Mardon, manufacturing Browns, Middles, Shops and Wrappers on one machine 78 inches in width, in 1885.[3] By 1910 Messrs Smith, Stone and Knight had taken over the mills, and the machinery and range of papers have been greatly increased since then.

6 AND 7, BITTON AND GOLDEN VALLEY

According to the Rev. H. T. Ellacombe[4] 'there used to be a small Paper Mill on the Boyd in Golden Valley, which was transferred to the village of Bitton, on the site of the mills belonging to the Brass and Copper Company. This mill was burnt down in 1849; the premises were purchased by Messrs Sommerville of Edinburgh, who in the same year erected very extensive machinery . . . .'

The existence of the first Bitton mill is confirmed by an advertisement in 1787,[5] stating that a 'very compleat paper mill' was to be sold. It was situated in the parish of Bitton, within half a mile of the upper road between Bath and Bristol, and it was then 'in full work.' This is apparently the mill which, having been a boring mill and a leather mill, was converted from paper making to cotton spinning, and re-converted to paper making about 1812.[6] It was known to the Excise authorities as No. 6, Bitton Mill, in the Bath Collection of

[1] *House of Commons Papers*, 1852, vol. LI, no. 128.
[2] *The Paper Mills Directory*, 1876.
[3] *The Directory of Paper Makers*, 1885.
[4] *History of the Parish of Bitton*, 1881, p. 232.
[5] *Gloucester Journal*, 24 December 1787.
[6] Gloucestershire Records Office, D. 184 (Sherwood MSS.). I am indebted to Mr Irvine E. Gray for this information.

Excise; in 1816 it was occupied by Thomas Bevan, who about 1824 was temporarily partnered by George Swayne. Mill No. 6 appears in Excise Letters up to 1832, but the same sources record another Bitton paper mill, No. 563, in the names of Bevan and Swayne in 1824; from 1831 to 1846 the paper-maker recorded was William Bevan, followed by Richard William MacDonnell in 1848. This was apparently the mill which was burnt down, and in the following year Mill No. 148 was built by W. Sommerville. In 1851[1] the Golden Valley Mill had two beating engines at work and one silent, and about 1876[2] the firm of W. W. and J. Sommerville was making writings and envelope papers, tub-sized, on two machines of 68 and 78 inches in width. The firm of Golden Valley Paper Mills Ltd. now occupies the mill and produces T.S. and Air Dried Ledger, Loose Leaf, Writing, Typewriting, Envelope and Speciality Papers, E.S. Account Book, Bond, Writing, Pasting and Tinted Papers, Rag Printings, T.S. and E.S. Cartridges, Base Papers, Telegraph Parchments, Special Finishes, Special Watermarked Papers.[3]

8, WICK AND ABSON

I have no final proof that there was a paper mill at or near Wick in this parish. Bigland's reference[4] (under Wick and Abson) to a paper mill near the cliffs adjoining the River Boyd seems to concern the old Bitton Mill. However, in 1810,[5] William Pook the younger, late of the parish of Wick and Abson, paper maker, dealer and chapman, was recorded as bankrupt.

9, WICK

The above could not possibly refer to another Gloucester-shire Wick, in the parish of Berkeley. There was a paper mill

---

[1] *House of Commons Papers*, loc. cit.
[2] *The Paper Mills Directory*, 1876.
[3] *Directory of Paper Makers*, 1948.
[4] R. Bigland's *Collections relative to the County of Gloucester*, 1786, II, p. 6.
[5] *London Gazette*, 8 May 1810.

in that parish in the 18th century. In 1739,[1] Edmund Smith, paperman of Berkeley, is recorded, and in 1764[2] a grist mill, late a paper mill, in the tithing of Alvington (? Alkington) near Stone in the parish of Berkeley, was to be sold. I. Taylor's Map of Gloucestershire, 1777, shows Wyck Mill near Berkeley.

Rudge[3] refers to the manufacture of coarser sorts of paper at Wick, but no other information about the types of paper made there has been found. The only Excise reference to Wick Mill is in the Letter of 1816, which records it as No. 98, occupied by Eli Gazard. This mill was in the Gloucester Collection of Excise, and this suggests that it was the Wick in Berkeley parish rather than a mill in Wick and Abson.

10, HACK (WOTTON-UNDER-EDGE)

The partnership of Thomas Reeve and James Ablart of Wotton-under-Edge, paper makers, was dissolved in 1773.[4] The newspaper notice states that all sorts of best press papers for clothiers, also fine Sugar Loaf Blue and Brown Papers were available. The paper manufacturing business 'in all its branches' was to be carried on by James Ablart separately, but he went bankrupt in 1774.[5] The paper mill was then for sale,[6] being described as a very complete and new-erected paper mill, in a good situation for vending great quantities of paper. There were two glazing engines for making press paper.[7]

The mill was still for sale in 1776 and 1777,[8] the business meanwhile being carried on by Mr Bence, stationer in Wotton-under-Edge. By the 1790's, Thomas Palser had set up as a paper maker, and advertised for a journeyman press paper

---

[1] *The Bristol Poll Book*, 1739.
[2] *Gloucester Journal*, 25 June 1764.
[3] T. Rudge, *General View of the Agriculture of Gloucestershire*, 1807.
[4] *Gloucester Journal*, 19 July 1773.
[5] *London Gazette*, 17 September 1774.
[6] *Gloucester Journal*, 14 March 1774.
[7] *Felix Farley's Bristol Journal*, 4 November 1775.
[8] *Gloucester Journal*, 2 September 1776, and 17 February 1777.

maker.[1] In 1798,[2] Hack paper mill was advertised to let, applications being invited by Thomas Palser, the proprietor. It is stated that there was every accommodation for manufacturing writing papers and glazed press papers for which the mill had been employed for more than the past seven years. There was a fine spring of water rising a few yards above the mill, remarkable for softness, which supplied the engine with water for washing, etc.

The Excise Letters refer to Hack Mill as No. 99, in the Gloucester Collection. A Thomas Palser was the occupier in 1816, followed by Joseph Palser about 1838, and Henry Cogswell about 1847, the date of my last reference to the mill. Members of the Palser family were engaged in making paper cards in Wotton-under-Edge between 1822 and 1844.[3]

11, WHITMINSTER

My first reference to this paper mill is in a newspaper advertisement of 1764,[4] when a foreman for a paper mill was wanted, applications being invited to Thomas Evans at Whitminster. The paper mill is marked on I. Taylor's Map of Gloucestershire, 1777.

Mr Joseph Smith senior, paper maker of Whitminster, died in 1791[5] and Mrs E. Smith carried on the business about 1797[6] (when one of her apprentices eloped), probably making the coarser sorts of paper.[7] In the Excise Letter of 1816 the mill is designated No. 101, in the Gloucester Collection. The paper maker then was Thomas Smith, followed by Hester Smith up to 1834, the date of the last reference in the Excise Letters.

[1] *Gloucester Journal*, 20 February 1792.
[2] Ibid., 10 December 1798.
[3] Pigot's *Directories*.
[4] *Gloucester Journal*, 2 April 1764.
[5] Ibid., 28 February 1791.
[6] Ibid., 20 February 1797.
[7] T. Rudge, op. cit.

12, DURSLEY

'An excellent and extensive paper manufactory' had been established close to the town of Dursley by the 1790's.[1] Joseph Smith was the paper maker responsible, and it thus appears that families of Smiths were connected with three paper mills— Wick, Whitminster and Dursley—at all of which, according to Rudge, the coarser sorts of paper were produced. In 1816, the Excise authorities numbered this mill 97, in the Gloucester Collection; Sally Smith was then the paper maker. She was followed by C. Dealy, who went bankrupt in 1826.[2] In 1827–8 Joseph White was in occupation, and the mill was then described as 'Rivers Mill'[3] by the Excise authorities.

13, NAILSWORTH

Mr L. E. Chamberlain kindly informs me that his family history (1896) states that Charles Ward made paper at Dunkirk Mills in 1767. This is possibly the mill referred to in the Excise Letter of 1816 as No. 100, Nailsworth, in the Gloucester Collection, the paper maker then being Thomas French. Mill No. 100 left off work in 1839.

14, ST. MARY'S (CHALFORD)

In 1813[4] a clothing mill of this name at Chalford was for sale. This mill was probably later converted for paper making, appearing as No. 96 in an Excise Letter of 1846,[5] when it was occupied by Samuel W. Wright and Robert Alexander Cochrane. In 1847 another Letter gives the names of paper and pasteboard makers here as Frederick Wiggins, R. A. Cochrane, Edward Arthur Cochrane, Charles Jackson, William Green and John Burrill.

[1] *Universal British Directory of Trade and Commerce*, II, p. 854.
[2] *Alfred*, 28 March 1826.
[3] Letter of 2 May 1827, in General Letters Book No. 13 of Tarporley 1st Ride.
[4] *Bristol Gazette*, 3 June 1813.
[5] Letter of 23 January 1846, in General Letter Book No. 19 of Tarporley 1st Ride.

15, VATCH OR HERMITAGE (STROUD)

William Ward, paper maker, late of Vatch Mills, is mentioned in a newspaper of 1794.[1] In that year Francis and John Ward were at Vatch Mills and the latter's name is recorded in the Excise Letter of 1816 at Mill No. 102, Hermitage, in the Gloucester Collection. Vatch Mill is shown on Greenwood's Map of Gloucestershire, 1824. Mr L. E. Chamberlain informs me that John Ward, 'one of the oldest paper makers in this county,' died at Hermitage Mills in 1826.

16, 17, 18 AND 19, WINCHCOMBE

The Postlip Mills of Messrs Evans, Adlard and Co. Ltd., celebrated their two-hundredth anniversary in 1949. The earliest paper makers here seem to have been the Durham family; perhaps one of them was the Mr Derham who in 1728[2] produced to the Royal Society some 'very good brown and whited brown paper, made of nettles and other weeds.' At any rate, the death of Mr James Durham, an eminent paper maker, at Postlip is recorded in 1760.[3] An interesting link with the industry at Winchcombe is that in 1756[4] William Clark, a millwright and engineer from there had settled in Gloucester and was making paper mills.

About this time there was a paper mill 'very near the town' of Winchcombe,[5] and I. Taylor's Map of Gloucestershire, 1777, shows three paper mills between Winchcombe and Postlip. Paper moulds as well as paper were made at Winchcombe, for in the 1790's[6] the following are recorded there:—William Durham and Samuel Timbrell, paper makers; Joseph Hughes, paper mould maker. This branch of the industry seems to have been continued in the same family for many years, for in 1834 and 1844 there is mention of Alfred Hughes, paper mould

[1] *Gloucester Journal,* 7 July 1794.
[2] *Farley's Bristol Newspaper,* 5 July 1728.
[3] *Felix Farley's Bristol Journal,* 9 February 1760.
[4] *Gloucester Journal,* 27 January 1756.
[5] *The Travels Through England of Dr Richard Pococke* (1757), II, p. 274.
[6] *Universal British Directory of Trade and Commerce,* 4, p. 770.

maker of Winchcombe, and in 1852–3,[1] Hughes and Tovey, paper mould makers there.

Rudder[2] states that Mr William Durham was one of the most considerable paper makers in the kingdom; this was probably the Mr Durham, senior, an 'eminent paper maker,' who died at Postlip in 1803.[3] The first Excise Letter of 1816 and another of 1832 record Nathaniel Lloyd and Co. at Mill No. 103, Postlip, in the Gloucester Collection. A paper mill of this number left off work in 1842, although it is still recorded (in the occupation of W. Townsend) in the *Paper Mills Directory* of 1860. Meanwhile Mill No. 633 (the number still borne by the Postlip Mills to-day) had appeared in the Excise Letters. From 1828 to 1835 it was occupied by paper makers named Tregent, in 1837 by William Searle Evans, in 1847 by Orwell Lloyd Evans and in 1851, when five beating engines were at work,[4] by James Robert Evans, William Gates Adlard and William Gilling. In 1860[5] the firm of Evans and Adlard was producing coloured and blotting papers, and in 1876[6] blottings, coloured papers and filterings, using one machine 60 inches in width.

The fact that only two Excise Numbers were allotted to Mills at Postlip suggests that two of the mills were operated as one. There is, however, the complication that a paper mill existed at Sudeley, close by. This is not named in any of the Excise Letters available, but proof of its existence is in the watermarks of paper made there, an example being 'Lloyd James, Sudeley Mill, 1841.'[7] This mill probably ceased work in the 1840's.

---

[1] Robson's, Pigot's and Slater's *Directory*.

[2] S. Rudder, *New History of Gloucestershire*, 1779, p. 828.

[3] *Salopian Journal*, 23 February 1803. Information from Mr L. C. Lloyd.

[4] *House of Commons Papers*, loc. cit.

[5] *The Paper Mills Directory*, 1860.

[6] Ibid., 1876.

[7] This watermark occurs on one of the papers from the Solicitors' Office of the late Mr George Potts, of Brozeley, now in the possession of Mr L. C. Lloyd.

20, BROMSBERROW

I. Taylor's Map of Gloucestershire, 1777, shows a paper mill on a stream to the north-west of Bromsberrow. The Rev. C. V. Colman, Rector of Bromsberrow, kindly tells me that there is a 'Pepper Mill' on the site (apparently the same as that which is named thus on I. Taylor's Map of Herefordshire, 1786), but neither he nor I has found any other reference.

21, HALL

Hall Farm, about a mile west-south-west of Awre, appears to be on the site of the paper mill shown on Greenwood's Map of Gloucestershire, 1824. In the Excise Letter of 1816 this is designated Mill No. 142, Hall, in the Hereford Collection. Joseph Lloyd was the paper maker then and also in 1829, followed by Thomas Newell in 1832 and Benjamin Small in 1834, the date of the last Excise reference.

22, 23 AND 24, GUNS

Bigland[1] states that Gun's Mill was converted into a paper mill from an iron furnace. This must have occurred before 1743,[2] when 'any Paper Man who is capable of undertaking a White Vat' might have heard of a master by applying to Joseph Lloyd at Gun's Mills where he would 'meet with all suitable encouragement.' Joseph, a son of Joseph Lloyd of Gun's Mills, is recorded in 1739, in the Parish Register of Flaxley.[3]

In 1746,[4] Joseph Lloyd of Abenhall, paper maker, took an apprentice named William Bayham of Newland. On the death of this Mr Lloyd in 1761[5] the paper making at Gun's Mill was to be carried on by the widow and son (Hannah and Joseph Lloyd). Further fragments of information[6] show that the

---

[1] op. cit., I, p. I. .
[2] *Gloucester Journal*, 19 July 1743.
[3] I am indebted to Brigadier L. S. Lloyd for this information.
[4] *The Apprentices of Great Britain* . . . Book 50.
[5] *Gloucester Journal*, 24 February and 22 December 1761.
[6] e.g. Rudder, op. cit., p. 209.

industry was carried on there throughout the second half of the 18th century.

In 1762 and 1766[1] apprentices eloped from Hannah and Joseph Lloyd respectively, paper makers at Gun's Mills. Mr Lloyd was married in 1771[2] to Miss Robinson of Little Deane, 'an amiable young lady with a genteel fortune.' The partnership between Joseph Lloyd the elder and the younger, paper manufacturers of Gun's Mills, was dissolved in 1816.[3]

The Excise Letter of 1816 records Joseph Lloyd at three mills, Nos. 143 (Guns), 144 (Middle Mill), and 145 (Upper Mill). Greenwood's Map of Gloucestershire, 1824, shows three mill symbols at Gun's Mills, and the Tithe Map and Apportionment of Abenhall parish, 1840, refer to the paper mill as the lowest of a group of mills there, some of the others upstream being 'washing mills'; both these and the paper mill, however, were then in the occupation of Joseph Lloyd. Thus it seems fair to assume that Gun's, Middle and Upper Mills were close together on this site. I have no reference to the Upper and Middle Mills, Nos. 145 and 144, after 1832, but board mills No. 144 are recorded as Clanna Mill, Lydney, and Soudley Mill, near Newnham, in 1885 and 1890 respectively.[4]

By 1847 Mill No. 143 had passed to George Lunnon, by 1860[5] to Aaron Goold, making printing papers, by 1866[6] to the Gun's Mills Paper Company, producing coloured papers and cart-ridges, and by 1876[7] to Henry Affleck, the products then being brown papers, made on one machine 53 inches in width. No later reference has been found.

25, RODMORE

This paper mill, in the parish of St. Briavel's, was advertised to let in 1774.[8] The newspaper states that there was 'a Constant

---

[1] *Gloucester Journal*, 23 March 1762, and 1 September 1766.
[2] Ibid., 5 August 1771.
[3] *London Gazette*, 2 November 1816.
[4] *Directory of Paper Makers*, 1885 and 1890.
[5] *The Paper Mills Directory*, 1860.
[6] Ibid., 1866.
[7] Ibid., 1876.
[8] *Gloucester Journal*, 12 December 1774.

Supply of fine Spring Water to serve the Engine and great Plenty of Water to work the Mill.' It was again advertised in 1789,[1] when it was described as 'on a modern construction' and adapted for the making of white or brown paper. I am indebted to the Rev. H. F. Heal, Vicar of St. Briavel's, for the information that William, a son of William Stevens, paper maker, was baptised in 1815. In the Excise Letter of 1816, the mill is numbered 140, in the Hereford Collection and in the occupation of William Stevens; in 1832 the paper maker was James Stevens. Elizabeth Stephens of Rodmore Paper Mills, aged 86, was buried in 1841. I have no later reference.

26, ROWLEY

It seems likely that Rowley Iron Forge (advertised for sale in 1797)[2] was converted to a paper mill. In 1809[3] the partnership between Joseph and Thomas Morris of Chepstow, paper makers at Rowley Forge, Gloucestershire, and Pandy Mill, Monmouthshire, was dissolved. The Excise Letter of 1816 designates Rowley Mill as No. 141 in the Hereford Collection, in the occupation of Thomas Morris. In 1820 the paper maker was Joseph Morris, to whose name that of Richard Morris is added in Excise Letters of 1829 and 1832; in 1841, John Lavender was the occupier. One beating engine was at work at Rowley in 1851.[4] By 1876[5] this had become a board mill. It closed down about 1930.

27, CONE

Richard Barrow, paper maker of Woolaston, is recorded in 1774.[6] He died in 1777, and Cone Paper Mill, lately in his possession, was advertised to be let.[7] It is described as a large

---

[1] *Gloucester Journal*, 15 June 1789.
[2] Ibid., 26 June 1797.
[3] *London Gazette*, 6 May 1809.
[4] *House of Commons Papers*, loc. cit.
[5] *The Paper Mills Directory*, 1876.
[6] *The Bristol Poll Book*, 1774.
[7] *Gloucester Journal*, 26 May 1777.

commodious paper mill, with convenient drying houses. Mr Barrow had for some years past employed the mill in manufacturing different sorts of writing and other papers.

The next paper maker here was probably the John Ward of 'Woollastone' who went bankrupt in 1793.[1] The mill appears to have been out of action for some years, as it does not appear in the Excise Letters until 1820, hence its high number, 519. It was then occupied by John Reece. The firm of Reece and Sandford (who also had paper mills in Monmouthshire) worked this mill up to the 1860's. In 1851[2] six beating engines were at work, and in 1876[3] news, printing and coloured printing papers were made on a machine 48 inches in width.

My last references to this paper mill appear in 1885 and 1890,[4] when the firm of T. P. Gillespie was making Printings, News, E.S. Writings, Envelope Papers, square and angular, and Tinted Papers on a machine 80 inches in width.

28, LONGHOPE

My only reference to this paper mill is in an Excise Letter of 1821,[5] when Benjamin Constance was the paper maker at Mill No. 244, in the Gloucester Collection.

29, QUENINGTON

In 1743[6] Thomas Clarke was apprenticed to Jos. Carby of Ludington, Gloucestershire, paper maker, who was possibly the Mr Joshua Carby who, at the age of 84, died in 1791,[7] described as an 'eminent paper maker and an honest man.' He was at Quenington, where a paper mill is marked on

---

[1] *London Gazette*, 30 March 1793.
[2] *House of Commons Papers*, loc. cit.
[3] *The Paper Mills Directory*, 1876.
[4] *Directory of Paper Makers*, 1885 and 1890.
[5] Excise General Orders, Printed, I, 1819–23. General Letter of 1st September 1821.
[6] *The Apprentices of Great Britain* . . . Book 50, fol. 217.
[7] *Gloucester Journal*, 14 February 1791.

I. Taylor's Map of Gloucestershire, 1777. Rudder[1] states that writing paper was made there and that this furnished employment for a few hands.

This paper mill was known to the Excise authorities as No. 229, in the Marlborough (and later the Oxford) Collection. In 1816 and up to 1833 the paper maker was Joshua C. Radway, and in 1841 Joseph Bence Palser. Four beating engines were at work there in 1851.[2] By 1860,[3] William A. West was making Straw Printings and News at Quenington, and the same firm was there in 1876,[4] the date of my last reference.

30, LITTLE BARRINGTON

According to the Excise Letters, this paper mill (No. 228, in the Marlborough Collection of Excise) appears to have been worked by George Ward from 1816 to 1842, and then by Henry Ward until it was discontinued in 1846.

ACKNOWLEDGMENTS

In addition to acknowledgments made in the above paper, I wish to express my gratitude to all who have helped me in this study and to the Council of the University College of the South West of England, Exeter, for a grant in aid of the research.

---

[1] op. cit., p. 617.
[2] *House of Commons Papers*, loc. cit.
[3] *The Paper Mills Directory*, 1860.
[4] Ibid., 1876.

XXVI

PAPER - MILLS IN HAMPSHIRE

ALMOST all the paper-mills which have been at work at one time or another in Hampshire were established before 1800. The well-known antiquity of the industry at Laverstoke and near Southampton prompted an inquiry into the origins of other paper-mills, and evidence has now been found of paper-making in six localities in the county before 1700. No doubt the powerful, clear streams were one factor attracting early paper-makers to various parts of the county, and by 1750 the industry was well scattered.

Unfortunately, evidence concerning the early paper-makers and paper-mills in the British Isles is extremely dispersed up to 1816, when the Excise authorities,[1] who had managed the duty on paper since 1712, issued what is apparently the first of a series of General Letters and Orders giving the names of paper-makers and the names and numbers of paper-mills in England. From these it is possible to reconstruct something of the history of many paper-mills between 1816 and 1852.

Most of the Hampshire paper-mills ceased work long ago, this process being part of the general contraction of the paper-making industry geographically from about 1830 to the present time. During this long period, hundreds of paper-mills, especially the smaller and more remote mills, went out of production, the adverse factors including increasing and effective competition from better-situated and better-equipped mills, changes in transport and raw materials, the paper duties and so on. As several Hampshire mills played an early and important part in the English paper industry, this article attempts to put on record an outline of the story of each mill based on all the available evidence.

1. Frog Mill (Curdridge).

My thanks are due to the Rev. F. H. Sargeant, Rector of Bishop's Waltham, for kindly searching all the records of that parish and for sending me extracts from the Rate Books, in which the paper-mill is first listed in 1663, at a rate of two shillings. Further entries appear up to 1668, then there is no mention of the paper-mill until 1679, the name " Cornelius " appearing in its stead. The paper-mill reappears from 1680 to 1693.

---

1. I am indebted to the Commissioners of Customs and Excise for permission to read in their library and to quote from their records.

2   PAPER-MILLS IN HAMPSHIRE

In 1738,[2] William Mears was apprenticed to Henry Ball of Bishop's Waltham, paper-maker, who insured his goods and stock, etc., there in 1739.[3] William Meers of Bishop's Waltham, paper-maker, was married in 1744.[4] From 1759 to 1764 the paper-mill was assessed for rates[5] in the name of John Houghton. No other relevant information has been found up to 1805, when Joseph Jellyman of Bishop's Waltham, paper-maker, was married.[6]

Frog Mill is listed in the first Excise Letter of 1816[7] as Paper-mill No. 157, in the Isle of Wight Collection of Excise and worked by John Gater. Other Excise Letters show that it was held by him up to 1835 at least and that it ceased work in 1841.

2. Bentley.

I am indebted to Mr. W. Hugh Curtis for drawing my attention to the fact that this paper-mill is marked on Ogilby's Road Map, 1675. Although it is sometimes referred to as Bentley Paper-mill, there are no references to the paper-making industry in the parish records of Bentley,[8] and in fact the mill was formerly in the parish of Binsted. The burials of Abraham Cawood, paper-maker, and of Elizabeth, wife of Abraham Cawood, paper-maker, of Binsted, are recorded in the Parish Register of Shalford[9] (Surrey) in 1721 and 1712 respectively.

Two early newspaper advertisements[10] state that this paper-mill was to be let in 1712 and 1713. In the first it is described as " Bentley Paper-mills near Farnham, standing on a Fair Streame, and lately fitted up to make fine White Paper " ; the second states that it was " to be Lett good Pennyworth, the Tenant being lately dead." It is marked on a map of 1759[11] as " Corn Mill olim Paper Mill," and its position is noted in two Travelling-books of that period.[12] The paper-mill is listed in the Binsted Parish Rate Book[13] at various dates between 1743 and 1775.

2. *The Apprentices of Great Britain*, 1710-62 (typescript) ; extracted from the Inland Revenue Books at the Public Record Office for the Society of Genealogists, 1921-8. Book 15, fol. 193.

3. *Sun Fire Insurance Policy*, No. 80592, April 24th, 1739. I am indebted to the Sun Insurance Office Ltd. for permission to search their old Policy Registers and to quote from these.

4. *Allegations for Marriage Licences in Hampshire*, 1689 - 1837, II. *Publications of the Harleian Society*, XXXVI, p. 27.

5. The series of rate books is imperfect.

6. *Allegations for Marriage Licences in Hampshire*, I, XXXV, p. 425.

7. General Letter of October 8th, 1816, in General Letter Book, No. 4, of the Ellesmere Division, Chester Collection.

8. Searched by kind permission of the Rector, Canon G. L. Cole.

9. Society of Genealogists' transcript from a microfilm copy by Major Y. Burges.

10. *The Post Boy*, September 2nd, 1712, and April 18th, 1713.

11. I. Taylor's Map of Hampshire.

12. *A New and Accurate Description of the Present Great Roads and the Principal Cross Roads of England and Wales*, 1755 ; and *Kitchener's Post Chaise Companion*, 1767.

13. Searched by kind permission of the Vicar, the Rev. A. Mackay.

3. Bedhampton.

I have found no absolute confirmation of a paper-mill here, but the existence of one seems more than possible in view of two early relevant references. In 1676[14] the will of Richard Roades was proved, and in 1700[15] Thomas Roades was married ; both are described as paper-makers of Bedhampton.

4. Up Mill (West End, South Stoneham).

In 1686[16] this paper-mill belonged to the Company of White Paper Makers and was one of the very few mills in England making white paper at that time. Samuel Willey, paper-maker, Covenant Servant to the Company, " left their Service " and went from their mill near Southampton called " Upp Mill " in July 1693.[17] Several French and probably also Dutch paper-makers were employed there. In the South Stoneham Registers[18] are recorded a Frenchman (daughter christened, 1687), Peter and Esther Jacques " belonging to the Paper Mills " (daughter christened, 1701), Nicholas Nowell " a Dutch Man at the Paper Mills " (daughter christened, 1702), " a frinch child at the paper mill " (christened, 1704), " a Frinch man at the paper mill " (children baptised, 1708), and Anne Roche of the Paper Mills (married, 1709/10). Richard Batt, of South Stoneham, paper-maker, was married in 1701.[19] Other people of the paper-mill mentioned in the early Registers are Beal (daughter buried, 1701) and John Robinson, paper-maker (married, 1731).

Daniel, son of Mr. Daniel Rousillon, was christened in 1699. On the death of the elder (who had been churchwarden at South Stoneham), the " great Paper Mills, Flock Mills and Corn Mill called Up Mills, with a new Brick dwelling-House, all in good repair . . . . within three miles of Southampton and nine of Winchester," late in his possession, were advertised in 1720[20] to be let or sold. His son seems to have carried on the business, however, as Mr. Roussillon was rated for the mills as late as 1756. From 1758 to 1766 the assessment was on Mr. (Harry) Ball who, when married in 1769[21] was described as a paper-maker of South Stoneham.

14. *Index of Wills proved in the Prerogative Court of Canterbury*, X, *The Index Library*, British Record Society, 71, 1948, fol. 94.

15. *Calendar of Sussex Marriage Licences, Archdeaconry of Chichester*, 1575 - 1730, Sussex Record Society, IX, 1909, p. 138.

16. *V.C.H., Hants*, III, 1908, pp. 479-480.

17. *London Gazette*, September 25th, 1693.

18. The Parish Registers and Rate Books were searched by kind permission of the Vicar, the Rev. C. R. Macbeth.

19. *Allegations for Marriage Licences in Hampshire*, I, XXXV, p. 36.

20. *The Daily Courant*, January 22nd, 1720, and *London Gazette*, March 26th, 1720.

21. *Allegations for Marriage Licences in Hampshire, loc. cit.*

In 1771[22] an advertisement referring to West-end Mills appeared in the following terms : " Wanted, a sober man at West-end Mills, that is capable of carrying on the Business of Paper-making." Applications were to be made to John Gater of Swaythling, Southampton.

The mill was known to the Excise authorities as No. 158, West End, in the Isle of Wight Collection, with John and Edward Gater, paper-makers, in charge.   In 1851[23] there was only one beating-engine at work, and my last reference is in 1860,[24] when John Gater and Company were said to be producing Writing Papers hand- and machine-made.

5. Bramshott.

My thanks are due to Mr. A. H. Salisbury for kindly sending me the results of his search of the early records of Bramshott parish.   The early Registers contain the following relevant details : George West " from ye Paper Mill " was buried in 1698/9 ; John Salter " ye paper man " was buried in 1711 ; John, son of John Smith, Paper-man, was baptised in 1714.   In 1709 John Porter was listed " for the paper-mill," but within a short time the mill seems to have passed to John Woods, of Bramshott, merchant, who in 1719[25] insured his goods and merchandise in his paper-mills and warehouses adjoining in Bramshott.   The possibility that the port of Chichester was the outlet for some of the paper made at Bramshott is suggested by the fact that Woods also insured[26] his goods and merchandise in his warehouse on Dell Key near the city of Chichester.

Shortly after this, however, the owner was Mary Streater of Bramshott, widow, who in 1725[27] insured her paper-mills only in the parish of Bramshott, including the wheels, hammers, engines and other utensils in the said mills, then in the occupation of John Graveat.   Later in the 18th century the mill was occupied by Richard Pim.   As a paper-maker of Bramshott, he took apprentices[28] in 1747, 1754 and 1757.   In 1761[29] " the warehouse and workshop belonging to Mr. Pim's paper-mill at Bramshott were wilfully set on fire by one of his apprentices.   There being a great quantity of pitched rope and rags in the warehouses, they were burnt to the ground in a few minutes, and the mill was with great difficulty

22. *Reading Mercury and Oxford Gazette*, September 2nd, 1771.
23. *House of Commons Papers*, 1852, Vol. 51, No. 128.
24. *The Paper Mills Directory*, 1860.
25. *Sun Fire Insurance Policy*, No. 12971, January 1st, 1719.
26. *Ibid.*, No. 24500, December 21st, 1721 ; but he also insured his Corn Mills at Nutbourn, near Chichester (Policy No. 24499, December 21st, 1721), and the corn trade may have been the link with the port.
27. *Ibid.*, No. 38051, February 28th, 1725.
28. *The Apprentices of Great Britain*, Book/Fol. 18/31, 19/199 and 21/30.
29. Capes, *Rural Life in Hampshire*. Information from Mr. A. H. Salisbury.

saved." The damage was computed at £600. In 1763,[30] 1786[31] and the 1790's[32] the paper-maker there was Henry Pim.

The Bramshott mill was known to the Excise authorities as No. 119, in the Hampshire Collection. In 1816 it was worked by John Elstone, and by 1832 William Warren. The firm of William Warren and Sons, followed by Warren Brothers, ran the mill for the remainder of the 19th century. In 1885 and 1890[33] the following products were advertised as made by this firm at Bramshott and Standford Mills : Cartridges, White and Coloured Royal Hands, Small Hands, Middles, Browns and Paper Bags. These were made on two machines 54 inches in width. Later Directories, up to 1920, state that Bank of England papers were made at Bramshott by Messrs. Portal on a machine 72 inches in width. The mill last appears in the 1924 edition of these Directories.

6. Clatterford (Isle of Wight).

Roscoe's reference[34] to this paper-mill is the only one I have found. He states "About the commencement of last century, an enterprising foreigner, an emigrant, erected a paper-mill near Clatterford ; but the undertaking did not succeed, and was eventually abandoned. Vestiges of the mill and pond are still seen, and the house is known at this time by the name of the Paper Mill." A paper-maker named Isaac Tipps, of Carisbrooke, was married in 1711.[35]

7. Bere Mill.

Shortly after 1711 Henri Portal, who had been trained as a paper-maker at the South Stoneham Mill, took a lease of Bere Mill, near Whitchurch.[36] He insured his goods and his merchandise in his dwelling house there in 1717.[37] This paper-mill is marked on I. Taylor's and T. Milne's Maps of Hampshire, 1759 and c. 1791.

8, 9 and 10. Romsey.

The earliest reference I have found to a paper-maker here concerns Math. son of Math. Plyer of Romsey infra, paper-maker, who was apprenticed to Robert Newlands of the same place, cloth-worker, in 1715.[38] There are several references to John Hockley,

30. Rate Assessments.
31. B.M. Add. MSS., 15054, fol. 14.
32. Universal British Directory of Trade and Commerce, 3, p. 92, wherein henry Pim is described as a paper-maker, maltster and miller.
33. Directory of Paper Makers, 1885 and 1890.
34. T. Roscoe, Summer Tour to the Isle of Wight, 1843, p. 8.
35. Allegations for Marriage Licences in Hampshire, II, p. 279.
36. V.C.H., Hants, V, 1912, pp. 489-490.
37. Sun Fire Insurance Policy, No. 8679, July 8th, 1717.
38. The Apprentices of Great Britain, Book 4, fol. 85.

paper-maker of Romsey, who was married in 1733.[39]   His name appears in the Romsey Poor Law Assessments[40] from 1745 to 1762, during which period he was rated for the paper-mill near the Abbey.   Another paper-mill was apparently rebuilt in 1759 and was then also assessed in Hockley's name.   In that year[41] he took an apprentice named John Edwards.   One of the chief paper-makers later in the 18th century was probably the William Sharp of Romsey, whose partnership with Joseph Everett of London, Stationer, was dissolved in 1783[42] ; the pasteboard and message-card manufactory was in future to be carried on by William Sharp in Worship Street, Upper Moorfields, on his own account.   It is probable that a third paper-mill had been added by the 1790's,[43] when John Dusautoy, W. Godfrey, James Skeats and William Sharp are listed as paper-makers at Romsey, and the third mill may have been the " newly erected paper-mill " in the occupation of Messrs. Godfrey and Skeats, advertised for sale in 1800.[44]   Another paper-maker, Benjamin Mitchell of Romsey, was married in 1812.[45]

The Excise Letter of 1816 records three paper-mills at Romsey, in the Salisbury Collection.   Nos. 340, 341 and 342 were occupied respectively by Stephen Sharp, John Skeats and Company, and Edward Jones.   By 1818 William Brookman had replaced the second firm at Mill No. 341 (Test Mill).   By 1850, Thomas Westcott was at No. 342 (Abbey Mill), and only one mill is recorded in 1851.[46] In 1860 William Brookman was making Printing Papers at Mill No. 341 and by 1866 this mill had passed to William Harvey, who was still there in 1876,[47] making Royal Hands, Small Hands and Browns on one machine 60 inches in width.

In 1885[48] William Harvey at Test Mill, No. 341, was making Thin Caps, Crowns, Royals, Thick and Thin Browns.   By 1930 a mill of the same number was called Drayton Mill, making Browns, Specialities and Toilet Papers.   Paper-making ceased at Drayton Mill in 1939.

In 1885 Randall and Company were making Browns, patent Compressed Leather and Leather Boards on two machines 60 inches in width and two vats, at Abbey Mills.   In 1910 the products were Leather Boards, Glazed Boards, Shank Boards and Stiffeners, and in 1948 Trunk and Suitcase Boards, Shoe Boards, etc.

39. *Allegations for Marriage Licences in Hampshire*, I, p. 386.
40. I am indebted to Sir Richard Luce for information from the Romsey Rate Books (imperfect series).
41. *The Apprentices of Great Britain*, Book 22, fol. 21.
42. *London Gazette*, May 13th, 1783.
43. *Universal British Directory of Trade and Commerce*, IV, pp. 352-4.
44. *Reading Mercury and Oxford Gazette*, May 5th, 1800.
45. *Allegations for Marriage Licences in Hampshire*, II, p. 38.
46. *House of Commons Papers*, loc. cit.
47. *The Paper Mills Directory*, 1860, 1866 and 1876.
48. *Directory of Paper Makers*, 1885, 1930, 1910, 1948.

11 and 12. Laverstoke.

Henri Portal acquired the lease of this paper-mill in 1718[49] and the contract for Bank of England paper in 1724. He insured his dwelling-house, paper-mill and outhouses adjoining at Laverstoke for £300 in 1719[50] and the early expansion of his concern is suggested by the facts that in 1727 he insured his buildings and stock at his paper-mill at Laverstoke for £1200, and in 1742 he also insured "one other little paper-mill situated in the same yard."[51]

In 1765[52] Jos. Portal was a signatory to a petition concerning the Excise duty on paper. By the 1790's[53] the firm had become Portal and Bridges, whose names appear at Mill No. 337, in the Salisbury Collection, in the Excise Letter of 1816. About this time[54] two vats were constantly employed all the year round. In 1832 the paper-maker was John Portal and in 1849 Wyndham Spencer Portal. In 1851[55] one engine was at work and two were silent. By 1876[56] six vats were being employed, and by 1885 nine vats. By 1890 a machine of 54 inches in width had been added and by 1910 the number of vats had risen to fifteen. This famous mill is, of course, still at work.

13. Warnford.

A paper-mill here is mentioned in an addition, dated January 2nd, 1619, at the end of the Will of John Knight of Chawton dated August 15th, 1617.[57] John Grivatt, paper-maker of Warnford, insured his houses in Hambledon in 1722 and 1724, and Francis Filer, paper-maker of Warnford, was a party to the insurance of the Faulcon Inn in Warnford in 1730.[58] I am indebted to the Rev. Charles A. Millen for the information that there is still a building in Warnford known as "Paper Mill," and that in the earliest Rate List of Warnford, 1732, ffrancis ffyler was rated 8d. for the mill and 2/6 "ffor the milles."

14. Down Mill.

In 1729, 1730, 1732 and 1739[59] policies were taken out to insure "Down Husband Mills" near Whitchurch. The first three contain the name of Tobias Butler, paper-maker, and the fourth

49. V.C.H., Hants, V, 1912, pp. 489-490.
50. Sun Fire Insurance Policy, No. 15682, November 6th, 1719.
51. Ibid., Policies No. 41551, April 24th, 1727, and No. 92086, July 26th, 1742.
52. Excise and Treasury Correspondence, May 24th, 1765.
53. Universal British Directory of Trade and Commerce, IV, p. 937.
54. C. Vancouver, General View of the Agriculture of Hampshire, pp. 403-4.
55. House of Commons Papers, loc. cit.
56. The Paper Mills Directory, 1876, and Directory of Paper Makers, 1885, 1890, 1910.
57. P.C.C. Dale 17. I am indebted to the Rev. Charles A. Millen, Rector of Warnford, for this information.
58. Sun Fire Insurance Policies, Nos. 21764, August 3rd, 1722 ; 31015, May 7th, 1724 ; 51312, August 17th, 1730.
59. Ibid., Nos. 48331, August 1st, 1729 ; 52002, October 20th, 1730 : 59812, January 17th, 1732 ; 80813, May 22nd, 1739.

Lawrence Turton, paper-maker, who is, however, described in the policy of 1729 as a shalloon-maker of Whitchurch, insuring his mills. Henry French, paper-maker, late of the parish of Downe Husband, was in debt in 1743.[60] The paper-mill, as also Laverstoke and Bere paper-mills, is shewn on several maps of Hampshire of the 18th and early 19th centures, including I. Taylor's (1759), T. Milne's (*c.* 1791), Mudge's (1817) and Greenwood's (1826).

Down Mill was numbered 335 by the Excise authorities and was in the Salisbury Collection. From the 1790's[61] to the 1820's William Allee was the paper-maker and he was followed by Thomas and William Slade in the 1830's and Charles Fuller in the 1840's. Fire consumed the mill in 1846.[62] It appears to have been rebuilt and the Rev. F. B. Allen, Vicar of Hurstbourne Priors, kindly tells me that the Parish Registers contain the name of Thomas Batt, paper-maker, married in 1850.

The rebuilt mill seems to have been given the number 338 and to have been called the Falcon Mill. In 1851[63] one beating-engine was at work and two were silent. In 1866 it was not at work, nor in 1876,[64] when its advertised product was printing paper, made on a machine 60 inches in width.

15. Standford.

I am indebted to Mrs. J. M. E. Stevens for sending me a complete list of the paper-makers mentioned in the records of Headley Parish ; some of the entries can be connected with Bramshott, Barford and Standford paper-mills, but others cannot be separately linked with any one of these. The first relevant entry, William Eade, paper-maker (daughter buried in 1739), may be connected with Standford, as may other entries of paper-makers in the 18th century : Richard Beck (daughter baptised, 1761), Sarah Wills, a paper-maker's daughter from Whitchurch (buried, 1762), John Gosling (examined, 1763). Standford paper-mill may be that shewn on I. Taylor's map, 1759, and it is probably that shewn on T. Milne's map, 1791. The Excise authorities numbered it Mill No. 120, in the Hampshire Collection, with paper-makers in occupation as follows : 1816, James Edds ; 1832, James West ; 1836, Robert Long ; 1842, William Warren.

The Headley Parish Registers record the following paper-makers at Standford : 1813, Richard Smith ; 1828, James Tilbury and Richard Curtis (1828-31) ; 1830, Robert Puttick ; 1832-6, Thomas Tilbury ; 1832, James Stubble ; 1836-41, James West ;

60. *London Gazette,* August 20th, 1743.
61. *Universal British Directory of Trade and Commerce,* IV, p. 938.
62. *The Devonshire Chronicle and Exeter News,* August 11th, 1846.
63. *House of Commons Papers, loc. cit.*
64. *The Paper Mills Directory,* 1876.

1849-57, George Elstone ; 1859, Edwin Eggar ; 1874, William Suter, senior, foreman in Messrs. Warren's Mill, Standford. My last reference is in 1890 (see Bramshott above).

16 and 17. Upper and Lower Barford.

Both these paper-mills are marked on J. Rocque's Map of Surrey, 1775. As stated under Standford, however, some of the early entries of paper-makers in the Headley Parish Registers may be linked with these mills. Allen Mills, of Barford, paper-maker, was bankrupt in 1777,[65] and one of the Barford paper-mills (" well adapted for making printing papers ") was to be let or sold in 1778.[66] A partnership between Abraham Harding senior and junior of Barford Mill, paper-makers, was dissolved in 1790.[67] Samuel Hale, paper-maker of Headley, is mentioned in the Parish Registers in 1814 ; a notice to his creditors appeared in 1816.[68]

The Barford paper-mills were known to the Excise authorities as Nos. 121 (Upper) and 122 (Lower), in the Hampshire Collection. In 1816 they were respectively occupied by Francis and Timothy Bryant ; the latter, however, is recorded in the Parish Registers as a paper-manufacturer of Barford Upper Mill in 1814, 1822 and 1825. The Upper Mill seems to have ceased work in the 1830's, my last reference, in an Excise Letter of 1829, being to James Harman there.

The Parish Registers contain other references to paper-makers at or of Barford as follows : 1816, William Eads ; 1821, William Boxall ; 1822, Thomas Thistle ; 1823, Richard Waller ; 1827, Henry Hobday (Barford Lower Mill) ; 1840 and 1842, Thomas Tilbury ; 1838, Thomas Puttick (Barford Mill) ; 1849, William Tilbury (Barford Mill) ; 1873, Henry Cropper (machinist, Barford Mill).

18. Hook.

This paper-mill, which was situated on the White Water at Wolson Bridge, is shewn on several old maps of Hampshire : I. Taylor's (1759), T. Milne's (c. 1791), Mudge's (1817) and Greenwood's (1826) ; it also appears on J. Andrews and Andrew Dury's Map of the Country 65 miles around London (1809 edition, probably compiled 1777). My first reference to a paper-maker (Thomas Andrews) is in 1749,[69] and the name of Edward Chamberlin appears in the Excise Letter of 1816, in which the paper-mill is numbered 338 in the Salisbury Collection. This is my last reference to it.

65. *London Gazette*, March 18th, 1777.
66. *Reading Mercury and Oxford Gazette*, April 6th, 1778.
67. *London Gazette*, July 13th, 1790.
68. *Ibid.*, December 21st, 1816.
69. *Sun Fire Insurance Policy*, No. 118494, October 27th, 1749.

19. Alton.

I am indebted to Mr. W. Hugh Curtis for his kind attempts to find information about this paper-mill in the 18th century or earlier. However, we have discovered no paper-maker here earlier than the 1770's, when William Barrett went bankrupt.[70] He seems to have been followed by Robert Myears who, described as a paper-maker of Alton, is named in a notice of 1778[71] referring to Barford Mill. Alton Mills were to be let in 1780,[72] when they were in his occupation. The advertisement states that he was ill and could not attend to the business ; he died later that year.[73] At that time the premises consisted of a two-vat paper-mill and a water grist-mill under one roof. The paper-mill was considered to be particularly capable of making fine goods, " from the purity of the water supplying the engine."

The next tenant was probably William King, who apparently gave his name to the paper-mill, and was there until 1796,[74] when the " very commodious and convenient paper-mill " at Alton, lately in his occupation, was to be let. The excise number of this mill was 339, in the Salisbury Collection. The letter of 1816 states that the paper-maker then was Thomas Easton. He was followed by John Edward Spicer (1826), with Cornelius Paulton (about 1842-4). The mill appears to have been idle for a short period from 1848, and a new number, 159, was assigned to it. The mill was known by this number until the firm of Spicers removed to Eynsford, Kent, in 1909, when it closed down. For many years the firm of H. and W. R. Spicer and Company produced hand-made writing and account book papers, drawing and parchment papers, bank notes, etc., using eight vats.[75]

20. Clatford.

My earliest reference to this paper-mill is in the Excise Letter of 1816, wherein it is numbered 336, in the Salisbury Collection. In 1816 and 1817 the paper-makers were John Titcombe, and Thomas and William Slade, whose mill was insured in 1817 for £1000 and in 1826 for £2000.[76] They were followed by John Bune about 1831. The only other early references to paper-makers at Upper Clatford occur in the Parish Registers, 1819, when children of Budd and Baker were baptised.[77]

70. *London Gazette*, November 23rd, 1773. William Barret took an apprentice in 1770. (*P.R.O. Apprenticeship Registers*, *I.R.I.*, Book 26, fol. 148.)
71. *Reading Mercury and Oxford Gazette*, April 6th, 1778.
72. *Ibid.*, January 17th, 1780.
73. *Ibid.*, March 27th, 1780.
74. *Ibid.*, June 27th, 1796.
75. *Directory of Paper Makers*, 1885 and 1890.
76. I am indebted to Mr. R. Baker for this information.
77. The Rev. R. Bridle, Priest-in-Charge, Upper Clatford, kindly sent me this information.

John Bune was succeeded by William Bune, then by James Bune, who was still at this mill about 1851,[78] when one beating-engine was at work and one was silent.[79] From 1860 to 1885 Francis G. Giles at Clatford is recorded in trade directories. The chief products were hand- or machine-made air-dried writing-papers made on one vat and one machine 40 inches in width.

21. Botley.

Botley paper-mill is recorded in an Excise Letter of 1832[80] as No. 79, in the Hampshire Collection, worked by William and James Clark. It ceased work in 1848.

22. Overton.

Directories from 1924[81] onwards record Messrs. Portals at Overton Mills, making Treasury Notes, Security Papers and Loans.

During the period of the geographical expansion of the paper-making industry in England, several other Hampshire mills were advertised as suitable for paper-making. The chief advantage of the sites thus advertised was the availability of fine, clear water from ponds and streams. These mills included Steep Mill near Peters-field,[82] Grewell Mill,[83] and Longparish Mill.[84] I have no evidence that any of these was taken up by paper-makers.

Acknowledgments.

In addition to the acknowledgments made in this article, I wish to express my gratitude to all who have helped me in this study, including many who could not be named in connection with any particular item of information. I am also grateful to the Council of the University College of the South-West of England, Exeter, for a grant in aid of my research.

78. Slater's *Directory*, Hampshire, 1852, p. 10.
79. *House of Commons Papers*, *loc. cit.*
80. General Letter of November 28th, 1832, in General Letter Book No. 15 of the Tarporley 1st Ride.
81. *Directory of Paper Makers.*
82. *Oxford Gazette and Reading Mercury*, May 18th, 1767.
83. *Ibid.*, June 19th, 1769.
84. *Reading Mercury and Oxford Gazette*, April 1st, 1800.

XXVII

PAPER-MILLS IN HEREFORDSHIRE

All the paper-mills which formerly worked in Herefordshire seem to have been established during the period of the expansion of the paper-making industry in England in the eighteenth century. As with Shropshire, Monmouthshire and Cornwall among others, the county has lost this industry, the distribution of which has shrunk in many parts of England since the 1830's. All the mills were quite small and were probably forced to close by the competition of bigger and better-placed mills where paper-making machines were installed, or by economic and geographical factors of a general nature, including taxation, the concentration of the industry into fewer and bigger units, and changes in types of transport and raw materials.

Up to 1816, information concerning paper-mills and paper-makers in this country has to be culled from many scattered local and " national " sources. In 1816, the Excise authorities, who had managed the duty on paper since 1712, issued what is apparently the first of a series of General Letters and Orders containing the names and numbers of paper-mills at work and the names of the paper-makers in possession. I am indebted to the Commissioners of Customs and Excise for permission to search and to quote from these records in their library.

Many of the old paper-mills were scattered through the countryside and were situated not on the major rivers but on tributary streams where there was enough water to drive the mills and a supply of clean water for the manufacture of paper from rags by the hand or vat process. Herefordshire had only a few mills, but none of them was on the Wye.

Further information about any of the paper-mills will be particularly welcome.

1. Grove Mill Near Presteigne

The only early information referring to this mill has been kindly provided by Mr. W. H. Howse, who searched the deeds of Grove House by permission of Mr. E. Davies. An indenture of 29th March, 1776, refers to some land attached to the house as Paper Mill Close, which was conveyed from the possession of Stansil Griffiths to Thomas Legge. An earlier indenture of 30th November, 1750, names four fields attached to the house, but none of them bore this name, so perhaps the paper-mill was established between 1750 and 1776. The next possible reference to this paper-mill occurs in an Excise Letter of 1822, when a " new " mill, No. 504, Grove, in the Salop Collection of Excise, was opened in the name of Benjamin Rowley. Mr. Howse tells me that a notice of sale in the *Hereford Journal* of 30th December, 1846, stated that Mr. Beebee of Willey Court was selling (among other property which was specified) " Grove House, Stapleton, near Lugg Bridge, Presteigne, with outbuildings and a paper-mill ". No later reference has been found.

2. HAY MILLS

This paper-mill was situated on the river Teme, about $4\frac{1}{2}$ miles west by south of Ludlow Castle. In 1740[1] it was advertised to be let and entered upon immediately. It was described as " a Paper Mill newly fitted up in the best manner " with engine, hammers, *etc.*, and was situated " upon a clear and fair-coloured water more than sufficient in the driest seasons and not flooding in the wettest ". There was said to be constant carriage to Bewdley by pack horses almost every day in the week, within a mile of the mill.

Three more advertisements of this paper-mill in the same newspaper[2] have been found. The first two state that it was to be let, and was a paper-mill with an engine for making white paper. The third also states that it was to let and in complete repair. My last reference, in 1771[3], is a newspaper notice referring to James Oliver, who had been apprenticed at the age of six to Mr. Thomas White, Master Paper-maker at Hay Mills and had served him upwards of seven years.

3. BILL MILLS

In 1731,[4] William Morris was apprenticed to Thomas Parker of Weston, Hereford, paper-maker. Mr. W. N. Wintle, the present owner of Bill Mills, kindly tells me that the deeds mention the paper-mill in 1736, when the occupier was a Mr. Bond, and in 1775, when the name of Thomas Parker appears. The latter is mentioned as the lessee in two advertisements in 1774,[5] when the paper-mill " in exceeding good repair, and constantly supplied with water ", was for sale. The paper-mill is shown on Taylor's Map of Herefordshire, 1786. It is listed in the first Excise Letter of 1816[6] as Paper-mill No. 146, Bill Mill, in the Hereford Collection of Excise, worked by Joseph Lloyd, paper-maker. My last reference to it is in 1821.[7]

---

[1] *The Gloucester Journal*, 15th April, 1740.
[2] *ibid.*, 26th July, 1748 ; 16th December, 1760 ; and 1st November, 1762.
[3] *The British Chronicle or Pugh's Hereford Journal*, 28th May, 1771.
[4] *The Apprentices of Great Britain*, 1710–1762 (typescript) ; extracted from the Inland Revenue Books at the Public Record Office for the Society of Genealogists, 1921–28. Book 49. Fol. 251.
[5] *The Gloucester Journal*, 14th March, 1774, and *The British Chronicle or Pugh's Hereford Journal*, 7th April, 1774.
[6] Letter dated 8th October, 1816, in General Letter Book No. 4 of the Ellesmere Division, Chester Collection.
[7] W. Cobbett, *Rural Rides*, I, 1821, p. 37.

4. TRESECK

This paper-mill was advertised for sale in 1776,[1] when it was said to be in excellent repair. A similar advertisement ten years later[2] stated that it was then in the possession of Thomas White. Several entries in the Excise Letters refer to Paper-mill No. 147, Tresick, in the Hereford Collection of Excise, with paper-makers as follows: 1816, Edward Williams; 1819, James Preece and Thomas Cary; 1825, Joseph Robinson; 1827, Richard Thornbury; 1832, John Johnson; 1838, Edward Johnson (?). The paper-mill is marked on Bryant's Map of Herefordshire, 1835, but it must have ceased work shortly after 1838.

5. MORTIMER'S CROSS

I am indebted to Mr. Rhys Jenkins for drawing my attention to Dr. R. Pococke's reference[3] to this paper-mill, situated " in a large plain ". It also is shown on Bryant's Map of Herefordshire, 1835, but the Excise Letters show that it had ceased work by then. It appears in the first Excise Letter as Paper-mill No. 148, in the Hereford Collection of Excise, worked by Henry Pearson Cooke, but the mill bearing this number was discontinued in 1824. Meanwhile in 1823, Paper-mill No. 536, Mortimer's Cross, is recorded in the occupation of John Wade, paper-maker, to whose name that of George Wood was added in 1824; this mill also was discontinued in that year. In an Excise Letter of 1832, Mill No. 148 is blank but No. 536 is listed in the possession of Henry Pearson Cooke.

6. CUSOP

My only information about this paper-mill is that it is marked on Bryant's Map of Herefordshire, 1835. The Rev. George Griffiths, Rector of Cusop, kindly informs me that there is a local tradition that many years ago three mills, flour, cider and paper, existed in Cusop Dingle, but he can find no confirmatory evidence. So far it has not been possible to identify this with any paper-mill named in the Excise Letters, and it is therefore rather likely that it worked before 1816, possibly even in the eighteenth century.

7. FURNACE, ST. WEONARDS

I have found only two references to paper-makers here. In 1808[4] Benjamin Street, paper-maker, of St. Weonards, took an apprentice named John Rogers. Street's name appears in the Excise Letter of 1816 in connection with Mill No. 126, called Furnace, in the Hereford Collection of Excise. This mill appears to have been at a place still bearing that name in the parish of St. Weonards.

---

[1] *The Gloucester Journal*, 22nd January, 1776 and *The London Evening Post*, 27th January, 1776.

[2] *The British Chronicle or Pugh's Hereford Journal*, 29th June, 1786.

[3] *The Travels through England of Dr. R. Pococke*, (1756), ii, p. 222.

[4] Records of the Office of Inland Revenue, Apprenticeship Books (in the Public Record Office), Book 72, Fol. 121.

XXVIII

EARLY PAPER MILLS IN KENT

The Kentish mills have played and still play a very important part in paper making in England, yet little is known of the history of some of them. This prompted an investigation into the origins of the early paper mills in the county. The information so far available has proved to be extremely fragmentary, but as is shown below, is sufficient to suggest that at least 20 paper mills worked in Kent in the period 1588-1738. The latter year is a convenient limit to the present study, for one of the very few early authoritative statements was then made as to the number of paper mills which existed in this country. In reply to an estimate by two paper makers, Samuel Galliott and Richard Parry (the first of whom was probably earlier and perhaps even in 1738 at Eynsford Mill in Kent'), that there were then 600 paper mills in England and Wales, the Commissioners of Excise stated that there were but 278². The evidence produced below suggests that Kent had about a score of these, but it is readily admitted that other paper mills in the county may have already come into existence. To these, however, no reference as early as 1738 has yet been found.

1 and 2. Dartford

No evidence has been found to challenge the general acceptance of John Spilman's mill at Dartford as the first of the Kentish paper-mills. This was in existence by 1588³ and was probably the mill which suggested to Shakespeare his topical reference to a paper mill in *Henry VI* (Part Two, Act IV, Scene 7). As the relevant words in the play are spoken by Jack Cade (who led the rebellion of 1450) it has sometimes been thought that Shakespeare had in mind a paper mill in England in the first half of the fifteenth century. One writer' connects Jack Cade's words with Bromley in Kent (where there was indeed a paper mill in the eighteenth century⁵ if not earlier), stating that in or about the year 1449 Lord Saye purchased

the mill and converted it into a paper mill. I have
found no documentary evidence in support of this.

After the death of John Spilman the younger, the
first Dartford paper mill seems to have been carried on
by paper makers named Blackwell, followed by Archer,
up to 1740. Ralph Blackwell, of Dartford, paper
maker, was married in 1666/7[6]. In 1736[7], William
Quelch, of Wrotham, paper maker, insured his house
and paper mill under one roof in Dartford parish, in
the tenure of Richard Archer. The latter, described
as "Richard Archer the elder, of Dartford, paper
maker," was declared a bankrupt in 1740[8], and the
paper mill and premises late in his possession were
advertised for sale in the same year[9]. Towards the
end of the seventeenth century another paper mill
had been established at Dartford and was used by
the Company of White Paper Makers[10]. An advertisement in 1700[11] states that a horse had been lost
from the paper-mill grounds near Dartford; this may
refer to either mill. There can be little doubt, however, that the second mill continued to work throughout the first half of the eighteenth century. In 1748
and 1749[12], John Collins and William Curd were apprenticed to William Quelch and John Terry respectively, paper makers of Dartford.

3. Eynsford

I am indebted to the manager of Eynsford Paper
Mills for the information that he possesses a document dated 1648 which shows that part of a flour mill
there was at that time converted to a paper mill.
Entries in the Eynsford Parish Registers [13] suggest
that families of paper makers named Galliott and
Johannot were at Eynsford Paper Mill in the 1690's
and for many years afterwards, in the case of the
Johannots. Andrew Johannot, Senior, died in 1737.
A paper maker of the same name, of Eynsford, who
went bankrupt in 1746[14], was probably his son, born
in 1706.

Two other sons of Andrew Johannot seem to have
occupied early paper mills at Tottenham and Deptford. In 1735[15], Israel Johannot of Tottenham, paper
maker, insured his mill and stock, etc. Josias Johannot, of Deptford, paper maker, went bankrupt in 1753[16].
These names appear in the baptisms recorded in the
Eynsford Parish Registers, in 1695 and 1706 respectively.

EARLY PAPER MILLS IN KENT

4. Shoreham

In 1719 and 1728 respectively, Alexander Russell
and John Russell of Shoreham, paper makers, insured
a paper mill here[17]. Samuel, son of Edward Sanders,
paper maker of " Shockham," Kent, was apprenticed
in 1721[18]. William Wilmott of Shoreham, paper maker,
insured his paper mill in 1737 and 1740[19], and took
an apprentice named Thomas Haynes in 1747[20].

5. Wrotham

In 1723 and 1731[21], William Buttershaw and James
Cripps, both of Ightham, were respectively apprenticed to William Quelch of Wrotham, paper maker.
These apprentices' names are interesting in relation
to the later development of the industry in Kent,
when they became very well known. We find William,
son of James Cripps, paper maker, baptised at West
Peckham in 1749[22], and apprentices taken by James
Cripps, of St. Pauls Cray, paper maker, in 1757, 1762
and 1766[23]. William Buttonshaw, paper maker of West
Peckham, took an apprentice in 1755[24].

6. Strood

John Hadds of " Stroud," Kent, paper maker, took
an apprentice named John Murfield in 1718[25]. I have
not been able to confirm the presence of a paper mill
at Strood.

7. Snodland

C. H. Fielding[26] refers to an entry in the Snodland
Parish Registers stating that a stranger at Snodland
Mill was buried on June 10, 1636, and comments " this
seems to point to Snodland having had a paper mill
pretty early, as the trade is mentioned about this
date." James Smith, paper maker, was buried at
Snodland in 1705[27].

8. East Malling

A newspaper notice in 1723[28] states that Matthew
Lane, apprentice to William Middleton of East
Malling, paper maker, had absented himself.

9. Tovil

Peter Musgrove, of " Tovill " in the parish of Maidstone, paper maker, insured his paper mill in 1727[29].
In 1731 it was reported that the powder mills at Tovil
had blown up[30], and that a paper mill and house ad-

joining were destroyed[21]. William Musgrove of Maidstone, paper maker, took an apprentice named John Jones in 1742[22]. This entry is probably connected with Tovil Mill.

10. Loose

In 1721[3], James Harris of Loose, son of William Harris, paper maker, was apprenticed to Thomas Wilds of Maidstone, paper maker. In 1741[24], William Quelch of Loose, paper maker, insured his house in Loose and his paper mill, etc., under one roof only, standing singly. He took as an apprentice in 1743[25] one Abraham Musgrave who later appears to have taken over the business at Loose, for as a paper maker there he had an apprentice in 1757[26].

11. Otham

William Keeble of Otham, paper maker, took apprentices named Isaac Jones and Ste(phen?) Curtis in 1722 and 1723 respectively[27]. He insured the mill in 1723[28].

12. Sandling

In 1716[29], William Gill of Maidstone, insured his paper mill at "Sandlin." Another policy was taken out in 1731[30] by Edward Rowe (near the East India House in Leadenhall Street, Stationer) on his paper mill known by the name of Sandlin Mill near Aylesford, in the tenure of David Dean.

13 and 14. Boxley

A deed of 1671[31] refers to premises, including a paper mill, in the parishes of Boxley, Burnham and Aylesford, the tenant then being Thomas Willard. No trace of a paper mill has been found in Burnham parish. If the reference concerns Boxley, this was very possibly the mill where John Hillier of Boxley, paper maker, in 1712[32] and 1715 took apprentices named James Bridgeland of Cranbrook and Robert Whetland of East Church, both in Kent. In 1716[33], William Gill, paper maker, insured his paper mill in the parish of Boxley; in a policy of 1722[34] this was stated to be in the tenure of John Hillier. William Gill went bankrupt in 1729[35]; "a large paper mill" was included in details given in the advertisement of his estate.[36]

If all these details refer to one and the same paper mill in Boxley, there was probably another in existence there by 1722. In that year[37] John Swinnock, of

Boxley, paper maker, took out a policy for his dwelling house and goods; he went bankrupt in 1727[16].

Further insurance policies support the idea that there were already two separate paper mills in Boxley some years before 1740, when James Whatman, a tanner's son of Boxley, married the relict of Richard Harris, paper maker of Hollingbourne[19]. In September and November, 1735[20], William and Joseph Cordwell, both of Boxley, paper makers, took out separate policies on a dwelling house and millhouse in Boxley. Joseph Cordwell was still in the paper making business in 1736[21], when a bag of fine white linen rags was stolen from his warehouse in the parish of Boxley. About that time Richard Harris of Hollingbourne, paper maker, insured his stock-in-trade in his paper mills and store rooms all in one building in Boxley[22].

In 1740[23], Edward Russell of Boxley, paper maker, insured his utensils, implements and stock-in-trade in his paper mill standing by itself near the house; shortly afterwards [24] James Whatman, of Boxley, insured his utensils and stock in his paper mill called the old Turkey Mill near his dwelling house but not adjoining.

15. Hollingbourne

James Whatman of Loose, tanner, insured a house and paper mill " being one entire building " in the parish of Hollingbourne in the possession of Richard Harris, paper maker, in 1733 and 1736[25]. Richard Harris of Hollingbourne, paper maker, insured his household goods and stock-in-trade in his dwelling-house, mills, drying lofts and warehouses all under one roof in Hollingbourne, in 1734[26].

The Hollingbourne mill, then in the occupation of John Terry, was insured by William Quelch of Loose and John Terry of Hollingbourne, paper makers, in 1739[27], and their household goods and stock-in-trade there were insured in 1740[28]. This was probably the same mill as that insured by James Whatman of Boxley, also in 1740[29], when it was still in the tenure of John Terry. In 1741[30], when the goods, mill, etc., were again insured, the policy was in the name of John Sanders, paper maker, who was declared an insolvent debtor in 1748[31].

16. Sittingbourne

Peter Archer of Sittingbourne, paper maker, was married in 1708[32]. William Stevens, late of Sittingbourne, millwright and paper maker, was bankrupt in 1749[33].

17. Chartham

In 1733[44], Peter Archer of " Siddingbourn," paper maker, insured his paper mill in Chartham parish " on the other side of the river." This " very good new-built paper mill " was advertised for sale in 1738[45].

18. Canterbury

The earliest reference found so far to a paper maker who was possibly at the Canterbury Mill gives the name of James Gillmore in 1665[46]. Two paper makers, John Moore and John Bailey, of St. Mary Northgate, Canterbury, were married in 1668 and 1690 respectively[47]. The Roll of the Freemen of the City of Canterbury contains three entries which certainly refer to Canterbury paper makers between then and 1741[48]:—Thomas Bannister of River, paper maker, apprenticed to Richard Wellard of Canterbury, in 1714; John Cooper, of London, paper maker, apprenticed to William Cook of Canterbury in 1734; and John Collier of London, silkweaver, son of Peter Collier of Canterbury, paper maker, in 1741. More entries in the period 1690-1747[49] very probably refer to the Canterbury mill:—Richard Wellard, paper maker, 1693; John Cooper and Richard Wellard, paper makers, apprenticed to Richard Wellard, 1704; Peter Collyore and John Hobbs, paper makers, apprenticed to Richard Wellard, 1708, as also Jonas Atkins, paper maker, 1714; James Cooke, paper maker, son of William Cooke, carpenter, 1714; Thomas Wilks, Thomas Cooke, James Hutt and Edward Welshe, all paper makers apprenticed to William Cook in 1722, 1741, 1741 and 1747 respectively.

In 1736[50], John Deane of the parish of Holy Cross next Canterbury, miller, insured the paper mills next the corn mill.

19. Goudhurst

Robert Wilson of Goudhurst, paper maker, was married in 1657[51]. No other reference has been found to the industry there, but a memory of it is preserved in field names in the parish. " Paper Mill " appears in the names of three fields close together, shown in the Tithe Apportionment and Map of Goudhurst, 1842.

20. Little Chart

Although the first reference to a paper maker here occurs just outside the period under review, it is so near as to be worthy of mention. In 1743[52], John

EARLY PAPER MILLS IN KENT

Mannings of Snarsdon, Kent, was apprenticed to Thomas West of Little Chart, paper maker (who was probably at Ford Mill).

21. Buckland

Thomas Chapman, of Buckland, near Dover, a paper maker aged about 23, was married in 1638[3]. There may have been here an interesting early link with the paper making industry in Shropshire, as the marriage was with the consent of the paper maker's father, Richard Chapman of Shropshire, and there was a paper mill near Ludlow called Chapman's Mill, to which my earliest reference is in 1718/19[1].

Another paper maker of Buckland, John King, was married in 1705[5]. A newspaper of 1733[6] contains a report of an accident at "Brookland" near Dover, when a boy belonging to a paper mill was hanged in going to put some paper to dry on the line.

22. River

Another early paper mill must have existed in the same area, as Thomas Bannister, of River, paper maker, is mentioned in 1714 (supra) and John Walter of River, paper maker, took an apprentice Thomas Langley, in 1719[7].

Acknowledgment

I acknowledge with gratitude the grant made by the University College of the South-West of England, Exeter, in aid of this research.

By permission of "*Notes and Queries.*"

1. Samuel Galliott's name first appears in the Eynsford Parish Registers (MSS. copy by F. C. Cowell from a transcript by Sir T. Colyer-Ferguson, Society of Genealogists) as the father of children baptised in 1699 and 1701. His occupation is not given.

2. Letter from the Commissioners of Excise dated 9th February, 1738, in *Excise and Treasury Correspondence*, 1715/6-1745, p. 247. I am indebted to the Commissioners of Customs and Excise for permission to read in their library and to quote from this source.

3. Thomas Churchyard, *A Description and playne Discourse of Paper*, 1588.

4. E. L. S. Horsburgh, *Bromley*, 1929, p. 445.

5. The paper mill is marked on the *Map of Kent*, by Andrews, Drury and Herbert, 1769. It was advertised for sale in the *Kentish Gazette*, January 30, 1789.

6. *Allegations for Marriage Licences issued by the Vicar-General of the Archbishop of Canterbury*, ed. G. J. Armytage, *Publications of the Harleian Society*, XXXIII, 1892, p. 199.

7. *Sun Fire Insurance Policy* No. 72,367, January 6, 1736. I am indebted to the Sun Insurance Office, Ltd., for permission to search their early Policy Registers and to quote from these.

There is no doubt, however, that its story down to 1932 is linked with that of Mill No. 315, below.

The third paper mill at East Malling must have been set up by 1798, when George Blunden was a master maker. In 1816 the Excise authorities gave the name of William Blunden at Mill No. 315[29]. George Blunden is recorded there in 1824[30] and as a manufacturer of brown paper in 1832-4[31]. Although he was bankrupt in 1829[12], he went into partnership with Francis Collins for a short time in the 1830's[33]. By 1836[14] Robert Tassell had taken over this mill (in 1838 he was partnered by Henry Smith[35]) and by 1850[36] it was in the hands of the two Busbridges who also held Mill No. 314, above. In 1860 Mill No. 315 was held by Busbridge & Hodge, and in 1866 and 1876 by G. F. Busbridge & Co.,[37] but each entry refers to East Malling *Mills*, so that Mill No. 314 was probably also included. In 1860 the products were fine writing and envelope papers; in 1866, tinted linear, cheque, drawing, writing and envelope papers; and in 1876, writing, drawing and account book papers from two machines of 60 and 70 inches. In the 1880's[38] two mills with one machine each are mentioned, and in later years they were working under the firm of Busbridge & Co. (1919), Ltd. They closed in 1932[39].

REFERENCES

1. T. Balston, *James Whatman Father & Son*, 1957, and *William Balston Paper Maker*, 1954.
2. A. H. Shorter, *Paper Mills and Paper Makers in England, 1495-1800*, The Paper Publications Society, Hilversum, Holland, 1957, especially pp. 184-196.
3. In 1765 the paper mill was insured by John and William May, and in 1804 by John May, gentleman of Snodland. *Sun Fire Insurance Policies* Nos. 217760, March 16, 1765, and 759217, January 30, 1804.
4. *Jackson's Oxford Journal*, May 2, 1807.
5. *Kentish Chronicle*, December 22, 1807.
6. *Excise General Letter*, October 8, 1816.
7. *Sun Fire Insurance Policy* No. 926387, January 22, 1817.
8. *Excise General Letters*, September 1, 1821, May 18, 1824, November 28, 1832, and February 3, 1836.

9. *Devonshire Chronicle and Exeter News*, September 15, 1840.
10. *Excise General Letters*, March 14, 1849, and May 16, 1850.
11. *House of Commons Papers*, 1852, 51, No. 128.
12. *Morning Chronicle*, August 11, 1858. Another partnership concerning the firm of C. Townsend Hook & Co., paper manufacturers, was dissolved in 1859. *Ibid.*, April 16, 1859.
13. *Paper Mills Directory*, 1860, 1866 and 1876.
14. *Paper Makers' Directory of All Nations*, and *Directory of Paper Makers*.
15. *Directory of Paper Makers*.
16. Information from the Rector of Ditton.
17. *Kentish Chronicle*, December 15, 1812.
18. *London Gazette*, January 30, 1816.
19. *Excise General Letters*, October 8, 1816, September 1, 1821, May 18, 1824, and November 28, 1832. In the 1821 entry the name of Stephen Golding is also given.
20. *Excise General Letters*, July 1, 1834, and May 13, 1847.
21. *London Gazette*, July 6, 1816.
22. *Excise General Letter*, October 8, 1816.
23. *Ibid.*, September 1, 1821. *Pigot's Directory*, 1832-4.
24. *Excise General Letters*, September 15, 1838, and June 29, 1848.
25. *Ibid.*, October 8, 1816.
26. *Ibid.*, December 2, 1819, May 18, 1824, September 15, 1838, and June 29, 1848.
27. *Morning Chronicle*, January 4, 1854.
28. *House of Commons Papers*, 1852, 51, No. 128.
29. *Excise General Letter*, October 8, 1816.
30. *Ibid.*, May 18, 1824.
31. *Pigot's Directory*, 1832-4.
32. *Alfred*, November 10, 1829.
33. *Excise General Letters*, November 28, 1832, and March 16, 1833.
34. *Ibid.*, February 3, 1836.
35. *Ibid.*, September 15, 1838.
36. *Ibid.*, May 16, 1850.
37. *Paper Mills Directory*, 1860, 1866 and 1876.
38. *Paper Makers' Directory of All Nations*.
39. Information from Messrs. Wiggins Teape & Co. (1919), Ltd.

PART II

Four paper mills were situated between Aylesford and Sandling; two of them were certainly established long before 1782, when Hasted[1] mentioned two paper mills on the west side of Boxley parish near Aylesford, "on the rivulet which takes its rise under the chalk hills." Unfortunately there are few references to the names of the paper mills before the early nineteenth century.

New Mill, Pratling Street

I have found no specific reference to New Mill before 1816, when the master paper maker was a Thomas Stroud. His name appears among the paper makers mentioned in apprenticeship records as early as 1774, but not until 1800-3 as a paper maker taking on apprentices[2]. There is a watermark STROUD & CO. 1802[3], and that company were master paper makers in 1803[4]. It is possible that some of these references should be connected with a Thomas Stroud who, during the period 1803-1812, was in partnership with Daniel Newman under the firm of Stroud and Newman at a paper mill (also called New Mill) at Eyhorne Street, Hollingbourne, but I am inclined to think that this was a different man, perhaps a Thomas Stroud, junior. In 1807[5] Thomas Strood was a paper maker of Hollingbourne, but there was also a Thomas Stroud, senior, paper maker of Maidstone, and the latter may have been the one who held the New Mill at Pratling Street. The name Stroud appears in a list of subscriptions from paper makers in 1813[6], and in 1816[7] Thomas Stroud was at New Mill, which had the Excise Number 318. Later references leave no doubt that the New Mill bearing this number was at Pratling Street. In 1821 it was occupied by Charles Wise, in 1825 by John Lavender and in 1832 by Joseph Moreton[8]; in the 1830's[9] there are references to Joseph Moreton, maker of white paper, at Pratling Street. The next occupier was John Mason[10], but by 1846[11] New Mill was in the hands of Samuel-Salkeld Knight, a millboard maker. His immediate successors were Thomas Compere[12], who was bankrupt in 1815[13], and George Mason, whose tenure lasted until about 1860[14]. The mill had only one beating-engine at work in 1851[15].

In the 1860s and 1870s[16] John Skelton Isaac was making patent carriage panels and millboards at Pratling Street; he was followed by Warwick Isaac & Co.[17], who appear to have been the last proprietors. They made patent panels for railway carriages, paper makers' press boards and millboards. According to local information in Boxley and Aylesford, the mill was pulled down in 1889.

Forestall (or Forstal)

It is probable that references in the Boxley parish records to a paper mill and its tenant Thomas Willard between 1671 and 1696 should be connected with this mill. The later history of the mill can be traced by comparing several scattered references with entries in the Boxley records and in the Excise Letters. The succession of master paper makers down to 1816 was: John Hillier, 1712-1724; William Russell, 1725-33; Edward Russell, 1733-62; Mrs. Russell or Hillyer Russell, 1781-1810; Clement Taylor Russell, 1811-16 (he was bankrupt in that year)[18].

In 1816[19] William Trindale was the occupier of a mill which bore the Excise Number 319; this is simply described as "Mill" in the available Excise records down to 1838, but other references make it certain that it was Forestall. In 1821 the occupier was John Pine, in 1824 Charles Wise, in 1832 George Fowle, and in 1838 John Lavender[20]. In 1832-4[21] George Fowle was described as a maker of white paper at Forestall Mill, Aylesford, and in 1839[22] a similar entry occurs, but John Lavender is also mentioned as a paper manufacturer at Forestall Mill. No later reference to paper making at this mill has yet been found.

Cobtree, Sandling

This appears to have been the paper mill which is marked on the *Boxley Tithe Map* (1844); it stood a little to the east of Cobtree and below a pond. Although the entries in the Excise Letters always refer to Cobtree, there seems to be little doubt that this mill was generally known as Sandling Mill during the eighteenth century. It can be traced through the tenures of families called Dean and Thomas as follows: David Dean, paper man, 1700-32; Thomas Dean, 1733-50; Mrs. Elizabeth Dean, 1750-80; William Thomas or Mrs. Thomas, 1781-1812. In 1813 the relevant entry in the *Boxley Rate Book* reads "Stacey Wise late Thomas" and the mill was probably owned or occupied by paper makers named Wise up to 1824.

In 1816, however, Florence Young is named as the occupier of Mill Number 299, Cobtree[23]; her name does not appear in the *Boxley Rate Book,* in which entries continue to refer to Stacey Wise, Messrs. Wise, then Charles Wise (from November, 1816). The last-named was at Mill No. 299, Cobtree, in 1819[24]; in 1824 he was declared bankrupt, and was referred to as a paper manufacturer of Sandling[25]. In 1826 an entry in the *Boxley Rate Book* reads "Mr. Allnutt late Wise," and this must refer to Henry Allnutt, who was already in partnership with John Wilson at Cobtree[26]. A few years later Thomas Smith and Henry Allnutt were the master paper makers[27], and they probably continued in possession until the mill ceased work in 1838[28].

Sandling

Sandling Mill is not recorded in the available Excise Letters until 1819, but it is possible that it was working before that year, perhaps in the tenure of a paper maker named Brenchley. That name appears in the *Boxley Rate Book* in the early 1800s, and there is a watermark C BRENCHLEY in a paper used in 1807[29]—some years before Charles Brenchley can be identified at either Otham (1812) or Padsole (1818). In 1819[30] William Peters and Thomas Chaplin were paper makers at Mill No. 513, Sandling, and this is confirmed by an assessment on Chaplin and Peters for a paper mill in the *Boxley Rate Book*, 1820-3. In 1823-4[31] they were known as Peters &

Co., paper manufacturers, Sandling. Their mill (No. 513) was recorded as "discontinued" in 1825[32], and no further references to paper making there have been found up to 1839, in that year William Hunt[33] and Reuben Hunt[34] were described as paper manufacturers at Sandling (the mill was re-numbered 329). In the December R. Hunt, paper manufacturer, Sandling Mills, was declared bankrupt[35], and that probably marked the end of paper making there.

Medway and Springfield Mills

The history of Springfield Mill from the time of its establishment by William Balston in 1806 and of Medway Mill from the beginning of this century (when it was taken over by W. & R. Balston) is so well known as to need no reference here. The earlier history of Medway Mill appears to date from 1860, when as Mill No. 329 it was worked by Uriah Robert Macey and James Eives[36]; in the 1860s[37] the products were browns, royal hands and mill wrappers. In the 1870s[38] Monckton & Co., at the Medway Paper Works, made air-dried browns on a machine of 57 inches. They were followed by the Medway Paper Mills Co., Ltd., who in the 1880s and 1890s[39] were making air and cylinder-dried browns and best mill wrappers, grey and coloured cartridges, royal hands, botanical papers, copying drying royal, fly papers, filter papers, sizing papers and many special papers to order. By 1895 there were two machines.

Padsole

Most of the paper mills on the River Len will be considered in a further instalment. Padsole was the lowest paper mill on that stream, and was begun by James Smythe and Finch Hollingworth in 1793. Their partnership did not last long, for in the following year Smythe alone insured the mill. Clement Taylor was another paper maker who had an interest in Padsole Mill, and when he was bankrupt in 1798 a moiety of the paper mill was for sale[40]. The next master makers here were John Hayes and John Wise; the former was bankrupt in 1804[41], and the mill was probably carried on for a time by John Wise. This

is suggested by the contrast between the watermarks
HAYES & WISE 1800 and JOHN WISE 1804[42].

By 1808[43] the proprietors were Stacey Wise and
Christopher Patch, who used the watermark S WISE
& PATCH[44]; their partnership was dissolved in
1810[45], but Stacey Wise continued, probably in
partnership with Charles Wise. Watermarks S & C
WISE are in papers from the period 1812-14[46], and
in 1816 Stacey Wise and Charles Wise, paper manufacturers of Maidstone, were bankrupt[47]. The
former's next partner was Charles Brenchley; in
1818[48] they were recorded as at Padsole (the mill
number was omitted) and in 1820[49] at Maidstone Mill,
Excise Number 515. That this mill was in fact
Padsole is confirmed by a reference to Wise &
Brenchley at Padsole Mill in 1823-4.[50] S. Wise and
C. Brenchley, described as paper makers of Maidstone, were bankrupt in 1824[51], and in the following
year Edw. Wise was the occupier of Mill No. 515[52].
By 1832 Stacey Wise had formed the last partnership at this mill—with Geo. Symes Knyvett[53]—and
they were making paper and pasteboard[54]. Their
partnership could only have been short-lived, for in
1839[55] Edmund Shaw was recorded at Padsole Mill;
paper making there ceased in 1846[56].

Bridge Mill

As with Aylesford Mills, the story of Bridge Mill
is well known from the time of its commencement
under the firm of Albert E. Reed & Co., Ltd. In
1904 fine printings were being made on one machine,
and by 1907 a second machine had been added[57].

PAPER MILLS IN THE MAIDSTONE DISTRICT

REFERENCES

1. E. Hasted, *The History and Topographical Survey of the County of Kent*, II, 1782, p. 132.
2. *Apprentices' List, Smythe Mss.*, Maidstone Museum.
3. *Whatman and Balston Archives.*
4. General Meeting of Master Paper Makers, June 13, 1803. *Papers from Springfield Mill.*
5. *Maidstone Poll Book*, 1807.
6. *Papers from Springfield Mill.*
7. *Excise General Letter*, October 8, 1816.
8. *Ibid.*, September 1, 1821, June 17, *1825*, and November 28, 1832.
9. *Pigot's Directory*, 1832-4 and 1839
10. *Excise General Letter*, October 27, 1837.
11. *Ibid.*, February 23, 1846.
12. *Ibid.*, March 14, 1849.
13. He was described as Thomas Compere of Aylesford, paper maker. *Morning Chronicle*, October 29, 1851.
14. He is recorded in *Paper Mills Directory*, 1860.
15. *House of Commons Papers*, 1852, 51, No. 128.
16. *Paper Mills Directory*, 1866 and 1876.
17. In 1883 the firm was William Warwick Isaac, and in 1885 Warwick Isaac & Co. *The Paper Mill Directory of the World*, 1883, and *Directory of Paper Makers*, 1885.
19. *Excise General Letter*, October 8, 1816. Trindale's name appears in the *Boxley Rate Book* in 1820.
18. *London Gazette*, November 30, 1816.
20. *Excise General Letters*, September 1, 1821, May 18, 1824, November 28, 1832, and September 15, 1838.
21. *Pigot's Directory*, 1832-4.
22. *Ibid*, 1839.
23. *Excise General Letter*, October 8, 1816.
24. *Ibid.*, December 2, 1819.
25. *Alfred*, July 12, 1824.
26. *Excise General Letter*, June 17, 1825.
27. *Ibid.*, November 28, 1832.
28. *Ibid.*, September 15, 1838.
29. *Whatman and Balston Archives.*
30. *Excise General Letter*, December 2, 1819.
31. *Pigot's Directory*, 1823-4.
32. *Excise General Letter*, June 17, 1825.
33. *Pigot's Directory*, 1839.
34. *Excise General Letter*, September 10, 1839.
35. *Devonshire Chronicle and Exeter News*, December 9, 1839.
36. *Paper Mills Directory*, 1860.
37. *Ibid.*, 1866.
38. *Ibid.*, 1876.
39. *Directory of Paper Makers.*
40. *Kentish Gazette*, April 6, 1798.
41. *London Gazette*, May 1, 1804.

42. In papers in the *Whatman and Balston Archives*. John Hayes is listed as a paper manufacturer at Padsole in *Holden's Triennial Directory*, 1805-7, but this information appears to have been out of date.
43. Stacey Wise & Patch were assessed for a mill in Maidstone. *Maidstone Rate Book*, 1808.
44. *Whatman and Balston Archives*.
45. *London Gazette*, August 14, 1810.
46. *Whatman and Balston Archives*.
47. *London Gazette*, March 26, 1816.
48. *Excise General Letter*, December 31. 1818.
49. *Ibid.*, March 3, 1820.
50. *Pigot's Directory*, 1823-4.
51. *Alfred*, May 11, 1824.
52. *Excise General Letter*, April 2, 1825.
53. C. S. Knyvett was a paper manufacturer in 1831. *14th Report of the Commissioners . . . Excise . . . Paper*, 1835. He was probably at Padsole then, with Stacey Wise. who is named in the same list.
54. *Excise General Letter*, November 28, 1832.
55. *Pigot's Directory*, 1839.
56. *Excise General Letter*, January 23, 1846.
57. *Directory of Paper Makers*.

PART III

This Part is devoted to the paper mills on or near the River Len above Maidstone. Padsole Mill, the lowest paper mill on the stream and within the town of Maidstone, was considered in the previous Part of this series. The history of the next two paper mills going upstream—Turkey (Excise Number 300) and Poll (No. 301) is so well known[1] as to require no detailed treatment here. Turkey Mill can be traced as a paper mill from the time of the tenure of George Gill, who was certainly a paper maker there in 1680 and possibly earlier. Poll Mill was converted from a fulling mill to a paper mill in or about the year 1718, and the first master paper maker there was John Swinnock. He was followed by William Gill, 1728-31; William Cordwell, 1731-5; Joseph Cordwell, 1735-56; Abraham Ferron, 1756-7; Edward Ferron, 1758-61; Clement Taylor, 1761-76; James Taylor, 1776-87. The mill was bought by James Whatman in 1785, and worked by him from 1787 until he sold it in 1794. Thomas Robert and Finch Hollingworth and William Balston, paper makers, continued the working of the mill until the dissolution of their partnership in 1805. Poll Mill was discontinued in 1825, the last proprietors there being Finch and Thomas Hollingworth[2].

Otham

Otham Mill stood on the boundary of the parishes of Otham and Maidstone; for many years it consisted of a corn mill and a paper mill, and several of the tenants were both millers and paper makers. The first known master paper maker at Otham was William Keeble; his tenure lasted from about 1700 to 1726. He was followed by William Hills, 1727-42, and Alexander Mathison, 1742-56, but during the latter's tenure Thomas Pine, paper maker, either owned or had an interest in the paper mill. During the second half of the eighteenth century the mill was worked by various members of the Pine family (or families), including Thomas Pine the elder; Thomas Pine, junior, John and Simon Pine; Messrs. Pine; Thomas Pine & Co.; John Pine & Co.; Simon Pine; Thomas and John Pine; Edward Pine. In 1801 Thomas and Edward Pine, paper makers and millers, insured their paper mill and corn mill situated between the parishes of Maidstone and Otham[3]. As no *Otham Rate Book* is available for the period 1767-1805, it is difficult to give the year in which Thomas Pine entered into a papermaking partnership with Russell and Edmet at Otham, but it was probably about 1802. In 1806-10 the names of Thomas Pine and of Messrs. Edmed & Co. appear in assessments at Otham[4], and in 1811[5] the death was reported of J. Hopfold, who "for many years" was engineer to Pine, Russell, Edmet & Co., paper makers of Maidstone.

A watermark RUSSELL & CO 1810[6] may have been that of the Messrs. Russell who replace Messrs. Edmed & Co. in the Otham assessments in 1811[7], or possibly that of the Russell family who held Forestall Mill at that time. Russell's tenure of Otham Mill did not last long, for in 1817[8] Joshua Russell, paper maker of Otham, was a bankrupt, and the mill appears to have been held by Charles Brenchley from 1812, when his name appears in the *Otham Rate Book*. The watermark C BRENCHLEY 1812[9] was probably used at Otham Mill, which was held by him in 1816 and bore the Excise Number 305[10]. In 1819 the assessment was on Brenchley & Wise[11], a partnership which is confirmed in the Excise records of that year[12]; similar assessments were made up to 1822, but in that year Thomas Pine and Ed. Davis took over the mill[13]. Assessments in 1824[14] include "late Brenchley & Wise" and also Thomas Pine, but in 1825 both the assessments and the Excise Letters[15] show that the mill was taken over by John Green. In 1832[16] Otham Mill, No. 305, was held by John Green, senior and junior, and another reference about that time[17] states that John Green & Son, of Otham and Hayle Mills, were making white, coloured and fancy paper.

PAPER MILLS IN THE MAIDSTONE DISTRICT

Otham Mill was later occupied by the proprietors of Turkey Mill; entries in the Excise records of 1846 and 1848[18] refer respectively to John, Thomas and John Hollingworth, and Thomas and John Hollingworth at Mill No. 305. In 1851[19] there was one beating-engine at work, but in 1859 a papermaking machine, which had been installed in the 1830's, was removed to Turkey Mill and "the building was converted to house a 2-engine washing machine for cleansing and beating rags[20]." A Directory reference in 1860[21] states that T. & J. Hollingworth made printings at this mill.

Bearsted Spot

The Ordnance Survey Six-inch map of 1870 shows a paper mill near Bearsted Spot and some way up the Len from what must have been the site of Otham Mill. Mr. R. H. Goodsall[22] states that "Three hundred yards or so upstream from Otham Mill is a cottage known as 'Mill House' close by a large store building which, however, is not hard against the river." He suggests that this was the site of a corn mill, but I am inclined to think that this was where Bearsted Spot paper mill stood.

The *Maidstone Tithe Map*, 1843, shows a paper mill in the corner of Maidstone parish on the boundary with Otham, and the *Apportionment* reveals that the mill was held by John Meek, maker of millboards. There can be no doubt that this was the mill known to the Excise authorities as Bearstedspot; in 1846[23] John Joseph Meek was making paper and millboard at a mill of that name which had the Excise Number 340. In 1851 there was one beating-engine at work[24], and in 1860[25] the name of Peter Warren is given as a maker of millboards and brown papers at Bearsted Mill. In 1866 Mill No. 340, Bearsted Mill, was "not in work[26]."

Hollingbourne Old Mill, Mote Hole

This paper mill was established by James Whatman, tanner, of Loose, in 1733, and until 1739 was in the hands of Richard Harris, paper maker. For a year or two it was held by John Terry, who was followed by John Sanders, 1741-5. From 1746 to 1749 James Whatman (who by then was in possession of Turkey Mill as a paper maker) held the mill himself. Henry French was the tenant from 1749 to 1770, then James Whatman (the Second) took over the mill until 1774. Clement Taylor held the property from then until about 1791. Whatman's lease ended in 1794 and the freehold passed to Hollingworth & Co.

My earlier suggestion[27] that the Hollingworths do not appear to have worked this mill themselves must now be disregarded in the light of further research. Entries in the *Leeds Rate Book* of "late Whatman" during the years 1795-7 give way to "Mr. Hollingworth" from 1798, and the Hollingbourne assessments for 1795 show Balston, Finch Hollingworth & Co. as owners and occupiers[28]. After the disruption of that firm, William Balston took a short lease of the mill from the Hollingworths in 1805[29].

I have found no reference whatever to a "Hollingbourne Mill" or an "Old Mill" there in the Excise records, nor do I know of any local use of "Mote Hole" as the name of this mill, but that is how it must have been known to the Excise authorities. In 1816[30] Mill No. 302, Mote Hole, was in the hands of Finch and Thomas Hollingworth, and their names are given as paper manufacturers of Hollingbourne in 1823-4[31]. In 1832[32] the mill was worked by John, Thomas and John Hollingworth, and the Hollingworths were still there in 1848[33]. According to the Excise records, Mill No. 302 left off work in 1850[34].

New Mill, (?) Cotterams Mill, Park Mill, Eyhorne Street

I now think it probable that my evidence about paper makers named Daniel Newman and John Crispe[35] should be associated with this mill rather than with Hollingbourne Old Mill. If so, the mill or part of it must have been for a time in the parish of Leeds, for the sequence of master paper makers can be traced from entries in the *Rate Books* of that parish. A Mr. Newman is recorded therein from

1791 to 1793, followed by Daniel Newman down to 1809, Stroud & Newman 1810-12, Daniel Newman to 1817, and Richard Barnard in 1819. In general, this fits in well with the following information about master paper makers.

In 1799 and 1801[36] Crispe and Newman were master makers, and there is a watermark CRISPE & NEWMAN 1800[37]. There was certainly a John Crispe in Leeds parish at that time[38] and he was probably in partnership with Daniel Newman at New Mill until 1803, when the firm of Stroud and Newman at Cotterams Mill is recorded[39]. Thomas Stroud was described as a paper maker of Hollingbourne in 1807[40] and 1812[41]. Only one reference to the name "Cotterams Mill" has been found, but that mill seems to have been identical with New Mill, Excise Number 307, which was occupied by Messrs. Daniel Denny Newman in 1816[42]. In 1819[43] it was in the hands of Richard Barnard, senior and junior. Richard Barnard, paper maker of Hollingbourne, was bankrupt in 1831[44], but a proprietor of the same name was at New Mill again in 1833[45] and he in turn was bankrupt in 1835[46]. Mill No. 307 "left off work" in 1836[47], but in the following year it was taken up by Edwin Horsenail[48], who by 1839 had been joined by Charles Horsenail[49].

No further reference to papermaking here has been found up to the 1880's[50], when Hollingbourne Mills and Park Mills were at work under the numbers 301 and 302 and the firm of Hollingbourne (The New) Paper Mills Co., Ltd. In 1885[51] the Hollingbourne Mills (probably Grove Mill, see below) were making superfine writings, banks, drawings and ledger papers, tub-sized and loft-dried, and Park Mills (probably on the site of New Mill, see above) were producing writings, envelope, account book and blotting papers, and using the watermark H B BARNARD, KENT. The New Hollingbourne Paper Mills Co., Ltd. was wound up in 1887[52].

Grove Mill, Eyhorne Street

The earliest reference which can so far be connected with this mill is in 1762, when James Austen of Chatham insured his new-built paper mill in the parish of Hollingbourne; from 1764 to about 1769 this mill was in the tenure of a paper maker named William Avery. He was followed by Robert Williams of Eyhorne Street, who probably held the mill from 1775 until his death in 1803. The next proprietor was probably Richard Barnard, whose name appears in the Hollingbourne records in 1813, in which year he was a master paper maker[53]. In 1816[54] he held Eyhorne Mill (Excise Number 306), and in 1819[55] Richard Barnard, senior and junior, are recorded there. Watermarks R BARNARD 1821 and 1826 appear in papers in the *Whatman and Balston Archives*, and probably emanated from this mill, where white paper was made by James Barnard in the 1830's[56]. Richard Barnard's bankruptcies have been noted under New Mill, above; as with New Mill, the Eyhorne Mill (No. 306) left off work in 1836, but was taken over by Edwin (or Edward) Horsenail later in that year[57]. Together with Charles Horsenail, he was the occupier in 1839, but Richard Barnard was still the owner[58].

In 1842 and 1846[59] Timothy Healey was making paper and millboard at the Eyhorne Mill. His name is given in a Directory of 1860[60], but as Mill No. 306 had been recorded as "left off" in 1849[61], that entry was probably out of date. If papermaking was revived at this mill it was probably only for a time in the 1880's (see New Mill, above).

References

1. Their early history is given in T. Balston, *James Whatman Father & Son*, 1957.
2. *Excise General Letter*, April 2, 1825.
3. *Sun Fire Insurance Policy* No. 726430, December 11. 1801.
4. *Otham Rate Book*.
5. *Kentish Chronicle*, August 2, 1811.
6. In a paper in the *Whatman and Balston Archives*.
7. *Otham Rate Book*.

PAPER MILLS IN THE MAIDSTONE DISTRICT

8. *London Gazette,* January 18, 1817.
9. In a paper in the *Whatman and Balston Archives.*
10. *Excise General Letter,* October 8, 1816.
11. *Otham Rate Book.*
12. Charles Brenchley and Stacey Wise. *Excise General Letter,* June 26, 1819.
13. *Ibid.,* October 9, 1822.
14. *Otham Rate Book.*
15. *Excise General Letter,* April 2, 1825.
16. *Ibid.,* November 28, 1832.
17. *Pigot's Directory,* 1832-4.
18. *Excise General Letters,* January 23, 1846. and June 29. 1848. In 1847 the following partnership of paper manufacturers was dissolved: John Hollingworth of Turkey Mill, and Thomas and John Hollingworth of Otham. *London Gazette,* March 5, 1847.
19. *House of Commons Papers,* 1852, 51, No. 128.
20. R. H. Goodsall, Watermills on the River Len, *Archaeologia Cantiana,* LXXI, 1957, p. 123.
21. *Paper Mills Directory,* 1860.
22. *Op. cit.,* p. 122.
23. *Excise General Letter,* January 23, 1846.
24. *House of Commons Papers,* 1852, 51, No. 128.
25. *Paper Mills Directory,* 1860.
26. *Ibid.,* 1866.
27. A. H. Shorter, *Paper Mills and Paper Makers in England* 1495-1800, 1957, p. 195.
28. T. Balston, *James Whatman Father & Son,* 1957, p. 130.
29. *Ibid.,* p. 131.
30. *Excise General Letter,* October 8. 1816.
31. *Pigot's Directory,* 1823-4.
32. *Excise General Letter,* November 28, 1832.
33. *Ibid.,* June 29, 1848.
34. *Ibid.,* May 16, 1850.
35. A. H. Shorter, *loc. cit.*
36. General Meeting of Master Paper Makers. June 12, 1799, and Meeting of Paper Makers of Kent and Surrey, April 30, 1801. *Papers from Springfield Mill.*
37. A. H. Shorter, *op. cit.,* p. 286.
38. *Ibid.,* p. 195.
39. Meeting of Master Paper Makers, September 19, 1803. *Papers from Springfield Mill.*
40. A. H. Shorter, *op. cit.,* p. 196. The other references to Thomas Stroud should be transferred to New Mill, Pratling Street (see Part II of this series).
41. *Ibid.*
42. *Excise General Letter,* October 8, 1816.
43. *Ibid.,* June 26, 1819.
44. *Alfred,* March 8, 1831.
45. *Excise General Letter,* July 1, 1833.
46. *Devonshire Chronicle and Exeter News,* March 16, 1835.
47. *Excise General Letter,* February 3, 1836.
48. *Ibid.,* October 27, 1837.

49. Ibid., September 10, 1839. *The Hollingbourne Tithe Map* (surveyed 1839) shows them as owners and occupiers.
50. In 1883-4 there seem to have been two mills: the Hollingbourne Mills, run by the Hollingbourne Paper Co., with one machine, and the Park Mills. worked by The New Hollingbourne Paper Mills Co., with two machines. *The Paper Mill Directory of the World*, 1883. and *The Paper Makers' Directory of All Nations*, 1884.
51. *Directory of Paper Makers*, 1885.
52. *Paper Trade Review*, May 13, 1887.
53. *Hollingbourne Parish Register*, Baptisms. List of subscriptions from paper makers, September 7, 1813. *Papers from Springfield Mill*.
54. *Excise General Letter*, October 8, 1816.
55. *Ibid.*, June 26, 1819.
56. *Pigot's Directory*, 1832-4 and 1839.
57. *Excise General Letter*, October 28. 1836.
58. *Ibid.*, September 10, 1839. *Hollingbourne Tithe Map* (surveyed 1839).
59. *Excise General Letters*, December 1, 1842, and January 23, 1846.
60. *Paper Mills Directory*, 1860.
61. *Excise General Letter*, March 14. 1849.

PART IV

Lower Tovil

The first known master paper maker at Lower Tovil was Peter Musgrove, 1686-1701; he was succeeded by his son of the same name, 1702-21, but from 1722 to 1727 William Gill and John Robbins appear to have run the mill. For the next hundred years or so members of the Pine family were directly concerned in the working of Lower Tovil, beginning with Thomas Pine from 1728 (Thomas Pine, junior, from 1745 to 1750), followed by Simon Pine, 1750-80, and John Pine from 1781 to about 1830. John Pine must have used the watermark I PINE 1802, but the mark J & T PINE 1809 probably indicates his partnership with Thomas Pine. Watermarks LOWER TOVIL 1806, L TOVIL 1808 and LOWER TOVIL MILL 1810 are also known[1], but by the last year another partnership is represented by the watermark PINE & THOMAS 1810[2]. Another example is known from 1812[3], but three years later the partnership of John Pine and William Thomas, paper makers at Basted and Tovil under the firm of Pine & Thomas, was dissolved[4]. In 1816[5] John Pine held the Tovil Mill with the Excise Number 311, and references in the 1820's[6] give his name in connection with Lower Tovil.

By 1832[7] Thomas Smith and Henry Allnutt were the occupiers of Mill No. 311 and were making white, coloured and fancy papers at Lower Tovil and Ivy Mills[8]. They were in possession in the 1840's[9], but by 1850 the master makers were Henry Allnutt, senior and junior[10]. A reference to five beating-engines at work at Tovil in 1851[11] seems to be connected with this mill, which continued in the hands of Henry Allnutt & Son. In the 1860's and 1870's[12] they were making tinted crayon and coloured papers on one machine. By 1890[13] the firm was working under the two numbers 308 (transferred from Ivy Mill) and 311 as Lower Tovil Mill, and the history of the mill since that time is well known.

Upper Tovil

From 1680 to 1720 Stephen Mantiloe was a paper maker in possession of a paper mill at Tovil, probably the Upper Mill. An entry "Peter Musgrove late Mantilow" in the *Maidstone Rate Book* for 1721 makes it almost certain that in that year Musgrove transferred from Lower to Upper Tovil Mill. In 1745 he was followed by William Wilkins, whose tenure lasted until 1772. His immediate successor was Clement Taylor, junior, who rebuilt and enlarged the mill. After Taylor went bankrupt in 1797 the mill was worked for about two years by Russell & Co. (Edward and Clement Taylor Russell, with the addition of William Edmeads for a short time). In 1799 Joseph Ruse took over the mill and used the watermark J RUSE until 1804[14]. The watermark RUSE & TURNERS 1805[15] must have been used by the firm of Joseph Ruse, Richard Turner and Thomas Turner, whose partnership ended in 1815[16] by the retirement of the last-named from the business. This watermark was used in papers made as late as 1838[17], but meanwhile one of TOVIL MILL 1815[18] also appears, probably emphasising the distinction between this mill and Lower Tovil.

In 1816[19] Mill No. 312 at Tovil was held by Messrs. Ruse, Turner & Welch, but by 1819 Joseph Ruse had retired, leaving the mill in the hands of Richard Turner and Samuel Welch[20]. By 1832[21] Richard Turner was on his own, as a manufacturer of white paper at this mill[22]. In 1850[23] Henry Allnutt, senior and junior, were the occupiers, but the mill soon changed hands again. In 1856 the partnership was dissolved between Samuel Hook and William Simpson, paper manufacturers of Tovil Upper Mills[24], and Samuel Hook was declared bankrupt[25]. In the 1860's[26] William Simpson was making straw news and printings at this mill, and by 1876[27] the Tovil Paper Co., Ltd. were producing news and printings on two machines of 54 and 83 inches. They had three machines in 1891, but shortly afterwards the mill was partially destroyed by fire and was not working in 1894[28]. In 1895 Albert E. Reed & Co. had three machines at Tovil Mills, in 1900 four and in 1901 five[29]. The modern history of the mill down to the present time is well known.

Hayle

The history of this hand-made paper mill from 1810 was outlined in *The Paper Maker*, November, 1949, and is so widely known as to need little reference here. It has been in the hands of the Green family ever since the time of the John Green who held it when it was first recorded by the Excise authorities as Mill Number 310[30], and it still bears this number.

The nearby Buckingford (or Bockingford) Mill is occasionally mentioned in the records as working in conjunction with Hayle. In 1832[31] the two mills were in the hands of John Green, senior and junior, and Buckingford Mill was used as a washing mill about that time[32].

Ivy Mill

The early master paper makers at Ivy Mill were Richard Burnham, 1685-1702; Thomas Mantiloe, 1703-12; Thomas Pine, 1712-18; 1719-23, Thomas Gilford. From that time until 1815 the Pine family were directly concerned in the working of this mill, and there are many references to master makers named Thomas Pine (senior and junior), Simon Pine and John Pine. In the 1780's Robert Edmeads joined Thomas Pine in a partnership which was variously known as Edmeads & Pine, Thomas Pine & Co., and Pine & Edmeads. This was dissolved in 1805[33], and the business was to be continued by William Edmeads, Thomas Pine the younger, John Pine and John Edmeads, under the firm of Edmeads, Pine and Edmeads. They must have continued to use the watermark EDMEADS & PINE, for an example is known with the date 1808[34], but this seems to have been soon replaced by the mark IVY MILL, of which there are examples dated 1809[35] and 1813[36]. The deaths at Ivy Mill of Thomas Pine (probably the elder) and John Pine, paper makers, are recorded in 1808 and 1810[37], and in the latter year the partnership between William Edmeads, Thomas Pine, John Pine deceased and John Edmeads, paper manufacturers of Maidstone, was dissolved[38]. The Edmeads (who held Little Ivy Mill, see below) were bankrupt in 1813, and an entry in the *Loose Rate Book* reads "Pine, Smith & Allnutt" in place of Pine & Co. The partnership between Thomas Pine, Henry Allnutt & Thomas Smith, paper makers of Loose, was dissolved in 1815[39], and that marked the end of the connection of Pine with this mill.

In 1816[40] Mill No. 308 was held by Messrs. Smith & Allnutt; for many years they used the watermark SMITH & ALLNUTT[41] and in the 1830's[42] they were making white, coloured and fancy papers. In 1850[43] they held both Great and Little Ivy Mills, but in 1851 only Great Ivy was at work, with six beating-engines[44]. It continued under the firm of Henry Allnutt & Son; in 1860[45] they were making drawing, chart, tinted and coloured papers, and in the 1870's and 1880's[46] they had one machine and one vat, producing crayon papers, handmade drying royals, white and coloured blottings, tinted cheque papers and chemically prepared cheque papers. By 1891[47] the mill was worked by the Ivy Millboard Co., who had six vats in 1900[48]; it ceased work in 1924.

Little Ivy Mill

This paper mill can be identified from about the same time as Lower Tovil, Upper Tovil and Ivy Mills. The succession of early master paper makers was: William Harris, 1689-1727; William Quelch, 1728-46; Stephen Scott, 1747-50; Abraham Musgrove, 1751-8; Abraham Hillier, 1759-60; Henry French, 1760-75; Thomas French, 1776-95; Taylor, Edmeads and Russell, 1797-1802; William Edmeads & Co., 1803-13.

In 1813[49] William and John Edmeads, paper makers of Loose, were bankrupt and an entry in the *Loose Rate Book* reads "Allnutt late Edmeads." The entry for 1814 reads "Henry Allnutt," who by 1816[50] was in partnership with Thomas Smith at Mill No. 309, Little Ivy. They must have worked Great and Little Ivy Mills in conjunction, and in 1850[51], the date of my last reference to Little Ivy, they held both mills under the number 308.

PAPER MILLS IN THE MAIDSTONE DISTRICT

Loose (two mills)

Although these mills were known as Loose Mills, the property was partly in Loose and partly in East Farleigh parish; this makes it possible to distinguish them from Little Ivy Mill (which was wholly within Loose Parish) and Ivy Mill (which was partly in Loose and partly in Maidstone). One of the Loose paper mills existed in 1745, when the stock in it was insured by Stephen Scott, paper maker. Definite reference to the next master paper maker comes from 1750, when John Farley held a paper mill, and in 1770 he held the new and the old paper mills. After Farley died in 1775, James Whatman bought one of the mills and worked it until the sale to Hollingworth & Co., in 1794.

In 1816[52] Messrs. Finch and Thomas Hollingworth were the master makers at Loose First and Second Mills, Excise Numbers 303 and 304. In the 1830's[53] John, Thomas and John Hollingworth held the mills, of which the upper one was used as a washing mill to serve the lower[54]. The Hollingworths' tenure is also recorded in 1848[55], but in the following year Mills Nos. 303 and 304 "left off work[56]." Mill No. 303 (the lower mill) was taken up by Henry Gurney, senior and junior, in 1851[57], as a millboard mill, with two beating-engines at work[58]. It continued as a millboard mill for many years under the firm of Henry Gurney & Son, but has long since been demolished.

References

1. All these watermarks are in papers in the *Whatman and Balston Archives.*
2. This mark is in I. Hewlett, 1378 *Varieties of Paper Marks,* 1879.
3. In a paper in the *Whatman and Balston Archives.*
4. *London Gazette,* December 26, 1815.
5. *Excise General Letter,* October 8. 1816.
6. *Pigot's Directory,* 1823-4.
7. *Excise General Letter,* November 28, 1832.
8. *Pigot's Directory,* 1823-4.
9. *Maidstone Tithe Map,* 1843.
10. *Excise General Letter,* May 16, 1850.
11. *House of Commons Papers,* 1852. 51, No. 128.
12. *Paper Mills Directory,* 1866 and 1876.
13. *Directory of Paper Makers.*

PAPER MILLS IN THE MAIDSTONE DISTRICT

14. A watermark J RUSE 1804 is in one of the *Papers from Springfield Mill.*
15. In a paper in the *Whatman and Balston Archives.*
16. *London Gazette,* September 2, 1815.
17. In papers in the *Whatman and Balston Archives.*
18. *Ibid.*
19. *Excise General Letter,* October 8, 1816.
20. *Ibid.,* December 2, 1819.
21. *Ibid.,* November 28, 1832.
22. *Pigot's Directory,* 1832-4 and 1839.
23. *Excise General Letter,* May 16, 1850.
24. *Morning Chronicle,* April 19, 1856.
25. *Ibid.,* April 30, 1856.
26. *Paper Mills Directory,* 1866.
27. *Ibid.,* 1876.
28. *Directory of Paper Makers.*
29. *Ibid.*
30. *Excise General Letter,* October 8, 1816.
31. *Excise General Letter,* November 28, 1832.
32. J. Smith (publisher), *Topography of Maidstone and its Environs,* 1839, p. 87.
33. *London Gazette,* November 26, 1805.
34. In a paper in the *Whatman and Balston Archives.*
35. I. Hewlett, 1378 *Varieties of Paper Marks,* 1879.
36. In a paper in the *Whatman and Balston Archives.*
37. *Reading Mercury and Oxford Gazette,* October 24, 1808, and *Kentish Chronicle,* March 23, 1810.
38. *London Gazette,* April 16, 1810.
39. *Ibid.,* August 22, 1815.
40. *Excise General Letter,* October 8, 1816. The Excise authorities always referred to this mill as "Great Ivy."
41. One dated 1816 is given by I. Hewlett, 1378 *Varieties of Paper Marks,* 1879, and others up to 1830 are in papers in the *Whatman and Balston Archives.*
42. *Pigot's Directory,* 1832-4 and 1839.
43. *Excise General Letter,* May 16, 1850.
44. *House of Commons Papers,* 1852, 51, No. 128.
45. *Paper Mills Directory,* 1860.
46. *Paper Mills Directory,* 1876, and *Directory of Paper Makers,* 1885.
47. *Directory of Paper Makers,* 1891.
48. *Ibid.,* 1900.
49. *London Gazette,* January 12, 1813.
50. *Excise General Letter,* October 8, 1816.
51. *Ibid.,* May 16, 1850.
52. *Ibid.,* October 8, 1816.
53. *Ibid.,* November 28, 1832.
54. J. Smith (publisher), *Topography of Maidstone and its Environs,* 1839, p. 87.
55. *Excise General Letter,* June 29, 1848.
56. *Ibid.,* March 14, 1849.
57. *Ibid.,* May 20, 1851.
58. *House of Commons Papers,* 1852, 51, No. 128.

PAPER MILLS IN THE MAIDSTONE DISTRICT

Acknowledgments
I am very grateful to the following for the facilities and advice they have given me in the course of the research work which made it possible to compile this series of articles: the papermaking firms in the Maidstone district; the incumbents of the parishes of Hollingbourne, Leeds. Otham, Boxley, Loose, Maidstone, Ditton, Snodland and East Malling; Mr. Thomas Balston (especially for allowing me to search various papers from the *Whatman and Balston Archives* and from Springfield Mill); Mr. L. R. A. Grove, The Maidstone Museum: the Commissioners of Customs and Excise; the Sun Insurance Office, Ltd., and the Tithe Redemption Commission.

XXX

PAPER-MILLS IN MONMOUTHSHIRE

INFORMATION concerning the paper-making industry in Britain before 1816 has to be culled from many sources, general, regional, and local, and much of it is fragmentary, consisting of scattered references to paper-makers and paper-mills. In 1816, the Excise authorities, who had managed the duty on paper from 1712, issued what is apparently the first of a series of general letters and orders, which give the names of the paper-mills and paper-makers in this country, the numbers which were allotted to the paper-mills and the Collection of Excise in which they were situated.[1] This series of letters and orders ended in 1852, but from about that time many directories and other sources of information about the paper-making industry are available.

The first known paper-mill in England was John Tate's at Hertford, which was at work in the 1490's. No evidence has been found of a paper-mill in Monmouthshire earlier than 1722, but as paper-mills existed in other western counties, including Shropshire,[2] in the seventeenth century it is possible that at least one of the Monmouthshire mills was working before 1700.

During the eighteenth and early nineteenth centuries many paper-mills were set up in the British Isles. All the western counties of England were represented in this expansion, and in Monmouthshire two minor clusters of paper-mills developed in this period, along the White Brook and the Mounton Brook. Paper-makers were obviously attracted to these streams by the prospect of sufficient water power for their mills and clear, clean water for the manufacture of paper.

From the 1830's a large number of the paper-mills in the western counties, and indeed in many parts of the country, gradually went out of action. Many of them were, of course, quite small, consisting originally of one or two vats and engines driven by water power. The use of paper-making machinery, which gradually spread and increased from the early nineteenth century, meant that better placed and better equipped mills could compete more successfully than small and remote mills, which

[1] I am indebted to the Commissioners of Customs and Excise for permission to read in their library and to quote from their records. All the Monmouthshire mills during the period 1816–52 were in the Hereford Collection of Excise.

[2] L. C. Lloyd, *Paper-making in Shropshire, Trans. Shropshire Arch. Soc.*, XLIX, 1937–38, pp. 121–87.

were also affected adversely by other factors in due course, e.g. the coming of railways, the duties on paper, and changes in the sources and types of raw materials.

As with Cornwall, Herefordshire, and Shropshire, the paper-making industry has disappeared from Monmouthshire. Devon, Somerset, Gloucestershire, and Worcestershire still have some paper-mills, but the total working today is small compared with the number which formerly existed. According to the evidence at present available, the period covered by the industry in Monmouthshire is 1722–1885. The following is a summary of the principal relevant facts about the mills and the paper-makers.

I. ROLLING

The earliest reference to a paper-maker in Monmouthshire is probably connected with the Rolling Mill, situated near Ruthlin, Rehlan, or Yrychlyn, in what was formerly part of the parish of Rockfield. In 1722,[1] Jeremy Wyett was apprenticed to William Vaughan, of Rockfield, paper-maker. This paper-mill is marked on I. Taylor's map of Herefordshire, editions of 1754 and 1786, on which it is shown on the River Monnow, between Llanrothal and Skenfrith. No further reference to it has been found up to 1806,[2] when the partnership of the following was dissolved : Edward Williams of Shirenewton, co. Monmouth, paper-maker, Joseph Morris of Chepstow, shopkeeper, and Richard Morris of Chepstow, accountant, carrying on business as paper-makers at Pandy Mill, Itton, and at the Rolling Mill, Rockfield, in the said county. The first of these was in debt in 1813,[3] when he was described as ' formerly of Itton, Co. Monmouth, paper-manufacturer.'

The first Excise General Letter[4] containing a list of paper-mills gives Rolling Mill No. 125, in the occupation of William Farr, paper-maker. In 1825[5] the occupier was Edward Johnson, who is listed in directories of 1835 and 1844[6] as a paper-maker of Whitebrook. A paper-mill is shown to the south of ' Rehlan ' on Greenwood's map of Monmouthshire, 1830, and ' Yrychlyn Paper-Mills ' appear on Bryant's map of Herefordshire, 1835. It appears, however, from further Excise Letters that the Rolling mill had ceased paper-making by then.

II, III, IV, V, VI, VII, AND VIII.   WHITEBROOK

My earliest references to paper-mills here are in two newspapers of 1774,[7] reporting respectively that Mr. William Jones of the parish of Landogaun (Llandogo), paper-maker, was married at Bristol, and that a labourer at Whitebrook Paper-mills near

[1] *The Apprentices of Great Britain*, 1710–62 (typescript) ; extracted from the Inland Revenue Books at the Public Record Office for the Society of Genealogists, 1921–8, Book 47, fol. 191.

[2] *London Gazette*, 29th April, 1806.

[3] Ibid., 18th November, 1813.

[4] Letter of 8th October, 1816, in General Letter Book No. 4 of the Ellesmere Division, Chester Collection.

[5] Letter of 4th November, 1825, in General Letter Book No. 13 of the Tarporley 1st Ride.

[6] Pigot's *Directory*.

[7] *Felix Farley's Bristol Journal*, 1st January, 1774, and *Gloucester Journal*, 14th March, 1774.

Monmouth had run away with money received from Mr. Williams of Monmouth for the use of the Company at the said mills. Perhaps the Mr. Morgan described in a newspaper of 1775[1] as a paper-maker of Monmouth, also worked there.

The paper-mills are also mentioned in works of 1787,[2] 1793,[3] and 1804[4]: the last gives the information that the owner was a Mr. Grove of Bristol. In 1810[5] the partnership was dissolved between Kingsmill Grove, John Brown, and Kingsmill Grove the younger, under the firm of John Brown and Company, paper-makers at Whitebrook.

The Excise Letter of 1816 records four paper-mills at Whitebrook. Nos. 136 and 137 were in the occupation of John Morris, and Nos. 138 and 139 were worked by John Brown. Between 1823 and 1850 further Excise Letters report the following paper-makers in occupation of the various mills : Nos. 136, 137—William Cowley, 1823 ; Nos. 136, 137, 138—Samuel Tipper, 1827–32 ; No. 139—John Brown, 1827 ; No. 139—James Welch, 1829, and William and Michael Welch, 1832 ; Nos. 136, 137— John Evans, 1839 ; Nos. 139, 137—George Lloyd, 1839 and 1841, respectively ; No. 136, Samuel Matthews, 1850.

Excise Letters also show that another paper-mill (No. 642—called Upper Mill), worked in this locality between 1828 and 1839, the chief paper-makers being W. Williams and George Lloyd. In 1847, Upper Mill was apparently temporarily given the number 137, and was worked by James and Joseph Dale and Samuel Matthew. Yet another paper-mill (New Mill—No. 351) also appears in the Excise Letters for the first time in 1828. The paper-makers here in 1828 and 1832 were James Welch and William and Michael Welch. In 1835 and 1844, directories[6] record the paper-maker here as William Williams, and in 1850 James Dale.

Paper-mills Nos. 138 and 139 appear to have ceased work about 1839, and others must also have been silent in 1851,[7] when only one beating engine was at work at Whitebrook. However, the Rev. W. R. Thomas, Rector of Llandogo with White-brook, kindly informs me that ' paper-maker ' is the occupation of the majority of the bridegrooms recorded in the Parish Register between 1837 and 1860.

In the 1860's, and up to about 1876, there must have been considerable activity at the mills. Miss L. K. Richards of Llandogo remembers that her mother, born in 1847, described how esparto grass was transhipped at Bristol to river-going craft which carried it to Llandogo. These tied up at a quay near the Holme Farm, and the grass was stored in large ' esparto sheds.' Large waggons drawn by two or three horses were used to carry the grass to Whitebrook and to bring back the rolls of paper for transport to Bristol. Later on the large expense which would have been

---

[1] *British Chronicle or Pugh's Hereford Journal*, 26th January, 1775.
[2] *Torrington Diaries*, I, 1787, p. 270.
[3] C. Heath, *Tintern*, 1793.
[4] C. Heath, *Accounts . . . of the Town of Monmouth*, 1804.
[5] *London Gazette*, 5th June, 1810.
[6] Pigot's *Directory*.
[7] *House of Commons Papers*, 1852, Vol. 51, No. 128.

involved in building a necessary siding from the G.W.R. line up the Wye Valley was probably one factor leading to the closure of the mills.

In 1876,[1] Nos. 136 (Clearwater Mill) and 137 (Fernside Mill) had one paper-making machine each, of 76 in. and 68 in., respectively; it was stated that neither was working. In the same year, Wye Valley Paper Mills Company, at Wye Valley Mill, were making Fine Printings, Small Hands, and Cartridges on two machines, each of 72 in. in width.

Newspaper advertisements[2] in the period 1867–74 offered for sale the Clearwater, Fernside, and Wye Valley paper-mills. At Clearwater there was a turbine driven by water and developing about 70 horse-power, equivalent to an annual saving of coal worth £2,000. With Wye Valley Mills was offered a wharf, and with Fernside Mills three barges used for trading from the mills to Monmouth and Chepstow.

In 1885[3] (my last reference), mills Nos. 136 and 137 were stated to be Fernside Mills, in the possession of William Wilson and Company, manufacturing brown papers on one machine, 72 in. in width, and one vat.

IX. SHIRENEWTON

A newly-built paper-mill in the parish of Shirenewton, called Little Mill, was advertised for sale in 1758.[4] This, or one of the other old paper-mills mentioned below, may have been working earlier, for the name of William Fry, paper-maker, Chepstow, is recorded in 1754.[5] Little Mill may have been the ' large, commodious paper-mill,' with drying-houses, rag rooms, etc., situated on a good, clear stream of water fit to make white paper, and in the parish of Shirenewton, advertised in 1781.[6]

Mill No. 132 (Shirenewton) is recorded in the Excise Letter of 1816, when it was worked by Thomas Reece. Further Letters of 1832 and 1834 refer to it as Little Mill, occupied by William and Thomas Edwards, and my last reference to it dates from 1835,[7] when the paper-maker was Thomas Ellis.

X. PANDY

Pandy Paper Mills, situated in the parishes of Itton and Shirenewton, three miles from Chepstow, were advertised for sale in 1768,[8] when they were occupied by Alice Window. The advertisement states that either of the mills could be easily converted into a snuff-mill, corn-mill, or tucking-mill, and this suggests that there may have been two paper-mills at that time. In 1809,[9] the partnership was dissolved

---

[1] *The Paper Mills Directory*, 1876.

[2] *Chepstow Weekly Advertiser*, November, 1867 ; May and September, 1873 ; and November, 1874. I am indebted to Mr. Ivor Waters for this information.

[3] *Directory of Paper Makers*, 1885.

[4] *Gloucester Journal*, 8th August, 1758.

[5] *The Bristol Poll Book*, 1754.

[6] *Gloucester Journal*, 26th November, 1781.

[7] Pigot's *Directory*.

[8] *Felix Farley's Bristol Journal*, 16th January, 1768, and *Gloucester Journal*, 1st February, 1768.

[9] *London Gazette*, 6th May, 1809.

between Joseph and Thomas Morris of the town of Chepstow, paper-makers at Rowley Forge, Gloucestershire, and the Pandy Mill, Monmouthshire. Pandy Mill was known to the Excise authorities as No. 127, with paper-makers as follows : 1816 and 1832—John Reece ; 1827—James Welch ; 1829—William and Thomas Reece ; 1834—Thomas Edwards. This mill left off work in 1839, though it is still recorded with the name of Thomas Edwards in a directory of 1860.[1]

XI. ITTON COURT

Excise Letters of 1816 and 1832 list Mill No. 128 (Itton Court), worked by John Reece, who in 1839 was partnered by John Sandford. In 1847 the latter's name appears alone, and in 1851[2] only one beating engine was at work here. The mill last appears in a directory of 1860,[3] with the name of John Reece.

XII. DYER'S

John Reece is also named as the paper-maker at Dyer's Mill, No. 129, in the Excise Letters of 1816 and 1832.

XIII AND XIV. ITTON

Advertisements of 1779 and 1780[4] probably refer to one of the Itton Mills. In the first a paper-mill in complete repair, lying on a good stream of water in the parish of Itton, was advertised to let, and in the second for sale. In 1794 and 1800,[5] partnerships of paper-makers at Chepstow were dissolved as follows: Samuel Jenkins the elder and William Jones, and Samuel Jenkins the younger and William Jones. The Excise Letter of 1816 refers to two mills at Itton, Nos. 130 and 131, both worked by Messrs. Jones and Company. In 1832, No. 130 (Itton Mill) was occupied by James Welch, and No. 131 (Goodbehind Mill) by James Jones and Thomas Brown. In 1834 the latter is similarly described, in the possession of James Jones. Entries in directories of 1830, 1835, and 1844[6] suggest that Goodbehind Mill was in fact White Mill, for the paper-makers' names given therein are the same.

Mill No. 130 left off work in 1839, and No. 131 in 1849.

XV, XVI, AND XVII. LADY, LARK, AND LINNET

For many years in the eighteenth and early nineteenth centuries one or more of these mills, which were situated close together on the lower Mounton Brook, was in the hands of William Hollis, paper-maker, whose name appears in two advertisements in 1776 and 1777.[7] In 1781,[8] William Hollis junior, at Mounton, advertised for two

---

[1] *The Paper Mills Directory*, 1860.
[2] *House of Commons Papers*, 1852, Vol. 51, No. 128.
[3] *The Paper Mills Directory*, 1860.
[4] *Gloucester Journal*, 8th November, 1779, and 8th May, 1780.
[5] *London Gazette*, 11th October, 1794, and 24th June, 1800.
[6] Pigot's *Directory*.
[7] *Gloucester Journal*, 20th May, 1776, and 29th September, 1777.
[8] Ibid., 14th May, 1781.

journeymen paper-makers (one to work at the vat, the other to couch), who had been used to blue, cartridge, and other heavy sorts of paper.

In 1813[1] the partnership of Warren Jane and John Reece, paper-makers at Mounton, was dissolved.   The latter's name appears in the Excise Letter of 1816, at Mill No. 135 (Linnet Mill).   In the same list appear Nos. 133 and 134 (Lady and Lark Mills), with John Proctor in occupation.   Further Excise Letters record the following paper-makers at the three mills, which kept their numbers as above : 1818—William Hollis at Nos. 133 and 134 ; 1821—James Birt at No. 133, John Reece at No. 134 ; 1832—James Birt at Nos. 133 and 134, John Reece at No. 135 ; 1839—John Reece and John Sandford at No. 135 ; 1847—John Sandford at No. 135 ; 1848—John Birt and Tudor Castle at Nos. 133 and 134.   In 1850 Edward Baldwyn was added to these, and in 1851 John Birt is not recorded.   All these mills were at work in 1851[2] as follows :

> Lady Mill : eight beating-engines at work, two silent.
>
> Lark Mill : one beating-engine at work.
>
> Linnet Mill : four beating-engines at work, two silent.

Later directory entries[3] may be summarized as follows :—

1860.   Lady Mill, No. 133 : Castle and Company.

> Lark Mill, No. 134 : Castle and Company.
>
> Mounton Mill, No. 135 : Reece and Sandford, making Browns, Glazed Browns, and Pressing Boards.

1866.   Lady Mill, No. 133 : John Birt—Best Browns, Glazed Browns, and Paper Bags.

> Lark Mill, No. 134 : John Birt—Best Browns.
>
> Linnet Mill, No. 135 : John Birt—Browns, Glazed Browns, and Pressing Boards.

1876.   Lark Mill, No. 134 : John Birt—Rope Browns.

According to this directory, Linnet Mill (which had a machine 50 in. in width) was closed.   Lady Mill had been given up and offered for sale by Messrs. Corns and Bartleet, paper-manufacturers, in 1873.[4]

Only one advertisement of any other possible paper-making site in Monmouthshire has been found.   In 1815[5] an iron forge at New Wear, on the banks of the River Wye, was advertised to be let.   There was a never-failing supply of water, well adapted for (among other things) paper-mills.

ACKNOWLEDGEMENTS.—In addition to the acknowledgements already made in this article, I wish to express my gratitude to all who have helped me, especially Mr. Ivor Waters and Mr. Rhys Jenkins ; and to the Council of the University College of the South-West, Exeter, for a grant in aid of the research.

[1] *London Gazette*, 31st July, 1813.

[2] *House of Commons Papers*, loc. cit.

[3] *The Paper Mills Directory*, 1860, 1866, and 1876.

[4] *Chepstow Weekly Advertiser*, 21st June, 1873.

[5] *Bristol Gazette*, 30th March, 1815.

XXXI

THE EXCISE NUMBERS OF PAPER-MILLS IN SHROPSHIRE

In 1946, long after the publication of Mr. Lloyd's original paper, I took up the study of the paper-making industry in England as a whole and found much valuable information in the library of H.M. Customs and Excise in London. I am indebted to the Commissioners of Customs and Excise for permission to quote the details which follow. I gladly contribute these notes in association with Mr. Lloyd, to whom I am very grateful for information about paper-mills and paper-makers in many parts of the country.

The first duty on paper to be managed by the Excise began in 1712, but so far only a little information has been found in the Excise Records which assists me in the compilation of a list of paper-mills in England in the eighteenth century. There is no trace of numbers being allocated to paper-mills until 1816. The numbering of all premises subject to Excise duties was made statutory by 58 Geo. 3 c. 65 (1818), but the Commissioners of Excise, acting in connection with the requirements of 56 Geo. 3 c. 103 (1816), had already compiled a list of paper-makers, paper-mills and the numbers by which these were to be known to the Excise authorities. This list was to be issued to the Collectors of Excise as a General Letter, the first of many which were sent out until 1852, when this method was discontinued.

Copies of these General Letters or General Orders exist in manuscript letter books of various local Excise officials and in five printed volumes, all in the Library of H.M. Customs and Excise. They were issued to the local Supervisors of Excise in all parts of the country, who were instructed to inform the Head Office when a new licence to make paper was taken out, so that a mill number could be allocated to the new or renewed concern. At first the Commissioners seem to have given an entirely fresh number to " new " paper-mills which began or recommenced work after 1816, but the scheme became more complicated as the practice was adopted of giving the number of a mill which had left off work to a new or re-opened paper-mill. As time went on, such amendments were frequent, occurring for example with a change of paper-maker or on the issue of a licence after a period when a mill had been idle. As this was the practice when large numbers of small paper-mills (many of them short-lived) were springing up in this country, it is not always easy to tell what happened to any given paper-mill. Nevertheless, the evidence is of great value in Shropshire in confirming and adding to much of Mr. Lloyd's original work on the many paper-mills in the county.

In the very first list[1] we see that it was the Excise scheme of " Collections " which determined the sequence of numbers allotted to the paper-mills which were then at work. For the purpose of the Excise generally, the whole country was divided into Collections, which often covered a large area, and further into Districts, Divisions and Rides, within which Excise duties were collected. In the General Letter of 1816 the Collections outside London (*i.e.*, the " Country Establishment ") were arranged alphabetically ; the Barnstaple Collection came first, therefore the paper-mills in that Collection were placed at the head of the whole list, with mills numbered 1 to 5, followed by the Bath Collection with mills 6 to 21, and so on.[2]

The Collections did not correspond to counties, so we find, for example, the Shropshire mills given in the following : those in the far north of the county in the Chester Collection, those in the north-east, east and south centre in the Salop Collection, those in the south-east in the Stourbridge and those in the extreme south in the Hereford Collection. From time to time the areas covered by certain Collections were altered, so that in later years we find some paper-mills appearing in Collections different from those given in earlier lists.

The 1816 list contains the following which have been identified as Shropshire paper-mills :—

Chester Collection

No.	44	Weston Rhyn	...	Thaymer Duckett, paper-maker	
No.	46	Drayton	... ...	John Charles,	do.
No.	47	Old Mill	... ...	Edward Charles,	do.

---

[1] Chester Collection, Ellesmere District, Ellesmere Division, General Letter Book No. 4, Letter dated 8th October, 1816.

[2] There are a few exceptions to the general sequence, *e.g.*, Mills No. 481 and 484 in Shropshire. These were possibly last-minute insertions after the original list had been prepared for issue in 1816.

Hereford Collection

No. 149	Hopton	... ...	Thomas Botfield,	do.
No. 150	do. ...	... ...	do.	do.
No. 151	do. ...	... ...	do.	do.
No. 152	Walford	... ...	Thomas Lambert Hall,	do.
No. 153	Langley	... ...	Henry Harris,	do.
No. 481	Sturts ...	... ...	do.	do.

Salop Collection

No. 346	Tiberton	... ...	William Briscoe,	do.
No. 347	Ellerton Mill	...	John Challenor,	do.
No. 348	Patcher's Mill	...	Josiah Harding,	do.
No. 484	Paper Mill	... ...	do.	do.
No. 349	Bouldon	... ...	Peter Medlicott,	do.
No. 350	Forge ...	... ...	William Hazledine,	do.

Stourbridge Collection

No. 373	Coton Spring ...	...	Mary Hardman,	do.
No. 374	Alveley Brook	...	Richard Crow,	do.
No. 375	Sutton	... ...	John Faulkner,	do.
No. 376	Charlcott	... ...	William King,	do.

In later Excise Letters and Orders, the following paper-mills (some of which, as has already been shewn by Mr. Lloyd, had worked long before 1816), appear for the first time in the records available :—

1817 Mill No. 495, Chapman's Mill. Philip Birt Adams and Thomas Colerick. Hereford Collection.

1820 Mill No. 514, Drayton. Alexander Thomson. Chester Collection.

1823 Mill No. 529, Morda. Thomas Jones. Chester Collection.

1826 Mill No. 613, Turley Mill. Alexander Thomson. Chester Collection.
(Paper and pasteboard).

1826 Mill No. 374, Crow Nest. Henry Harris. Stourbridge Collection.

1829 Mill No. 661, Cleobury Mill. Thomas Lambert Hall. Hereford Collection.

1829 Mill No. 665, Cound. Benjamin Bates. Salop Collection.

It is unnecessary to quote extensively from the Excise Letters in the case of some of the above mills, as this would merely duplicate what Mr. Lloyd and I have already written up from other sources. The following is simply the most important information about certain of the above mills, given in the Excise Letters.

No. 44 Weston Rhyn

Further paper-makers here are recorded as follows :—1825, Tamer Duckett and Thomas Godfrey Duckett ; 1842, Thomas Jones ; 1846, John Gittens Hughes.

Nos. 46, 47, 514 and 613 Market Drayton

The details of Drayton and Old Mill, given in the Letters of 1816, fill part of the gap in our information noted on p. 168 of Mr. Lloyd's original paper. The new paper-mill at Drayton recorded in 1820, No. 514 worked by Alexander Thomson, was discontinued in 1826 ; in that year Turley (Tyrley) Mill appears as No. 613, also with the name of Alexander Thomson. I think that these mills were probably one and the same at Tyrley.

Nos. 149, 150 and 151 Hopton Wafers

A letter of 1824 confirms that the three paper-mills here had by then passed to Richard, William and Henry Nicholls.

Nos. 152 and 661 Walford and Cleobury

Mr. Lloyd tells me that Walford's Mill is the name still given to the disused mill on the Rea immediately north of Cleobury Mortimer. On their first appearance in the Excise Letters, both Walford and Cleobury Mills were worked by Thomas Lambert Hall.

No. 153 Langley

This is apparently the site of the Milson paper-mill at Langley, dealt with on p. 170 of Mr. Lloyd's original paper. In 1817 the paper-maker was Hugh Davies. It had ceased by 1832.

No. 481 Sturts

The Excise Letter of 1816 confirms Mr. Lloyd's evidence of a paper-mill at Sturts in the parish of Neen Sollars. When, in 1831, it was discontinued, the paper-makers were given as Joseph and Henry Harris.

No. 346 Tibberton

The Excise Records show that this paper-mill was in existence in 1816 and that in 1832 and 1838 respectively Thomas Wood and John Brittain were the paper-makers.

No. 347 Ellerton

The Excise Letters of 1816 and 1832 shew that Ellerton Mill was then used by a paper-maker named John Challenor, but it is not known when the mill was rebuilt after the fire of 1789, noted by Mr. Lloyd (pp. 157-8 of his original paper). It ceased work in 1834.

Nos. 348 and 484 Shifnal

In 1832 Mill No. 348 is recorded again as Patcher's Mill, worked by Peter Harding, and Mill No. 484 is called Evelith, worked by Thomas Picken.

No. 349 Bouldon

In the same Letter of 1832 (my last reference to this mill), Simon Cox is named as the paper-maker here.

No. 350 Forge

The Excise Letter of 1816 contains my only reference to this mill. Mr. Lloyd informs me that the name of the paper-maker in that year, William Hazledine, is that of a celebrated iron-founder, one of whose forges was at Upton Magna. This almost certainly confirms the reference to a paper-mill at Upton Magna noted by Mr. Lloyd on p. 179 of his original paper.

No. 373 Coton Spring

The evidence produced above by Mr. Lloyd establishes that this mill was in Alveley. According to the Excise Letters, it was worked by Mary Hardman in 1816 and by William Hardman in 1818. Thomas James is the paper-maker named in a Letter of 1839 ; the mill had ceased work by 1846.

No. 374 Alveley Brook and Crow Nest

The paper-mill at Alveley Brook mentioned in the Excise Letter of 1816 is recorded as discontinued in 1826, but in that year another Letter gives a new paper-mill, Crow Nest, worked by Henry Harris ; this mill, which had ceased work by 1832, may have been on the same site, for Mr. Lloyd tells me that " Crow's Mill " is half-a-mile east-south-east of Hampton Loade in the parish of Alveley, and that " it is not identical with the site described on p. 147 of my paper, but is one of the two mills mentioned as standing higher up the brook." It is possible that Alveley Brook and Crow Nest were two separate paper-mills here, both distinct from Coton Spring ; on the other hand, they may refer to the same site.

No. 375 Sutton

The Excise Letters of 1816 and 1832 record John Faulkner and William Faulkner respectively as the paper-makers here. The additional evidence quoted by Mr. Lloyd above establishes that Sutton Mill was the paper-mill in Claverley parish. It ceased work in 1837.

No. 376 Charlcote

My only reference to this mill, in the Excise Letter of 1816, confirms Mr. Lloyd's particulars of the mill in Aston Botterell, given above.

No. 495 Ludlow

An Excise Letter of 1817 records this paper-mill as Chapman's Mill, the name by which it was known in 1747 (see below). Another Letter, of 1831, quotes the same Excise Number as applied to Ludlow, with George Wood and Thomas Wade, paper-makers. The same number at Ludlow is also given in a Letter of 1832, when John and Thomas Wade were the paper-makers.

No. 529 Morda

This mill does not figure in the Excise Letter of 1816 and by its appearance as late as 1823 it bore the high number 529.

151 THE EXCISE NUMBERS OF PAPER-MILLS IN SHROPSHIRE

Nos. 665 and 350 Cound

This is another paper-mill which does not appear in the Excise Letter of 1816. In other Excise Letters, No. 665, Cound, is listed in 1829 but is absent from a comprehensive Letter of 1832. No. 350, Cound, was a " new entry " in 1836 ; in 1839 it was worked by Thomas James. It ceased work in 1841.

SUMMARY

In view of the amount of additional information contained in our papers, Mr. Lloyd and I think it advisable to give in summary form at least the first and last years of our combined references to the Shropshire paper-mills as such. The following list is arranged so that reference can easily be made to the map of the distribution of paper-making centres on p. 128 of Mr. Lloyd's original paper and the sequence is roughly clockwise around the county, beginning in the north-western corner.

Name of Mill	First and last years as a paper-mill
1. Morda	1823–1876
2. Maesbury (?—Maesbrook)	1744–1747
3. Selattyn	1741–1811
4. Weston Rhyn	1712–1879
5. Market Drayton, Old Mill	1816–1846
6. do. Walk Mill	1755–1846
7. do. Tyrley Mill	1820–1846
8. Besford	Before 1750
9. Ellerton	1738–1834
10. Great Bolas	1665–1762
11. do. (second mill)	1665–1762
12. Tibberton	1813–1912
13. Longnor	1803–1812
14. Cound	1655–1841
15. Upton Magna, Forge	1808(?)–1816
16. Patcher's Mill, Shifnal	1759–1840
17. Evelith Mill, do.	1808–1840
18. Chesterton	1728–1753
19. Claverley	1729–1837
20. Alveley, Coton Spring	1686–1846

	Name of Mill	First and last years as a paper-mill
21.	Alveley Brook—Crow Nest ...	1816–1832
22.	Walford, near Cleobury Mortimer ...	1816–1860
23.	Cleobury Mill	1829–1890
24.	Hopton Wafers 1	1723–1840
25.	do. 2	1816–1840
26.	do. 3	1816–1840
27.	Langley, Milson	1650–1832
28.	Sturts, Neen Sollars	1816–1831
29.	Chapman's Mill, Ludlow	1747–1861
30.	Bouldon	1803–1832
31.	Charlcote, Aston Botterell	1791–1816

Unconfirmed Paper-Mills

32. Hanwood
33. Cressage

XXXII

PAPER-MILLS IN SUSSEX

Sussex is one of several English counties from which an old paper-making industry has disappeared. Two of the paper-mills which worked in the county appear to have been in existence shortly after 1700, if not before. From then until the 1820s there was a fairly general geographical expansion of the industry in or into almost every county in England and several paper-mills in Sussex appear to have begun work during that period. No evidence has been found of any paper-mill established in Sussex after 1825.

The early paper-makers usually tried to place their mills where abundant supplies of water for power and of clean water for the paper-making process were available. In Sussex we find the Iping and Duncton mills on or near the River Rother; those at Lindfield, Isfield, Lewes and in the parish of Barcombe were on or near the River Ouse.

Although the English paper-mills which have survived from the period of general expansion up to the present day are still fairly scattered, the geographical distribution of paper-making in many parts of the country has shown a marked contraction since the 1830s. Among the factors which in time tended to eliminate many of the small mills were competition from better-placed and bigger mills equipped with up-to-date machinery, changes in transport and raw materials.

The following account is simply a summary of my present information about each paper-mill and the paper-makers concerned. Further evidence relating to the early days of the industry in Sussex will be particularly welcome, for information about paper-mills is scattered and fragmentary up to the nineteenth century. The Excise authorities managed the duty on paper from 1712, but there is no trace of any complete list of paper-mills or paper-makers in England before 1816. From Excise General Letters and Orders of the period 1816-1852 it has proved possible to trace part of the history of many mills, and I am indebted to the Commissioners of Customs and Excise for permission to read in their Library and to quote from their records relating to this subject.

1. HOOE

The only known reference to a paper-mill here dates from 1704[1] when tenements called " The Paper Mills " were in dispute.

2. BARCOMBE

It seems very probable that there were two paper-mills at different times and places in this parish. A newspaper advertisement of 1706[2] states that a paper-mill, a corn-mill and lands in the parish of " Barcomb " were to be sold " by vertue of Commission of Bankrupt ". If the paper-mill and corn-mill were together it is possible that the site was in the south of the parish rather than at Sharps, but unfortunately the advertisement gives no details of the mills, their site or equipment.

3. SHARPS (formerly Barcombe, now Newick)

No further information about paper-making in Barcombe parish has been found up to 1813, when property called Sharps was purchased by James Pim, of Lindfield, paper-maker[3]. It appears that he erected a paper-mill at Sharps between 1813 and 1816, for in the latter year a mill of that name appears in an Excise Letter[4] as Paper-mill No. 392, in the Sussex Collection of Excise. The paper-maker's name in this entry is James Pim. The Tithe Map Apportionment of Barcombe Parish, 1841[5], shows that he was still the occupier then. The Tithe Map shows the mill in the small field behind Sharps Bridge House; and one site can still be identified. One beating engine was at work in 1851[6]. The paper-mill is named in deeds of 1859 and 1860, when it was surrendered to Charles Ellis, of Franklands, Keymer, farmer. A conveyance of 1867, however, refers only to the site of a paper-mill, among other property.

4. IPING

This, the last paper-mill to work in Sussex, is the only one about which many details are so far available. My first definite reference to the paper-mill occurs in 1725[7], when a Paper Mill and Corn Mill in " Ippen " in the County of Sussex were insured against fire by James Mills, paper-maker there. In 1746[8] John Edds of Worplesdon, Surrey (where there was a paper-mill called Bowers Mill[9]) was apprenticed to John Bigg, of Iping, paper-maker. Another apprentice to the same paper-maker eloped from his service in 1756[10], and in 1773[11] James Billinghurst, aged about 19, apprentice to Susannah Bigg, paper-maker at Iping, also eloped. Susannah was the widow of the Mr. John Bigg who was buried at Iping in 1772.[12] A second paper-maker of the same name, probably a son, must have carried on the business later, as a daughter of Mr. John Bigg, paper-maker, was baptised at Iping in 1778, and the Rate Book for 1780[13] includes an assessment on John Bigg for the Paper Mill House and Grounds. In 1795 he took out Patent No. 2040 for bleaching paper.[14]

The paper-mill was advertised for sale in 1800.[15] It is described as a capital paper-mill, well planned and commodious, in a most eligible and desirable situation at Iping. The advertisement states that it had been established more than 60 years, and continues :—"A regular and valuable trade is attached to the Mill, which has a constant and powerful supply of water, and is never flooded. The works are in substantial repair, with three water-wheels and six white vats, presses, frames, stuff chests, fixtures and every apparatus for carrying on a trade of the first consequence, with remarkably fine spring water. . . . The stream is sufficient to work two more vats." John Bigg was then "about to retire from business," and the mill was probably taken over shortly afterwards by the firm of Messrs. Harrison and Company (William Devaynes and Thomas Harrison) for this partnership of paper-makers at Iping was dissolved in 1808.[16] They were followed by Henry Cooke, who went bankrupt in 1814.[17] The Excise Letters and County Directories show that Iping Mill, No. 123, in the Hampshire Collection of Excise, was worked by paper-makers as follows :—1816, Smith and Warner; 1822-23, William Dodd Wells; 1825, Charles Venables; 1826-1839, Thomas and Benjamin Pewtress and James Low.

Richard Smith, paper-maker, appears in entries in the Iping Parish Registers between 1797 and 1814 and (presumably the eldest son of the same name) between 1820 and 1822. Other paper-makers recorded in the Registers during the period 1796-1828 are :—William Challen (entries from 1796-1813); William Brown, 1802-1813; Thomas Dudman, 1813; William Saunders, 1813; William Marshall, 1819; George Webb, 1824; Joseph Wright, 1828.

In 1851[18] seven beating engines were at work at Iping and one was silent. Further entries of paper-makers occur in the Parish Registers as follows :—Joseph Moseley, 1856; James Ayling, 1864; George Hill, 1874. In 1866 the mill was not working; at some time between 1860 and 1876, however, it passed from the occupation of Messrs. Pewtress and Company (producing News and Printings) to William Edward and John Chalcraft Warren (making Printings White and Coloured, News and Blotting Papers on one machine 60 inches wide).[19]   In 1885 and 1890 the products advertised were White and Coloured Blottings, Filterings and Middles, to which by 1930[20] (my last reference) were added Banks and Stereos and "other Rag Papers." The paper-mill was burnt down about that time and although a new mill was built it has not been used for paper-making.

5. LINDFIELD

Horsfield[21] implies that the manufacture of paper here had been carried on from about 1735 by a family called Pym. Very little information has been found. A newspaper of 1776[22] mentions Thomas Newland, a paper-maker born at "Linfield" in Sussex. The Excise Letter of 1816 shows that Lindfield paper-mill, No. 381, in the Sussex Collection of Excise was then occupied by Francis Pim. My last reference, in 1832-34[23], gives the name of James Pim, paper-maker, Lindfield. Mr. F. Bentham Stevens kindly informs me that the Lindfield Tithe Map, 1848, shows "Pim's Mill" on the site of Dean's Mill, but the Apportionment does not mention a paper-mill.

6. DUNCTON

The earliest reference to this paper-mill is noted in *V.C.H. Sussex*[24]. From the latter part of the eighteenth century, when it was established by Lord Egremont, this mill, known to the Excise authorities as No. 124, in the Hampshire Collection, worked up to the 1830s. In 1816 the paper-maker was George Edds and in the period 1827-1832 Thomas Austin.

7. ISFIELD

The Excise Letter of 1816 lists this paper-mill as No. 391, in the Sussex Collection, worked by Messrs. George Molineux and Thomas Johnston, whose names appear in the Excise Letters and County Directories up to the closure of the mill in 1850. Horsfield[25] describes it as "a large and handsome paper mill on the bank of the river, belonging to Messrs. Johnston, Molineux and Munn of Lewes," and states "it has recently undergone much improvement, and the finest paper is there manufactured." According to the same writer in 1835[26], some excellent paper was produced. The tithe map shows that the mill was due west of Isfield Place.

8. LEWES

The name of Thomas **Savage**, paper-maker, appears in the *Lewes Poll Book*[27] of 1803, but my first reference to the paper-mill in Lewes occurs in the Excise Letter of 1816, by which time the firm of Molineux and Johnston was in occupation, this mill being known as No. 390, in the Sussex Collection of Excise. With a short break about 1821-23, when the paper-maker was James Edds and paper was said to be the only manufacture of any note carried on in or near Lewes[28], this firm seems to have continued until about 1850.

9. WEST ASHLING

The proximity of Chichester and Westbourne to West Ashling suggests the possibility that the early paper-makers mentioned under those places below may have worked at a mill there. My first reference to West Ashling paper-mill, however, dates only from 1825[29], when an Excise Letter records it as a " new mill," No. 582 in the Hampshire Collection, worked by William Dodd Wells. Further relevant entries in the Excise Letters show that the paper-makers were as follows :—1832, Thomas Warren; 1842, William, Henry and Solomon Savage; 1850, Robert Chorley. Warren's name, in connection with this mill, appears in the list of Professional Gentlemen and Tradesmen Subscribers to Horsfield's *History*.... in 1835. My last reference to this paper-mill shows that its two beating engines were silent in 1851.[30]

10. CHICHESTER

I have not been able to confirm the presence of an early paper-mill here, but that possibility is suggested by the recorded marriage of a paper-maker named Noah Flower of Chichester in 1713.[31]

11. WESTBOURNE

Similarly the possibility of the former existence of a paper-mill at or near Westbourne is suggested by two entries of the marriages of paper-makers in 1731 and 1732,[32] the first John Blackwell and the second Henry Ball, both of "Westborne." Again, no confirmation has been found.

ACKNOWLEDGEMENTS

In addition to acknowledgements in the text and footnotes, my best thanks are due to Mrs. Maud A. Sampson Miss Helena Hall and all who have helped me in collecting material for this study, and to the Council of the University College of the South West of England, Exeter, for their grant in aid of the research.

[1] *V.C.H. Sussex,* II, 1907, p. 238. Exchequer Deposition. E.134/1 Anne, Easter 21. This authority has been verified at the Public Record Office.

[2] *The Post Man,* 12th December, 1706.

[3] For this information I, am indebted to Mr. F. Bentham Stevens, who kindly searched the title deeds of Sharps by courtesy of the present owner, Colonel Douglas Bate.

[4] Letter dated 8th October, 1816, in General Letter Book No. 4 of the Ellesmere Division, Chester Collection.

[5] Information from Mr. F. Bentham Stevens, who kindly searched the Tithe documents of several Sussex parishes for evidence relating to paper-mills.

[6] *House of Commons Papers,* 1852, Vol. 51, No. 128.

[7] Sun Fire Insurance Policy No. 37128, 26th October, 1725. I am indebted to the Sun Insurance Office Ltd., for permission to search and to quote from their Policy Registers.

[8] *The Apprentices of Great Britain,* 1710-1762 (typescript); extracted from the Inland Revenue Books at the Public Record Office, for the Society of Genealogists, 1921-1928. Book 17, Fol. 195.

[9] Sun Fire Insurance Policy No. 61267, 5th July, 1733, whereby Thomas Hillyer, paper-maker at Bowers in the parish of " Webblestone," insured his paper-mill called Bowers Mill.

[10] *Oxford Gazette and Reading Mercury,* 2nd August, 1756.

[11] *Reading Mercury and Oxford Gazette,* 21st June, 1773.

[12] The Iping Parish Registers were searched by the Rev. H. V. Saunderson, Rector of Iping-cum-Chithurst, who kindly sent me all details relevant to paper-makers.

[13] This information was kindly supplied by Miss E. M. Gardner.

[14] I am indebted to Mr. Rhys Jenkins for this reference.

[15] *Sussex Weekly Advertiser,* 2nd June, 1800, also *Gloucester Journal,* same date. An advertisement in similar terms, without mentioning Iping by name, appears in *Jackson's Oxford Journal,* 8th March, 1800.

[16] *London Gazette,* 7th May, 1808.

[17] *ibid,* 26th November, 1814.

[18] *House of Commons Papers,* loc. cit.

[19] *Paper Mills Directory,* 1866, 1860, 1876.

[20] *Directory of Paper Makers,* 1885, 1890, 1930.

[21] T. W. Horsfield, *The History, Antiquities and Topography of the County of Sussex,* 1835, I, p. 385.

[22] *The London Evening Post,* 3rd September, 1776.

[23] Pigot's *Directory.*

[24] II, 1907, p. 238.

[25] T. W. Horsfield, *History of the Environs of Lewes,* 1827, p. 142.

[26] *History, Antiquities* . . . . . I, p. 371.

[27] *V.C.H. Sussex,* II, 1907, p. 238.

[28] Pigot's *Directory,* 1823-24.

[29] Letter dated 17th June, 1825, in General Letters Book No. 13 of the Tarporley First Ride.

[30] *House of Commons Papers,* loc. cit.

[31] S.R.S. xii. 146.

[22] S.R.S. xxxii, 2, 10.

XXXIII

PAPER-MAKING IN WILTSHIRE

THE comparatively rapid increase in the number of paper-mills at work in Wiltshire in the 18th and early 19th centuries paralleled similar developments in many parts of England.[1] Most of the Wiltshire mills, which were quite small, closed down in the 19th century, probably owing to the operation of factors such as the competition of better-placed or better-equipped mills and changes in the nature and sources of raw materials. The number of people employed in the manufacture of paper in Wiltshire was never large, the highest figures recorded in the *Census; Occupation Tables* being those for 1901, when there were 45 men and 34 women in the industry.

The Wiltshire paper-mills were mostly in the north-west of the county, especially along the By Brook, and the south-east, within ten miles of Salisbury. A primary requirement of paper-makers —a good supply of water powerful enough to drive the mill and clear enough to be used in the paper-making process—was satisfied here, but the industry was probably also attracted to these areas by the proximity of Bristol and Bath, and Salisbury respectively, both as sources of raw materials and as markets. In some cases, paper-makers seem to have taken over mills formerly used by cloth-makers or corn-millers. For example, the 'Veverne' mill owned by a clothier in the 16th century[2] was probably on or near the site of the corn-mill which became the Weavern paper-mill (see below, p. 246). In 1744[3] a clothier is recorded at Widdenham mill in Colerne which was probably on the site of the later paper-mill.

There is little concentrated information about the paper-making industry in England up to the 19th century, but between 1816 and 1852 the Commissioners of Customs and Excise issued lists of paper-mills in the form of General Letters and Orders.[4] These usually recorded the Excise Numbers allotted to the paper-mills, the names of the paper-makers and mills, and the Collection of Excise in which the mills were situated. The paper-mills which worked in north-west Wiltshire during this period were in the Bath Collection of Excise; that at Calstone was in the Marlborough, and the Bulford, Bemerton, and Downton mills were in the Salisbury Collection.

The paper-mills

Probably the first paper-mill to be established in Wiltshire was at Bemerton (actually the mill is in the parish of West Harnham) and there are several early references to it;[5] it was working from either 1554 or 1569 until well into the 19th century. In 1726 George Thompson, paper-maker, took out a fire insurance policy[6] in respect of his household goods and stock in his dwelling house and paper-mills all under one roof in West Harnham. Later, the following were apprenticed[7] to paper-makers at West Harnham: James Thorn (1751) to George Thompson; and John Tull (1761), James Randall (1765), John Strugnal (1770), William Thompson (1773), and John Loader (1777) to James Wilkinson. A tablet in Bemerton church commemorates a child James Wilkinson at the paper-mill in 1779, and the name of James Wilkinson, of Bemerton paper-mills, appears in a notice in 1793.[8] The names of five paper-makers —Thomas Ketchen, Robert Wells, William Collens, James Randel, John Tull—are recorded in the Bemerton Registers of Marriages and Banns between 1763 and 1777. Excise Letters of 8 October 1816,[9] and 28 November 1832,[10] list Mill No. 344 at Bemerton. The name of the paper-maker concerned, James Forward, appears in the Wiltshire Poll Book in 1819, and in the Bemerton Rate Book up to 1845. The last known reference to this paper-mill is in a directory of 1860,[11] under the name of J. W. Towards (probably a mis-spelling of Forward), but as it is not mentioned in a list of paper-mills in 1851[12] it had probably ceased work before then.

There is a tradition that there was a paper-mill in St. Ann's Street, Salisbury. This was possibly the mill at which Ambrose Curtis, of Salisbury, paper-maker, worked about 1686.[13] A paper-mill east of the cathedral is shown on an 18th-century plan of Salisbury.[14]

The possibility that a paper-mill existed at or near Nunton is suggested by the recorded marriage of Henry Bacon of Nunton, paper-maker, in 1666.[15]

The earliest reference to the paper industry at Downton is the marriage of William Snelgar, of Downton, paper-maker, in 1740.[16] Samuel Snelgar of Downton, paper-maker, took apprentices named John Berryman (in 1755),[17] Joseph Snelgar and John Davis (in 1766), and John Snelgar (in 1768).[18] He insured the paper-mill in 1756.[19] It seems likely that at least one paper-mill in Dorset was started by paper-makers from Downton, as by the 1750's Samuel Snelgar and Anthony Berryman, paper-makers of Downton, had leased Carey paper-mill near Wareham.[20] About 1791[21] Downton had 'a good paper-mill' where Joseph Jellyman was the paper-maker. He had insured the mill in 1781.[22] The mill building still stands in the centre of the town. The manufacture apparently ceased for a time in the 1840's[23] and 1850's,[24] but in 1855[25] the name of W. Stradling, paper-manufacturer at Downton, is recorded, suggesting that the mill was not long out of action. For many years up to the closure after the First World War, this mill was equipped with two vats, producing hand-made writing and account-book papers. In 1885 and 1890[26] it was operated by Messrs. Wiggins, Teape, Carter, & Barlow, who were followed by Mark Palmer & Son, the last paper-makers to work it. Another mill at Downton, probably an adjacent building but a separate mill, was apparently used by the Jellyman family from about 1830 to 1860 for the manufacture of paste-board.

The paper-mill at Bulford was insured by Wingfield Hillman and Thomas Noyce, paper-makers, in 1765.[27] In 1784 Mary Mould, paper-maker, insured her goods, utensils, and stock.[28] The mill worked for nearly a century from 1786,[29] when the paper-maker was Thomas Mould. Members of this family seem to have migrated to Dorset,[30] where Carey mill was let to Joseph Mould, paper-maker of Bulford, in 1810, and Wimborne paper-mill was also worked by him in 1816. From 1786 to 1790 Isaac Brodribb was the master paper-maker at Bulford. In 1786 he insured his utensils and the stock in his paper-mill.[31] In 1790, when he was bankrupt, he was described as a paper-maker, late of Durrington.[32]

In 1791 Lawrence Greatrake, paper-maker, insured the utensils and stock in the paper-mill and in a warehouse at Andover (Hants).[33] In 1793 he was described as a paper-maker of Bulford.[34] Excise Letters show that Bulford mill (No. 345) passed through many hands in the 19th century. In 1866[35] A. Southby was recorded as the paper-maker, producing blottings, filterings, and small hands. The mill was dismantled about 1880.[36]

The paper-mill at Calstone was probably that advertised in 1791[37] as a valuable new overshot paper-mill near Calne. It was said to be esteemed for workmanship and strength, and one of the most complete in the kingdom. Among its advantages were that it was on a constant and one of the best streams of water for writing paper in England, that rags were collected in large quantities nearby, and that it was the first mill on the stream. The Excise Letter of 1816 records it as Mill No. 230, worked by John Huband. The last known reference to it is in 1876[38] when it was owned by William John Dowding & Sons, and was equipped with one machine 48 inches wide, making small hands and caps. A Directory of 1860[39] lists Daniel Huband at Mill No. 200 at Calne, but no other reference to this mill has been found.

Most of the other Wiltshire paper-mills were placed on or near the By Brook, west of Chippenham. Aubrey[40] states that in 1635 a paper-mill was built at Long Dean (Yatton Keynell) by a Mr. Wyld, to supply Bristol with brown paper. In 1746[41] this 'well accustomed' paper-mill, then occupied by Roger Lewis, was advertised to be let or sold. It was insured in 1753 and 1763[42] by John Lewis, described in the first policy as a paper-maker of Long Dean and in the second as a victualler of Wootton Bassett. In 1808[43] the partnership of Richard and Charles Barrow, paper-makers of Long Dean, was dissolved, and in 1809[44] Richard Barrow was declared a bankrupt, a fate which also befell his successor, D.

Husband, in 1814.[45] Excise Letters of 1816–47 refer
to this mill as No. 16. The products during this
period were paper, pasteboard, and millboard. The
last known reference to a paper-maker here is in
1860,[46] when John Sellick was stated to be manufacturing browns, royal hands, and cartridges.

The dissolution of the partnership of Sarah and
William Hill, paper-manufacturers of Widdenham
mill in Colerne, is recorded in 1813.[47] William Hill
was declared a bankrupt in 1814.[48] This mill was
much lower down the valley. It bore the Excise
Number 19 and was apparently in operation until
1866[49] when it was worked by W. Perrin, making
brown, blue, and sugar papers.

Charles Ward of Doncombe is named in a list
of paper-makers compiled about 1793[50] and in the
Wiltshire Poll Book, 1819. He was probably at
Doncombe mill in Colerne, which is listed in the
Excise Letter of 1816 as No. 17, occupied by Messrs.
Cottle & Ward. The first of these partners was
presumably the J. Cottell, paper-maker of North
Wraxall, whose bankruptcy is recorded in 1817,[51]
and the second Charles Ward of Doncombe paper-
mills, who died in 1825.[52] It passed through the
hands of at least four other paper-makers, producing
variously paper, pasteboard, and millboard before
it fell silent about 1847.

Weavern mill, which seems to have lain north of
Widdenham mill on the Colerne and Biddestone
parish boundary, was advertised for sale in 1793,
when it was described as an excellent two-vat
paper-mill, occupied by John Butler.[53] In 1794 this
paper-mill was equipped with two engines.[54] It
appears in the first Excise Letter in 1816 as No. 13,
occupied by Henry Garner, who about that time also
had an interest in Widdenham mill. The Excise
Records show that Weavern mill had ceased work
by 1834.

In the Excise Letter of 1816, Chaps mill, in
Slaughterford, is listed as No. 14, occupied by
Henry Garner the younger. It is the only paper-mill
now (1956) working in Wiltshire and it still bears this
number. A Directory of 1859[55] lists J. W. Dowding,
paper-manufacturer at Slaughterford; this family

still owns the mill. In 1860[56] it was producing blue and white royal hands. For many years it has been equipped with one machine (now 70 in. in width) making grocery papers, royal hands, bag papers, square-bottom, rose and satchel sugar bags, imitation Kraft bags, mill wrappers, fruit papers, jacquards, middles, pastel and cover papers, backing papers, browns, and straw paper.[57]

At least one other paper-mill worked at Slaughterford. William Duckett paper-maker of the parish of Slaughterford was bankrupt in 1792.[58] He appears to have been followed by James Bryant, to whom George Emery and Charles Curtis were apprenticed in 1802 and 1803 respectively.[59] According to the Excise Letter of 1816, Mill No. 15 there was occupied by Thomas Bevan, but the mill bearing this number had ceased work by the 1830's. Mill No. 631, Slaughterford, is recorded in an Excise Letter of 1827,[60] and was occupied by four different paper-makers in turn up to 1849. The industry at Slaughterford seems to have experienced a check in the 1840's, as both Chaps mill and Mill No. 631 are recorded in Excise Letters as 'left off'. The 1851 *Census Report* noted that the cessation of work at two paper-mills had caused a decrease of population at Slaughterford.

Other mills in this area were advertised as being attractive to paper-makers during the period of the geographical expansion of the industry. In 1784[61] Ford grist mills, in the parish of North Wraxall, were said to be calculated for adding a paper- or fulling-mill under the same roof, having been built for that purpose. There were fine crystal springs of water rising nearby, fit for making the finest white paper.

A reference has been found to supplies of cartridge paper from Trowbridge to the parliamentary garrison at Chalfield in 1645,[62] but no evidence of a paper-mill there has been discovered.

A notice in 1738[63] states that William Coles, paper-maker, kept a warehouse in Devizes where any person could be served with 'all sorts of paper, coarse or fine, as cheap and as good, as by any maker whatsoever'. The location of William Coles's mill is not known, but paper-makers named Coles were at Wookey Hole in Somerset for many years; the earliest relevant reference is to James Coles, paper-maker there, who insured his paper-mill in 1758.[64]

[1] The author's thanks are due to all who have helped him in the preparation of this article, and especially to the incumbents of the parishes containing the mills, to the editor of the *Wilts. Gaz.* and to the directors of the Sun Insurance Office Ltd. who kindly granted him permission to search and quote from their policy registers. Gratitude is also due to the Council of the University of Exeter for a grant in aid of the research.

[2] Ramsay, *Wilts. Woollen Industry*, 15.

[3] *London Gaz.* 22 Sept. 1744.

[4] MS. and printed volumes in the library of H.M. Customs and Excise, London, were consulted and are quoted by kind permission of the Commissioners.

[5] Rhys Jenkins, *Collected Papers*, 160.

[6] Sun Fire Insurance Policy No. 40105, 11 Nov. 1726.

[7] 'The Apprentices of Great Britain, 1710–62' (TS. at Soc. of Genealogists); IR 1/51/86, /23/29, /24/95, /57/173, /27/200, and /60/149.

[8] *London Gaz.* 23 Apr. 1793.

[9] General Letter Bk. No. 4 of the Ellesmere Division, Chester Collection (Libr. H.M. Customs and Excise).

[10] General Letter Bk. No. 15 of the Tarporley 1st Ride, Northwich Collection (Libr. H.M. Customs and Excise).

[11] *Paper-Mills Dir.* (1860).

[12] *Return of numbers of Paper Mills*, H.C. 128, p. 553 (1852), li.

[13] He is recorded as a bondsman to a marriage in 1686. 'Salisbury Marriage Licences' (TS. at Soc. of Genealogists, 1938).

[14] W. Naish, *Plan of Salisbury* (1751).

[15] *Marriage Licences of Salisbury, 1615–82*, ed. E. Neville and R. Boucher.

[16] 'Salisbury Marriage Licences' (TS. at Soc. of Geneal. 1938).

[17] IR 1/20/146.

[18] Apprentice Indentures in Downton Parish Chest; IR 1/56/205.

[19] Sun Fire Insurance Policy No. 152346, 17 May 1756.

[20] A. H. Shorter, 'Paper-Mills in Dorset', *Som. and Dors. Notes and Queries*, xxv. 145.

[21] *Univ. Brit. Dir.* (1791), ii. 845.

[22] Sun Fire Insurance Policy No. 438591, 23 Jan. 1781.

[23] *Pigot's Nat. Com. Dir.* (1844).

[24] *Slater's Dir.* (1852–3); *Return of numbers of Paper-Mills*: the mill is listed as having three beating engines at work in 1851.

PAPER-MAKING IN WILTSHIRE

[25] *Kelly's Dir. Wilts.* (1855).
[26] *Dir. of Paper-Makers* (1885, 1890).
[27] Sun Fire Insurance Policy No. 223612, 12 Aug. 1765.
[28] Ibid. No. 489264, 2 Feb. 1784.
[29] B.M. Add. MS. 15054, f. 13.
[30] *Som. and Dors. Notes and Queries*, xxv. 146.
[31] Sun Fire Insurance Policy No. 523473, 26 Oct. 1786.
[32] *London Gaz.* 24 July 1790.
[33] Sun Fire Insurance Policy No. 582560, 20 Apr. 1791.
[34] Archives of Stationers' and Newspaper Makers' Co., London. MS. list in notebook of Richard Johnson, Stationer.
[35] *Paper-Mills Dir.* (1866).
[36] Local information.
[37] *Kentish Gaz.* 24 May 1791.
[38] *Paper-Mills Dir.* (1876).
[39] Ibid.
[40] J. Aubrey, *Natural Hist. of Wilts.* ed. J. Britton, pt. II, v. 95.
[41] *Gloucester Jnl.* 24 June 1746.
[42] Sun Fire Insurance Policies Nos. 136179, 23 June 1753, and 202726, 27 Sept. 1763.
[43] *London Gaz.* 12 Oct. 1813.
[44] Ibid. 5 Dec. 1809.
[45] Ibid. 9 Aug. 1814.
[46] *Paper-Mills Dir.* (1860).
[47] *London Gaz.* 12 Oct. 1813.
[48] Ibid. 12 July 1814.
[49] *Paper-Mills Dir.* (1866).
[50] Archives of the Stationers' and Newspaper Makers' Co., London. MS. list in notebook of Richard Johnson, Stationer.
[51] *London Gaz.* 9 Aug. 1817.
[52] *Bath Chron.* 10 Mar. 1825.
[53] *Kent. Gaz.* 4 June 1793.
[54] *Glouc. Jnl.* 31 Mar. 1794.
[55] *Kelly's Dir. Wilts.* (1859).
[56] *Paper-Mills Dir.* (1860).
[57] *Dir. of Paper-Makers* (1948).
[58] *London Gaz.* 5 May 1792. It is possible that this reference should be connected with the Weavern mill.
[59] IR 1/70/207, /39/60.
[60] Letter dated 2 May 1827, in General Letters Bk. No. 13 of Tarporley 1st Ride (Libr. H.M. Customs and Excise).
[61] *Felix Farley's Bristol Jnl.* 29 May 1784.
[62] *Accts. of Parliamentary Garrisons of Gt. Chalfield and Malmesbury*, ed. J. H. P. Pafford (W.A.S. Rec. Brch. ii), 78.
[63] *Glouc. Jnl.* 4 Apr. 1738.
[64] Sun Fire Insurance Policy No. 162563, 8 May 1758.

XXXIV

PAPER-MILLS IN WORCESTERSHIRE

The history of paper-making in Worcestershire is concerned with an industry active more or less continuously over the past 350 years or so. Up to 1816, however, there is little concentrated information about paper-mills in England, and fragmentary details from many sources have to be pieced together. From 1816, when the Excise authorities, who had managed the duty on paper from 1712 onwards, issued what is apparently the first[1] of a series of lists of paper-mills and paper-makers in this country, the story can be told with greater certainty.

Documentary evidence has been found concerning thirteen paper-mills which have worked at one time or another in Worcestershire; there may well have been more, but I have discovered no evidence to support the statements that there were paper-mills at Inkberrow and Hoobrook.[2]

As was characteristic in the early phases of the industry, the mills were small and scattered. None was situated on the River Severn but there were several on its tributaries, including small streams or brooks. This probably reflects the paper-makers' desire to use sites where clean water was available for the paper-making process, provided sufficient water-power could be developed to drive their mills.

With the geographical and economic expansion of the paper-making industry in England in the eighteenth and early nineteenth centuries, paper-mills were thus scattered up and down the country, while in certain localities quite a swarm of paper-mills developed e.g. in the Wye Valley in Buckinghamshire, the Exeter region and around Maidstone. No such cluster developed in Worcestershire. From the 1830's onwards we note the disappearance of many small paper-mills adversely affected by factors hostile to the survival of the industry in the more rural areas of England. It is interesting that two of the oldest paper-mills in the West of England, Hurcott and Beoley, survived so long.

1. HURCOTT

It is possible that this paper-mill was established by 1600. I have not inspected the relevant documents, but the Secretary of Hurcott Paper Mills Ltd., kindly informs me that he has seen a photostat copy of the

---

[1] General Letter dated 8th October, 1816, in General Letter Book No. 4 of the Ellesmere Division, Chester Collection. I am indebted to the Commissioners of Customs and Excise for permission to read in their library and to quote from their records.

[2] *V.C.H. Worcs.*, III, 1913, pp. 418-9, 167 and 210.

Will of one Blount who died at the Paper Mill House at Hurcott in 1630, and that the mill was owned by one of the Blount family in 1597. Robert Gough died at "Hurcote Papar Myll "in 1653.[1] The next piece of evidence which is probably connected with this mill is dated 1715,[2] when James Simmons was apprenticed to Richard Heath of Kidderminster, paper-maker. A watermark "Heath" has been noted from 1743[3] and if this refers to the Hurcott paper-maker he must have been making white paper about that time.

Peter Rivers, late of the parish of Kidderminster, paper-maker, is mentioned in *Berrow's Worcester Journal*, 13th October, 1763. The same newspaper, 10th January, 1765, contains a notice relating to the estate and effects of Mr. Charles Heath, late of "Hurcourt" in the parish of Kidderminster, paper-maker, deceased. His widow proposed to carry on the paper-making business.

The paper-mill is marked on Taylor's Map of Worcestershire, 1772. About 1786[4] it was in the possession of Harriet Lea, and in 1790,[5] when it was described as a very eligible paper-mill where a very extensive business had been carried on for more than fifty years, it was advertised "to be disposed of and entered upon immediately", applications to Mr. Lea, of Hurcott, being invited. This advertisement gives much interesting information about the mill, which was then in full work and had a well established trade. Its equipment included two engines, two vats, four iron presses and a wood screw. There were very convenient warehouses, spacious drying-rooms, a rag house four storeys high, two large rooms with stoves for finished paper, and two "sols" (sorting rooms?)[6] with stoves. The accommodation included seven tenements for the workmen. The power was developed by an overshot water-wheel fed from a pool twelve acres in area. It was claimed that there was sufficient water in the driest season, that there was no possibility of being flooded and that there was exceedingly good soft washing water. The advantages of the situation of Hurcott were said to be that it was in the centre of a rich mercantile and manufacturing country, only one mile from the Staffordshire and Worcestershire Canal, and served by excellent turnpike roads to Kidderminster, Bewdley, Stourport, Stourbridge, Bromsgrove, Dudley, Worcester, Birmingham and Wolverhampton.

[1] *ibid*, II, 1906, p. 255.

[2] *The Apprentices of Great Britain*, 1710-62 (typescript); extracted from the Inland Revenue Books at the Public Record Office for the Society of Genealogists, 1921-28. Book 44, Fol. 81.

[3] W. A. Churchill, *Watermarks in Paper in the Seventeenth and Eighteenth Centuries*, 1935, p. 41.

[4] *B.M. Add. MSS.*, 15054, Fol. 13.

[5] *Gloucester Journal*, 26th April, 1790.

[6] Possibly "sol"=soler, or upper room, garret or loft. Common in leases till quite recently (Halliwell. *Dict. of Archaic Words*)—*Ed.*

36

It appears that as a result of this advertisement the business was taken up by John and Thomas Holl of the City of Worcester, paper manufacturers, stationers, etc., whose partnership was dissolved in 1792.[1] It was then stated that the manufactory would in future be carried on by John Holl. When he was declared bankrupt in 1793[2] he was described as a paper-maker, dealer and chapman, of Hurcott.

The next paper manufacturer here was probably Robert Vaughan Brooke. He also was declared bankrupt in 1806,[3] but his certificate was allowed and confirmed in 1810.[4] The Excise Letter of 1816 records his name at Mill No. 372, Hurcott, in the Stourbridge Collection of Excise. For many years after that paper-making was carried on by or in the name of Thomas James, who in 1860, 1866 and 1876[5] was manufacturing Superfine Writing and Book Papers, handmade, with four vats. Two beating engines were at work in 1851[6].

According to the *Directory of Paper Makers* the mill was worked in the 1880's by John James and in 1890 by Thomas James and Co., followed by the Hurcott Paper Mills Ltd. In 1910 the products were handmade Account Book, Writing, Drawing, Loan, Bank Note, Cheque and Printing Papers, from best linen and cotton rags only, and in 1915 and 1948 the firm advertised special loft air-dried papers and boards.

2 AND 3. BEOLEY

The earliest references to paper-mills here occur in 1650[7] when there were held with the manor a paper-mill in the occupation of Nicholas Clows and another called Seales Mill. The former is probably that shewn on Beighton's Map of Warwickshire, 1725.[8] By the 1790's it had passed to John and Matthew Mills,[9] who are named in the Excise Letter of 1816 as the paper-makers at Mill No. 473, Beoley, in the Worcester Collection of Excise. By 1850[10] the mill was in the possession of Thomas Parr, and in 1851[11] one beating engine was at work. In 1860 and 1866[12] H. and E. Parr were manufacturing needle and fish-

[1] *London Gazette*, 21st June, 1792.

[2] *ibid*, 9th November, 1793.

[3] *ibid*, 7th January, 1806.

[4] *ibid*, 3rd March, 1810.

[5] *The Paper Mills Directory* for those years.

[6] *House of Commons Papers*, 1852, Vol. 51, No. 128.

[7] *V.C.H. Worcs.*, IV, 1924, pp. 15-16.

[8] I am indebted to Mr. Rhys Jenkins for this information.

[9] Paper-makers listed in Richard Johnson's address book, 1793, in the archives of the Stationers' and Newspaper Makers' Company, to whom I am grateful for permission to quote this source.

[10] Slater's *Directory*, 1850. The present firm state that Henry Parr and Sons started in 1830.

[11] *House of Commons Papers*, 1852, Vol. 51, No. 128.

[12] *The Paper Mills Directory*, 1860 and 1866.

hook papers, while in 1876[1] and 1885[2] needle papers only were being made, in the last of these years on a machine 48 inches in width. An advertisement of 1910[3] gives the products as needle papers and rope browns made on a machine of 60 inches. The machine ran until 1941, producing needle papers.[4]

4. HEWELL

I am indebted to Mr. Rhys Jenkins for much of my information concerning Hewell paper-mill, Tardebigge. From the Perambulation of 1645[5] it appears that this was even older than the Beoley paper-mill which is therein referred to as the new paper-mill. Lord Plymouth put an assessment on the paper-mills in Tardebigge in 1691.[6]

The paper-mill is marked on Beighton's Map of Warwickshire, 1725, and on W. Yates' Map of Warwickshire 1787-9. A relevant reference occurs in 1752, when a set of paper-mills in the parish of Tardebigge, in very good repair, were to be let and entered upon immediately.[7] Particulars were available from the Steward to the Earl of Plymouth at his house at Hewell.

References to two paper-makers at Hewell have been found. John Holyoake (who was there in 1771[8]) advertised for three or four Journeymen Paper-makers "for writing work" at Hewell Paper-mill in 1768.[9] Holyoake's Will was proved at London in 1782.[10] Robert Lloyd of Tardebigge, paper-maker, was a party to deeds dated 26/27 March 1782[11] concerning property at Cleobury Mortimer, Salop.

5. ASTLEY BROOK.

In July 1728 several newspapers[12] reported that two corn-mills, a paper-mill and a house were swept down Astley Brook, following a thunderstorm and cloudburst. The paper-mill seems to have been replaced fairly quickly, for a newspaper of 1735/6[13] contains an advertisement that there was to be let for 21 years or a longer term "a very good

[1] *ibid*, 1876.
[2] *The Directory of Paper Makers*, 1885.
[3] *ibid*, 1910.
[4] Information from Henry Parr and Sons, Ltd., Beoley Paper Mills.
[5] Perambulation of the bounds and limits belonging to the parish or chapelry of Bordesley, 24th July, 1645, quoted in Nash, *Worcestershire*, II, 1782, p. 404. J. M. Woodward, *The History of Bordesley Abbey*, 1866.
[6] M. Dickins, *A Thousand Years in Tardebigge*, 1931, p. 651.
[7] *The Worcester Journal*, 16th January, 1752.
[8] M. Dickins, *loc. cit.*
[9] *Berrow's Worcester Journal*, 21st July, 1768.
[10] P. C. C. *Gostling*, 455, quoted in *Notes and Queries*, 195, 1950, p. 504.
[11] Purton, *MSS. Calendar of Deeds and Charters* in Shrewsbury Public Library, II, Nos. 850-2. I am indebted to Mr. L. C. Lloyd for this information.
[12] e.g. *Gloucester Journal, The Daily Post*, 16th July, 1728, and *The Weekly Journal or The British Gazetteer*, 20th July, 1728.
[13] *The Weekly Worcester Journal*, 9th January, 1735/6.

38

Paper-Mill, containing one Engine and Ten Hammers", situated "on a Brook never wanting Water sufficient for the Mill," which was situated in the parish of Astley, within a quarter of a mile of the River Severn, 4 miles from Bewdley and Kidderminster, 6 from Worcester and about 7 from Bromsgrove. This seems to be the same paper-mill as that referred to in a lease of 1739.[1] No later reference has been found.

6. ALFRICK

The name Papermill Coppice has survived near Leigh Brook.[2] I am indebted to the Rev. J. Hurford, Vicar of Alfrick, for identifying this paper-mill as Gunnex Mill. Mr. William Purshall of "Gunnix Mills" in the parish of Suckley and in the hamlet of Alfrick is mentioned in a newspaper of 1758.[3]. He took apprentices in 1752, 1762[4] and 1781,[5] and is described in the indentures as a paper-maker.

This paper-mill appears in Excise Letters of 1816 and 1832 under the name of Gunnex, Mill No. 475, in the Worcester Collection of Excise. In 1816 it was occupied by Henry Jones and in 1832 by James Jones.

7 AND 8. OVERBURY

Two indentures of 1724 and 1729[6] show that Conan Strait and Henry Cotton were respectively apprenticed to Ben Davis, paper-maker at Overbury. The apprentice named in the second indenture was stated to be of Ashton, Gloucestershire, and may have been the Henry Cotton who later was a paper-maker in Bristol.[7] Taylor's Map of Worcestershire, 1772, shows "Paper Mills" immediately north of Overbury and more than one mill symbol there. In 1795, Mr. Nind, paper-maker of Overbury, was married at Tewkesbury.[8]

The Excise Letter of 1816 records Overbury paper-mill as No. 472, in the Worcester Collection, occupied by Edward Robinson, whose business was discontinued for a time in 1821. When he resumed work the mill was renumbered 256, and this mill appears to have ceased work about 1834.

According to Mrs. Berkeley[9] there were two paper-mills at Overbury. The Red House was a paper-mill belonging to the Nind family, and Silver Rill was the paper-mill worked by the Robinsons, who have now built up a big paper and bag business in Bristol.

---

[1] *V.C.H. Worcs.*, IV, 1924, p. 234.
[2] *ibid.*, p. 355.
[3] *Berrow's Worcester Journal*, 14th December, 1758.
[4] *The Apprentices of Great Britain* . . . Book/Fol. 51/162 and 54/207.
[5] Alfrick Apprentice Indenture; details kindly given by the Rev. J. Hurford.
[6] *The Apprentices of Great Britain* . . . Book/Fol. 48/163 and 49/86.
[7] *The Bristol Poll Book*, 1739.
[8] *Felix Farley's Bristol Journal*, 24th January, 1795.
[9] *Old Worcestershire Water Mills, Trans. Worcs. Arch. Soc., XI*, N.S., 1934, pp. 24-5.

9. Wychbold

The paper-mill here was apparently that situated two miles north of Droitwich on the River Salwarpe. In 1777[1] it was advertised to be let and entered upon immediately, being described as a brown paper-mill, with plenty of water on the stream. The premises were "in exceeding good repair and made very convenient for carrying on the business of paper-making."

W. A. Churchill[2] notes a watermark "J. Corbett" of 1805 and this may refer to a paper-maker here, as in the Excise Letter of 1816 Margaret Corbet is listed as the paper-maker at Wychbold Mill, No. 474, in the Worcester Collection of Excise. Further Excise Letters show that in 1823 the paper-maker was Elizabeth Corbett, in 1824 and 1832 Luke Evans. In 1836 John Evans was making pasteboard there. The paper-mill is mentioned in a newspaper of 1841,[3] my last reference.

10. Stoke Prior

A newspaper notice in 1761[4] states that an apprentice to Joseph Shallard, paper-maker at Stoke Prior, had absented himself. The only other evidence I have found of a paper-mill there is that the field-name "Paper Mill Close" occurs in the Tithe Apportionment of the parish, 1845. It is possible that both these references are really connected with the Wychbold paper-mill.

11 and 12. North Littleton and Harvington

I am indebted to Mr. E. A. B. Barnard for drawing my attention to his contributions to the *Evesham Journal*[5] which give very full information about these mills. Mr. Barnard shows that the North Littleton paper-mill was erected in 1717 or thereabouts by John Washborne, and the Harvington paper-mill by John Gould in or shortly before 1803. The two mills were so close together that sometimes the proper name of one seems to have been applied to the other. Thus a newspaper advertisement in 1737[6] refers to a new paper-mill with twenty hammers and a glazing engine at Harvington. According to Mr. Barnard's evidence, this must have been the North Littleton paper-mill, and this conclusion is supported by the facts that it is this mill which is marked on Taylor's Map of Worcestershire, 1772, and that in 1787[7] Harvington Mills were described as Water Corn Mills.

[1] *Berrow's Worcester Journal*, 13th March and 12th June, 1777.
[2] *op. cit.*
[3] *Shrewsbury News*, 6th February, 1841. I am indebted to Mr. L. C. Lloyd for this information.
[4] *Berrow's Worcester Journal*, 1st October, 1761.
[5] 1939, Nos. 828-836 inclusive.
[6] *Gloucester Journal*, 14th June, 1737.
[7] *ibid.*, 10th December, 1787.

40

The venture at Harvington Paper-mill did not last long, John Gould being bankrupt in 1804[1], a bankruptcy that was superseded however in 1811.[2] The Littleton paper-mill seems to have worked through the first half of the nineteenth century. Mr. Barnard's information may be supplemented from Excise Letters between 1816 and 1846 in which the mill number 471, in the Worcester Collection, appears with reference sometimes to Harvington, sometimes to Littleton Mill. In 1816 the paper-maker was John Phillips, who was bankrupt in 1819.[3] Further paper-makers are recorded as follows: 1820, Edward James Flint and Patrick Tregent; 1825, Patrick Tregent; 1828, John White and James Grice; 1832-3, John Ibbotson; 1838, Joseph Bramwell; 1846, Abraham Day.

13. WYRE MILL (NEAR PERSHORE)

I have no information about a short-lived paper-making venture here other than that recorded by Mrs. Berkeley.[4] In 1705 William Lloyd, Bishop of Worcester, and his three sons re-erected the mill. "The Bishop was anxious to emulate the Sudeley paper-mill near Winchcombe. He had all the rushes cut at Wyre for pulp and a great well was sunk, but the project failed, as the water was too hard."

Acknowledgment

I acknowledge with gratitude the research grant made to me by the Council of the University College of the SouthWest of England, Exeter, for the pursuance of this study.

[1] *London Gazette*, 10th January, 1804.
[2] *ibid.*, 14th October, 1811.
[3] *ibid.*, 10th July, 1819.
[4] *op. cit.* p. 22.

XXXV

HURCOTT PAPER MILL

Hurcott is one of the oldest paper mills still at work in England; indeed it may be the oldest, for there is a possibility that it was established even before John Spilman's well-known mill at Dartford (Kent) began work in 1583. This possibility arises from two pieces of evidence. The first is that in 1601, in reply to a letter from the Lords of the Council on the subject of Spilman's rights in respect of the collection of rags for paper making, the Lord Mayor and Aldermen of the City of London stated that Spilman's mill was not the first paper mill in England, in that before his there were paper mills at Osterley (Middlesex), at Cambridge, in Worcestershire and elsewhere.[1] The second piece of evidence, which supports the suggestion that this Worcestershire paper mill might have been Hurcott, is that the Paper Mill House there is mentioned in 1630;[2] this is the earliest known reference to any Worcestershire paper mill by name. The only other available evidence about Hurcott Paper Mill during the seventeenth century is that Robert Gough died there in 1653.[3]

Most of the master paper makers at Hurcott from 1715 on have now been identified. In that year Richard Heath, paper maker of Kidderminster, took an apprentice James Simmons,[4] and the name Heath appears in a watermark of 1743.[5] His successor was Charles Heath, paper maker, who insured the paper mill in 1756[6] and probably worked it until his death in 1764[5], when a newspaper notice[7] referred to the estate and effects of Mr Charles Heath, late of "Hurcourt" in the parish of Kidderminster, paper maker, deceased, and stated that his widow proposed to carry on the business. Only one reference has been found to the next master maker, William Mainwaring, who insured the paper

1. A.H. Shorter, *Paper Mills and Paper Makers in England, 1495–1800*, The Paper Publications Society, Hilversum, Holland, 1957, pp. 29 and 45, quoting *State Papers Domestic*, Elizabeth, CCLXXIX, 88.
2. One Blount died at the Paper Mill House in that year. Information from Mr G.W. Aylward, Secretary, Hurcott Paper Mills Ltd., referring to Blount's will.
3. *V.C.H. Worcs.*, II, 1906, 255, quoting *Hurcott Parish Register* and Burton, *History of Kidderminster*, 1890, 187.
4. *Apprentices of Great Britain*, 1710–62, (typescript); extracted from the Inland Revenue Books at the Public Record Office for the Society of Genealogists, 1921–8, Book 44, fol. 81.
5. W.A. Churchill, *Watermarks in Paper in Holland, England, France etc., in the Seventeenth and Eighteenth centuries and their interconnection*, 1935, 41.
6. *Sun Fire Insurance Policy*, No. 150632, 21st Jan., 1756.
7. *Berrow's Worcester Journal*, 10th. Jan., 1765.

mill in 1769.[8] About 1786 it was in the possession of Harriet Lea,[9] and in 1790, when it was described as a very eligible paper mill where a very extensive business had been carried on for more than 50 years, it was advertised "to be disposed of and entered upon immediately", applications to Mr Lea of Hurcott being invited.[10] This advertisement gives much interesting information about the mill, which was then in full work and had a well established trade. Its equipment included two engines, two vats, four iron presses and a woodscrew. There were very convenient warehouses, spacious drying-rooms, a rag house four stories high, two large rooms with stoves for finished paper, and two sols with stoves. The accommodation included seven tenements for the workmen. The power was developed by an overshot water-wheel fed from a pool twelve acres in area. It was claimed that there was sufficient water in the driest season, that there was no possibility of being flooded and that there was exceedingly good soft water. The advantages of the situation of Hurcott were said to be that it was in the centre of a rich mercantile and manufacturing country, only one mile from the Staffordshire and Worcestershire Canal and served by excellent turnpike roads to Kidderminster, Bewdley, Stourport, Stourbridge, Bromsgrove, Dudley, Worcester, Birmingham and Wolverhampton. (The situation of the paper mill is shown clearly on a county map of 1772.[11])

It appears that as a result of this advertisement the Hurcott Paper Mill was taken over by John and Thomas Holl, stationers of Worcester. In 1791 they advertised for a "Foreman and Manager" in a paper mill in Worcestershire, and required one who had been "regularly brought up in the knowledge of manufacturing writing papers".[12] Their joint tenure of the mill did not last long, however, for in 1792 a notice appeared that the partnership between John and Thomas Holl, paper manufacturers, stationers etc. of Worcester, was dissolved.[13] It was stated that the manufactory would in future be carried on by John Holl, but he was declared a bankrupt in 1793;[14] he was then described as a paper maker, dealer and chapman of Hurcott. In the following year the paper mill "late in the possession of John Holl" was advertised for sale; it was stated that a spring of the purest water had been conveyed to the mill by an aqueduct, at a

8. *Sun Fire Insurance Policy* No. 276877, 2nd Nov., 1769.
9. Her name is given in a list of paper makers in *British Museum Add. Ms. 15054, Myvyrian Mss.,* 1786.
10. *Gloucester Journal,* 26th Apr., 1790.
11. Taylor's *Map of Worcestershire.*
12. *Kentish Gazette,* 11th Oct., 1791.
13. *London Gazette,* 21st June 1792.
14. *Ibid.,* 9th Nov., 1793.

considerable expense to the late occupier.[15] This suggests that Holl had made an effort to improve the manufacture of good quality papers at Hurcott.

The next proprietor certainly made such papers. Robert Vaughan Brooke was a stationer of Cheapside, London, in 1788,[16] and in 1803 a man of that name, described as a paper maker of Hurcott, insured the paper mill for £500.[17] Among the watermarks in papers made by him are R V BROOKE 1804[18] and R V B 1806.[19] He was declared bankrupt in 1806,[20] but his certificate was allowed and confirmed in 1810,[21] and in 1816, when the Excise authorities issued the first known numerical list of paper mills in England,[22] his name is given under Mill No. 372, Hurcott, in the Stourbridge Collection of Excise. During his bankruptcy, however, and again after 1816, the mill appears to have been worked by Thomas Garmston & Co. Described as paper makers of the city of Worcester, they insured the stock and utensils in their paper mill at Hurcott in 1806,[23] and the name of Thomas Garmston as the proprietor at Hurcott is recorded in an Excise Letter of 1818.[24]

A few years later the mill was taken over by Thomas James, whose name in connection with Hurcott Mill is given in an Excise Letter of 1826.[25] Papers watermarked T JAMES must have been made at Hurcott and dated examples are known from 1844 and 1852.[26] Two beating engines were at work at Hurcott in 1851,[25] and in the 1860s and 1870s the firm of Thomas James was manufacturing superfine writing and book papers, with four vats.[28] In the 1880s the mill was worked by John James and in 1890 by Thomas James & Co., who by 1900 were followed by the Hurcott Paper Mills Ltd. In 1910 the products were handmade account book, writing, drawing, loan, bank note, cheque and printing papers from best linen and cotton rags only, and from about 1915 up to the 1950s the firm advertised special loft air-dried papers and boards.[29]

15. *Aris's Birmingham Gazette*, 3rd March 1794.
16. *Sun Fire Insurance Policy* No. 543229, 18th Apr., 1788.
17. *Ibid.*, No. 755627, 1st Nov., 1803.
18. In a paper in the possession of Mr L.C. Lloyd, Shrewsbury.
19. In a paper in the *Whatman and Balston Archives*.
20. *London Gazette*, 7th Jan., 1806.
21. *Ibid.*, 3rd March 1810.
22. *Excise General Letter*, 8th Oct., 1816.
23. *Sun Fire Insurance Policy*, No. 796018, 27th Oct., 1806.
24. *Excise General Letter*, 31st Dec., 1818.
25. *Ibid.*, 15th May 1826.
26. In papers in the possession of Mr L.C. Lloyd, Shrewsbury.
27. *House of Commons Papers*. 1852, 51, No. 128.
28. *Paper Mills Directory*, 1860, 1866 and 1876.
29. Information from 1855 on is derived from the *Directory of Paper Makers*.

ACKNOWLEDGEMENTS

I gratefully acknowledge the kind permission of the following, who allowed me to search and quote from the records in their possession: Sun Insurance Office Ltd., Commissioners of Customs and Excise, Mr Thomas Balston and Mr L.C. Lloyd.

XXXVI

PAPER MILLS IN SCOTLAND IN 1800

Although the history of many of the Scottish paper mills is well documented and widely known, there appears to have been little attempt to study the distribution of the mills which existed about the year 1800.   An exception is found in the work of Mr. Robert Waterston[1], who has traced the mills near Edinburgh; but by 1800 several other mills had been established in different parts of Scotland.   The number of Excise licences issued to Scottish paper makers rose from 27 in 1785 to 39 in 1795; in 1800 there were 32[2].   Some help in identifying these paper makers and their mills has been afforded by Mr. Waterston's notes, the records of individual firms, Bushnell's references to Scottish paper makers in the eighteenth century[3], and the well-known list of paper mills in Scotland in 1832[4].

The chief purposes of this contribution are to supplement the established facts about the history of the paper mills by new evidence from about 1800, much of which is derived from sources in England (no doubt this could be greatly augmented from local sources in Scotland), and to show the geographical distribution of most of the 35 to 40 paper mills which must have been in existence.   As with England[5] and Ireland, the distribution in Scotland shows a major concentration near the capital city (especially on the Water of Leith and the North Esk), and smaller concentrations around other important centres such as Glasgow and Aberdeen (compare the groups of mills around, say, Belfast, Exeter and Cork). Several other mills were scattered through southern Scotland, but there was nothing like the general dispersal of mills in England—the difference being to a great extent a reflection of the contrast in the distribution of population in the two countries.

PAPER MILLS IN SCOTLAND

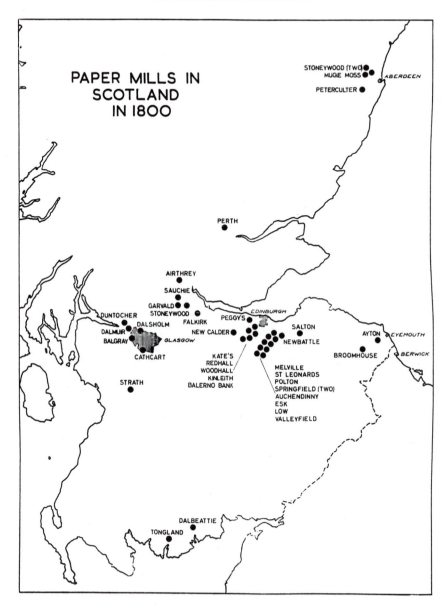

PAPER MILLS IN
SCOTLAND
IN 1800

STONEYWOOD (TWO)
MUGIE MOSS
ABERDEEN
PETERCULTER

PERTH

AIRTHREY
SAUCHIE
GARVALD   STONEYWOOD
DUNTOCHER   FALKIRK   EDINBURGH
DALSHOLM   PEGGY'S
DALMUIR   NEW CALDER   SALTON
BALGRAY   GLASGOW   NEWBATTLE   AYTON   EYEMOUTH
CATHCART   BROOMHOUSE   BERWICK
                 KATE'S
                 REDHALL
STRATH   WOODHALL   MELVILLE
                 KINLEITH   ST LEONARDS
                 BALERNO BANK POLTON
                             SPRINGFIELD (TWO)
                             AUCHENDINNY
                             ESK
                             LOW
                             VALLEYFIELD

DALBEATTIE
TONGLAND

I have had to include a few mills of which the earliest known dates are a little later than 1800, because it is possible that they had been set up by that year. Mills which are known to have been established shortly after 1800 have, of course, been omitted — examples are Ferryhill, near Aberdeen (1803), Rothes (1804) and Auchmuty (1809). I am grateful to many Scottish paper makers for the information they have given me, and to the Sun Insurance Office Ltd. and the Commissioners of Customs and Excise for permission to quote from their records.

Mugiemoss
The mill was started by Charles Davidson in or shortly after 1796[6] and was held by that firm under the Excise Number 66 in 1832. It is still worked by C. Davidson & Sons Ltd.

Stoneywood, Aberdeen (two mills)
A paper mill was established here in 1770 by John Boyle, a bookseller, and Richard Hyde, a dyer, both of Aberdeen[7]. In 1772 the mill was insured by Thomas Spark and Alexander Smith[8], and in 1787 the latter insured his two paper mills at Stoneywood[9]. In 1832 the mills, Numbers 7 and 8, were worked by Alexander Pirie and Charles Smith & Co. respectively. No. 7 is still working under the firm of Alex. Pirie & Sons Ltd.

Peterculter
This mill was set up by Bartholomew Smith in 1750. It still bears the Number 9 and is worked by the Culter Mills Paper Co. Ltd.

Perth
The Woodend mill near Huntingtower (about four miles north-west of Perth) was probably at work in the eighteenth century[10]. In the early years of the nineteenth century it held by Henry Lindsay and in 1832 by John Lindsay & Co. under the Excise Number 12.

Airthrey, Bridge of Allan

It is probable that one or more paper mills had been set up here by 1800 and that the proprietor was Robert Ferguson, paper maker of Bridge of Allan, who insured a house in Stirling in 1803[11]. Three mills, Airthrey First (Excise No. 40), Second (No. 38) and Third (71), were working in the early nineteenth century. The Second was the last to close down, in 1947.

Sauchie

Sauchie paper mill was in the parish of St. Ninian's, Stirlingshire. It is mentioned in insurance policies taken out by James and Robert Liddle, paper makers, in 1787, and by Robert Liddell, merchant and paper maker of the Milnholm of Sauchie, in 1791[12]. These are my only references, but the mill may have been in existence in 1800.

Garvald

This mill may have been at work before 1800. In 1806 and 1807 William Smail, paper maker of Garvald, near Denny, Stirlingshire, insured the paper mill[13]. John Muirhead was the occupier in 1832, when the mill bore the Excise Number 42.

Stoneywood, Denny

The paper mill can be traced from 1800[14]. Mill No. 39, Stoneywood, was held by Robert Weir in 1832. It is worked today by John Collins Ltd.

Falkirk

The only reference I have to this paper mill is that it was insured by William Kay & Co., paper makers, in 1799[15].

New Calder

1764 is the accepted date for the establishment of this mill[16]. It was being worked by William Robertson under the Number 5 in 1832 and it is still working under the firm of Adam Robertson & Co. Ltd.

Peggy's Mill

This mill was on the River Almond. It was in the hands of William Cadell, one of the founders of the Carron Iron Works, from 1782[17]. In 1807[18] William Cadell, Sons & Co. of Cramond, paper makers and iron forgers, insured their house at Peggy's Mill, and in 1832 Mill No. 57 was held by Phillip Cadell. Papermaking ceased in 1881, when the building was taken over by a firm of manufacturing chemists[19].

Kate's Mill, Colinton

This mill was rebuilt for papermaking in 1783[20] and was worked by John Balfour & Sons, who insured a paper mill at Colinton in 1798[21]. Known to the Excise authorities as No. 56, it was held by Alex. Cowan & Son in 1832. It was destroyed by fire in 1890[22].

Redhall

The paper mill can be traced from 1718[23]. Among the early paper makers was Robert Murdoch, who was at Redhall Mill in 1727[24]. The mill was insured by Gavin Hamilton, bookseller of Edinburgh, in 1758 and 1764, and by John Balfour & Sons, paper makers, in 1798[25].

Woodhall

A lease to Mark Stark in 1792 included the fall of water of the paper mill[26]. In 1832 Woodhall Mill, No. 54, was held by John Milne. It is still working under the Woodhall Paper Co. Ltd.

Kinleith

According to A. D. Spicer[27], the paper mill started work about the middle of the eighteenth century. Among the proprietors before 1800 were Walker & Co.,[28] and by 1832 the mill was in the hands of Russell, Kerr & Co. and bore the Number 53. It is still working under the firm of Henry Bruce & Sons Ltd.

Balerno Bank

Robert Douglas, paper maker, insured Balerno paper mill in 1776[29]. Twenty years later it was insured by Nisbett, McNiven & Co., paper makers, who had a warehouse for their stock and utensils in Blair Street, Edinburgh[30]. By 1832 there were three Balerno paper mills, working under the Numbers 51, 52 and 61, and also Balerno Bank mill, under the Number 50. In 1841[31] James Craig & Son held Balerno Bank Mill as No. 15, and by 1860[12] Hill, Craig & Co. were probably working two mills merged into one under the Numbers 15 and 51. Balerno Bank Paper Mills are still at work under the firm of John Galloway & Co. Ltd.

Melville

Established about 1750[33], this mill was for many years held by John Hutton. In 1764[34], described as a merchant of Edinburgh, he insured the machinery in the paper mill, and in 1792 he was referred to as "a very respectable paper manufacturer[35]." In 1797[36] Melville mill was insured by John Pitcairn, paper manufacturer, from whom it was acquired as a six-vat mill by Alexander Cowan in 1814[37]. It bore the Number 25, and was given up by Messrs. Cowan shortly after 1825[38].

St. Leonard's, Lasswade

In 1792 William Simpson, paper maker, of Polton, insured a house at St. Leonard's, and in the following year his paper millhouse, vathouse, etc., there[39]. He was still a paper maker at Lasswade in 1806[40], but by 1832 the mill was held by William Brookes under the Excise Number 26. Since 1843 it has been owned by the Tod family and is still worked by John Tod & Son Ltd.

Polton

A five-vat mill was erected here in 1768[41]. About 1784 it was taken over by William Simpson, who insured a new drying house and had a stock of rags in a warehouse at Leith[42]. In 1801[43] the mill was insured by Christopher Proven, paper maker, and shortly afterwards it passed to Alex. Annandale & Son, who worked it under the Number 28. Held by Annandale & Son Ltd., it ceased work in 1949[44].

Springfield (two mills)

Papermaking at Springfield started about 1742[45]. In 1796 Strachan & Cameron, paper makers, insured their paper mill at Springfield and the little paper mill near, also their stock and utensils in a warehouse in Fish Market Close, Edinburgh[46]. The little mill is mentioned in later policies; in 1813 both mills were held by Robert Cameron & Son[47]. One mill was at work in 1832, when it was occupied by John Cameron & Co. under the Number 29. It is still worked by William Tod, Junior & Co. Ltd.

Auchendinny

This paper mill dates from about 1716[48]. In 1786 it was insured by William Cadell of Carron Park and in 1803 by William Cadell & Co. There were then four vathouses, and this firm had warehouses in Edinburgh and Leith[49]. In 1832 Mill No. 24 at Auchendinny was held by Phillip Cadell & Co.

Esk Mills

This mill started in 1790[50] and was for a time held by John White, senior and junior, paper manufacturers; a notice to their creditors was published in 1814[51]. They were followed by James Brown & Co., who were working under the Excise Number 31 in 1832. The mill is still carried on by James Brown & Co. Ltd.

Low Mill, Penicuik

A Mr. Nimmo, of Edinburgh, converted this mill from fulling to papermaking in 1749[52]. In the 1790's[53] the lower paper mill at Penicuik was insured by William Simpson, paper maker of Polton, and was possibly held for a time by R. Walker who, as a paper maker at Penicuik, urged journeymen of Kent to come to his mill[54]. In 1815 it was purchased by Messrs. Cowan and, known as No. 27, Low Mill, it worked until 1892, when the firm's production was concentrated at Valleyfield Mill.

Valleyfield

The history of this paper mill is well known from the beginning (1709) to the present time. It was given the Excise Number 60 and is still worked by Alex. Cowan & Sons Ltd.

Newbattle

In 1796 Archibald Keith, paper maker of Newbattle, insured the paper mill and he and/or his sons worked it until 1815 at least[55]. By 1832 Mill No. 20, Newbattle, was occupied by James Craig, and it closed in 1890, when the proprietors were Robert Craig & Sons[56].

Salton (East Lothian)

In 1787 Robert Laing, paper maker of Salton Barley Mill, insured the paper mill. From 1790 to 1803 it was insured by William Cadell & Co., paper manufacturers of Carron Park, Stirlingshire[57].

Broomhouse

A printed advertisement, undated but probably issued between 1765 and 1775, states that Robert Taylor, bookseller in Berwick, had erected a large paper mill at Broomhouse[58]. For some years the mill was worked by Henry Taylor who, variously described as a paper maker and stationer of Berwick and a paper maker of Gibshaugh in the parish of Edrom, took several apprentices[59] and insured the paper mill[60]. He was bankrupt in 1786[61] and the lease of the "large and valuable mill" at Broomhouse on the Whitadder was for sale in 1788. The mill, which had five working vats[62], was taken over by Young Trotter who, as a paper maker of Broomhouse, insured his goods in 1801[63]. The following year the mill, which by then had eight vats, was insured by the Broomhouse Paper Mill Co.[64], and by 1832 it was being worked by Young Trotter & Son under the Excise Number 34. The mill was closed in 1842[65], when the firm moved to Chirnside Bridge Mill, No. 61, which is still worked by Y. Trotter & Son Ltd.

Millbank, Ayton

In 1785 John Taylor, paper maker of Ayton, Berwickshire, insured his paper mill[66]. A notice to his creditors appeared in 1793[67], and in that year his successors, Charles & Robert Kerr, paper makers, insured the mill[68]; they had stock in warehouses at Berwick and Eyemouth[69]. In 1803 Robert Kerr, paper maker and farmer of Millbank, insured his stock and utensils[70]. He was followed by the Martin family who worked the mill under the Number 36. Martin & Co. are recorded at Millbank in 1866[71], but meanwhile Bleachfield Mills near Ayton, No. 59, had begun work under William Martin in 1842[72].

Duntocher

This mill may have been established by 1800, but the first known reference is from 1808, when Joseph Combe, paper maker of Duntocher in Dumbartonshire, insured the paper mill. In 1817, the date of the last known reference, James Watson, paper maker, insured the machinery and utensils in his paper mill[73].

Dalmuir

Edward Collins established this paper mill in 1747. It later bore the Number 21 and was dismantled in 1857 after the firm of Edward Collins had gradually concentrated their business at Kelvindale[74].

Dalsholm

In 1800 James Russell & Co., paper makers, insured the stock and utensils in the paper mill. A similar policy was taken out in 1808[75] by James McArthur, who was still working the mill, Number 37, in 1832. Dalsholm Paper Co. Ltd. are the present proprietors.

Balgray

This paper mill was insured by James Duncan, paper maker, in 1790; it was in the parish of Govan, Lanarkshire. In 1804 it was held by Joseph Combe and in 1812 by William Combe[76].

Cathcart

In 1763 James Hall was a paper maker at the New Paper Mill, Cathcart[77]. In 1815 and 1816 Messrs. D.

& A. Campbell of Millholm, Cathcart, insured their paper and snuff mill[78]. This mill, known as No. 18, was working up to 1930, the last proprietors being Wiggins, Teape & Co. Ltd. Another Cathcart mill, No. 19, was worked by Robert Weir in 1832. Late in the nineteenth century it was in the hands of Solomon Lindsay, who appears to have been the last to work it.[79].

Strath Mill, Galston (Ayrshire)

The mill was insured by John Carson, paper maker, in 1786. Four years later a similar policy was taken out by William Finnie of Kilmarnock, trustee for the creditors of John Carson[80]. In 1832 the mill was held by Alexander Finnie under the Number 17. It appears to have ceased about 1876, the date of my last reference[81].

Tongland

In 1772 this paper mill, which included a glaze mill, was for sale[82]. The master paper makers were Allan McLauchlan[83], followed by John McLauchlan[84], and then by George Craig & Co.[85] It is possible that the mill was working in 1800 and later.

Dalbeattie

At least one paper mill here was probably working in the late eighteenth century. In 1805 William Cuchtree, paper maker, insured a paper mill at Dalbeattie[86]. In 1832 there were two paper mills there, Numbers 45 and 46, and the former was at work until about 1924[87].

REFERENCES

1. Early Paper Making near Edinburgh, and Further Notes on Early Paper Making near Edinburgh, *Book of the Old Edinburgh Club*, XXV, 1946, and XXVII, 1949.
2. *British Parliamentary Papers*, Reports from Commissioners (1857), IV, First Report of the Commissioners of Inland Revenue, 177, App. 30. lxix.
3. G. H. Bushnell (on Scotland), *A Dictionary of the Printers and Booksellers who were at work in England, Scotland and Ireland from 1726 to 1775*, published 1932.
4. Published in *The Paper Maker*. May. 1915.

PAPER MILLS IN SCOTLAND

5. A. H. Shorter, *Paper Mills and Paper Makers in England* 1495-1800, The Paper Publications Society, Hilversum, Holland, 1957, especially Chap. III.
6. Information from the present firm.
7. Information from the present firm.
8. *Sun Fire Insurance Policy* No. 313288, July 9, 1772.
9. *Sun Fire Insurance Policy* No. 528115, February 28, 1787.
10. I have an unidentified reference to a paper mill near Perth before 1800, given me by the late Mr. Rhys Jenkins.
11. *Sun Fire Insurance Policy* No. 755996, November 10, 1803.
12. *Sun Fire Insurance Policies* Nos. 526164, January 12, 1787, and 592319, November 17, 1791.
13. *Sun Fire Insurance Policies* Nos. 793723, August 20, 1806, and 805470, June 24, 1807.
14. Information from the present firm.
15. *Sun Fire Insurance Policy* No. 696236, November 23, 1799.
16. *The Paper Maker*, December, 1952.
17. Waterston, 1946.
18. *Sun Fire Insurance Policy*, No. 801018, February 10, 1807.
19. Information from John Galloway & Co. Ltd., Balerno Bank Paper Mills.
20. Waterston, 1949.
21. *Sun Fire Insurance Policy* No. 681673, September 29, 1798.
22. Waterston, 1949.
23. Waterston, 1949.
24. Bushnell, p. 338.
25. *Sun Fire Insurance Policies* Nos. 161124, February 19, 1758, 206106, January 14, 1764, and 681673, September 29, 1798.
26. Information from the present firm.
27. *The Paper Trade*, 1907, p. 216.
28. Waterston, 1946.
29. *Sun Fire Insurance Policy* No. 372819, August 27, 1776.
30. *Sun Fire Insurance Policy* No. 651503, January 26, 1796.
31. *Excise General Letter*, January 18, 1841.
32. *Paper Mills Directory*, 1860.
33. Waterston, 1949.
34. *Sun Fire Insurance Policy* No. 211333, August 7, 1764.
35. Letter, *Papers from Springfield Mill*, Kent. Information from Mr. Thomas Balston.
36. *Sun Fire Insurance Policy* No. 671703, October 28, 1797.
37. Waterston, 1949.
38. Information from Alex. Cowan & Sons Ltd., Valleyfield Mill.
39. *Sun Fire Insurance Policies* Nos. 608376, November 24, 1792 and 615222, May 27, 1793.
40. *Sun Fire Insurance Policy* No. 793716, August 20, 1806.
41. Waterston, 1949.
42. *Sun Fire Insurance Policies* Nos. 494619, July 12, 1784, 596402, February 9, 1792, and 608454, November 27, 1792.

43. *Sun Fire Insurance Policy* No. 716519, March 7, 1801.
44. *The Paper Maker*, September 1949.
45. Waterston, 1949.
46. *Sun Fire Insurance Policy* No. 651527, January 26, 1796.
47. *Sun Fire Insurance Policy* No. 880501, February 25, 1813.
48. Waterston, 1949.
49. *Sun Fire Insurance Policies* Nos. 514493, January 20, 1786, and 742129, January 6, 1803.
50. A. D. Spicer, *The Paper Trade*, 1907, p. 214.
51. *London Gazette*, November 5, 1814.
52. Information from Alex. Cowan & Sons Ltd.
53. *Sun Fire Insurance Policies* Nos. 592541, November 21, 1791, and 638878, March 14, 1795.
54. Letter, April 5, 1796, *Papers from Springfield Mill*, Kent.
55. *Sun Fire Insurance Policies* Nos. 651485, January 26, 1796, 729110, February 2, 1802, and 902339, January 2, 1815.
56. Information from Robert Craig & Sons Ltd., Caldercruix.
57. *Sun Fire Insurance Policies* Nos. 531913, June 19, 1787, 568836, April 24, 1790, 579776, February 4, 1791, and 742129, January 6th, 1803.
58. Information from H. G. Carter, University Press, Oxford.
59. *Apprenticeship Books*, P.R.O., I.R.1, 63/9, /41 and /220 (1783, 1784 and 1786).
60. *Sun Fire Insurance Policy* No. 481962, August 26, 1783.
61. *London Gazette*, April 11, 1786.
62. *Newcastle Courant*, July 19, 1788.
63. *Sun Fire Insurance Policy* No. 722362, September 29, 1801.
64. *Sun Fire Insurance Policy* No. 737137, September 29, 1802.
65. Information from Y. Trotter & Son Ltd.
66. *Sun Fire Insurance Policy* No. 501464, February 3, 1785.
67. *Newcastle Courant*, May 4, 1793.
68. *Sun Fire Insurance Policy* No. 622172, November 11, 1793.
69. *Sun Fire Insurance Policies* Nos. 629184, June 28, 1794, and 636475, January 12, 1795.
70. *Sun Fire Insurance Policy* No. 756669, December 1, 1803.
71. *Paper Mills Directory*, 1866.
72. *Excise General Letter*, January 24, 1842.
73. *Sun Fire Insurance Policies* Nos. 817960, June 13, 1808, and 928380, March 14, 1817.
74. *The Paper Maker*, July, 1949.
75. *Sun Fire Insurance Policies* Nos. 703288, May 24, 1800, and 820110, August 11, 1808.
76. *Sun Fire Insurance Policies* Nos. 577974, December 30, 1790, 758616, January 14, 1804, and 876479, November 10, 1812.
77. Bushnell, p. 316.

78. *Sun Fire Insurance Policies* Nos. 903800, March 7, 1815, and 916053, February 16, 1816.
79. *Directory of Paper Makers.*
80. *Sun Fire Insurance Policies* Nos. 524465, November 16, 1786, and 570080, May 31, 1790.
81. *Paper Mills Directory,* 1876.
82. *Newcastle Journal,* May 23, 1772.
83. *Apprenticeship Books,* P.R.O., I.R.1, 60/92 (1777).
84. *Apprenticeship Books,* P.R.O., I.R.1, 63/219 (1786) and *Sun Fire Insurance Policy* No. 525845, January 3, 1787.
85. *Sun Fire Insurance Policy* No. 651507, January 26, 1796.
86. *Sun Fire Insurance Policy,* No. 773918, February 13, 1805.
87. *Directory of Paper Makers.*

XXXVII

PAPER MILLS IN WALES

Little is known about early papermaking in Wales, and so far only five paper mills have been identified up to the year 1770. As there is no separate record of the numbers of licences issued by the Excise authorities to paper makers in Wales[1], it is impossible to get an official check on the number of Welsh mills before 1816, when the first Excise list of paper makers and mills in England and Wales was compiled on a numerical basis. There is little doubt, however, that the number of mills increased from about five in the 1770's to a maximum of about twenty during the 1820's. As in England, this peak period was followed by an almost continuous decrease in the number of mills at work, decade by decade, down to the 1920's.

There were no great concentrations of early paper mills comparable with the clusters which grew near London, Edinburgh and Dublin, for Wales lacked a large, dominant commercial centre which could act as a source of materials and a wholesale market for paper. Several of the early mills were in or near towns, for example, Haverfordwest, Carmarthen Crickhowell and Wrexham, but there were also a number of comparatively remote rural sites. The absence of paper mills from mid-Wales reflects the relative poverty, inaccessibility and low density of population of that area; but it must be remembered that there were mills in the counties of Cheshire, Shropshire, Herefordshire and Monmouthshire from which paper was probably supplied to many places in Wales, and that the western towns such as Aberystwyth may have obtained paper by sea transport.

It is probable that most of the early Welsh mills made only common papers, but during the first half of the nineteenth century the manufacture of white paper was established in Denbigh and Flint. Indeed

PAPER MILLS IN WALES

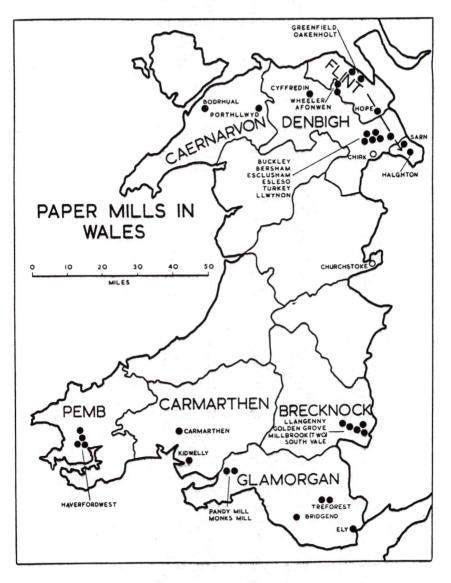

PAPER MILLS IN
WALES

GREENFIELD
OAKENHOLT

FLINT

CYFFREDIN

WHEELER/
AFONWEN

HOPE

BODRHUAL

PORTHLLWYD

CAERNARVON

DENBIGH

SARN

BUCKLEY
BERSHAM
ESCLUSHAM
ESLESO
TURKEY
LLWYNON

CHIRK

HALGHTON

0   10   20   30   40   50

MILES

CHURCHSTOKE

PEMB

CARMARTHEN

BRECKNOCK

LLANGENNY
GOLDEN GROVE
MILLBROOK (TWO)
SOUTH VALE

CARMARTHEN

KIDWELLY

GLAMORGAN

HAVERFORDWEST

TREFOREST

BRIDGEND

PANDY MILL
MONKS MILL

ELY

in 1841 these were the two leading counties in terms of numbers employed in the manufacture of paper; according to the Census Returns, there were 84 persons so employed in Denbigh and 26 in Flint, while Brecknock, Caernarvon and Pembroke had only seven each. During the period of decline in the numbers of mills, most of the small and remote units (whether vat or machine mills) ceased work; the chief causes of this geographical contraction of the industry were the competition of larger, better-equipped and better-placed mills, the advent of railways, and changes in the use of power and raw materials and in the production of types of paper. The only sites which have survived from before 1850 are at Abbey Mills (Flint) and the South Vale Paper Mill (Brecknock).

The story of the Welsh papermaking industry in the nineteenth century is, however, by no means one of overall decline. New mills were established at Cardiff in 1867 and at Oakenholt in 1871 and were well situated in relation to the availability of fuel and power and to transport by land and sea. The growth of these mills and the survivors from earlier days mentioned above is reflected in the numbers of people employed in papermaking in Wales in 1921: 168 in Flint, 76 in Glamorgan and 31 in Brecknock. More recently, mills have been set up at Treforest and Bridgend (Glamorgan) and their history is well known.

The notes which follow give the first and last known dates and proprietors in respect of each mill, with special reference to the earlier and less familiar sites. The map shows the distribution of all the mills, and the notes refer first to the sites in North Wales, considered from west to east, and then to those in South Wales, in the same general direction. I am indebted to the Sun Insurance Office Ltd. and the Commissioners of Customs and Excise for permission to quote from their records.

Bodrhual

In 1812 it was reported that a paper mill had been set up in the parish of Llanrug[2]. In 1816 Bodrhual paper mill was held by John Haslam under the Excise Number 443[3], and the proprietor in 1827, when work ceased, was Thomas Lloyd[4].

Porthllwyd

In 1816 this mill, No. 445, was in the hands of Robert Wynne[5]. Paper, buttonboard and pasteboard were being made there in 1846 by John Lloyd[6]; his name also appears in a Directory of 1850[7], but no later information about him has been found.

Cyffredin

The only known references to paper makers here are from 1819 and 1827, when Owen Lloyd and William Parsons respectively were the proprietors of Mill No. 508[8].

Wheeler, Afonwen

The earliest known record of a paper mill on the River Wheeler is in 1786[9]. This appears to refer to the Wheeler Mill, No. 444, which was held by William Smedley & Co. in 1816[10], but in later years the site was usually described as Afonwen, Caerwys. The mill closed in 1918; the last proprietor was J. R. Jones, who made best quality hand made writing and account book papers, loans, cheque and banknote papers, from seven vats[11].

Afonwen

Mill No. 501, also called Afonwen, was at work from 1822 (when the master paper makers were John Mather, senior and junior, and John Roberts[12]) to about 1860, when the name of Edward Parry was given there[13].

Abbey Mills, Greenfield, Holywell

A pin mill at Holywell was converted to a coarse paper mill by 1770[14]. In 1821 the Greenfield Mill was recorded as No. 193, in the possession of William Hill[15]. The Abbey Mills, Holywell, are still working under the firm of Grosvenor, Chater & Co. Ltd.

Oakenholt

This mill was established in 1871 and is still worked by the North Wales Paper Co. Ltd.

Hope Mills, Cefnybedd

In 1803 Edward Bage, paper maker, insured a paper mill in the township of Cummey in the parish of Hope[16]. This appears to have been the Hope Mill, Excise Number 39, which was held by Samuel Price in 1816[17]. By 1842[18] the Number had been changed to 551 and the site was known as Hope or Cefnybedd Mills. The last proprietor was S. Pickard, who up to 1890 was making biscuit caps and other machine glazed papers[19].

Buckley

In 1816 this mill, which bore the Excise Number 45, was held by John Lewis, and in 1825 by Edward Tomkins[20]. No later reference has been found.

Bersham

Harris & M'Murdoe were paper makers at "Wrexham Mills" in 1818-22[21]. This firm was probably the William Harris and William Dick M'Murdo who were the proprietors of Bersham Mill, No. 524, in 1823[22]. By the 1860's the mill had been renumbered 26, and the last known master makers were the Bersham Paper Co. Ltd., who made printings and news of straw and fibre[23].

Esclusham

Damage estimated at £3,000 was caused when the Esclusham Paper Mills near Wrexham were destroyed by fire in 1810[24]. The mill was in action again by 1816, when it was held by William Harris & Co. under the Excise Number 41[25]. The last master maker was probably W. H. Harris of "Wrexham Paper Mills," who is mentioned in 1848[26].

Escles or Esleso

This appears to have been the "Bromley's paper mill" of which Hughes & Co. (Hughes & Phillips) were the proprietors from 1816 to 1820[27]. Escles Mill was No. 40 in 1816 and No. 525 from 1823 to 1832, when the master maker was William Harris[28].

Turkey

In 1844 Harris Brothers were the proprietors[29]. By 1860 this mill, No. 46, was held by Henry Methold Greville, who made superfine vat book paper[30]. The last firm to work the mill was James Greville & Son, who are recorded up to 1916[31].

Llwynon

In 1797 Edward Bozley, paper maker of Llwynon in the parish of Wrexham, insured his stock and utensils in a paper mill[32]. This is the only known specific reference to Llwynon, but it appears to be connected with a site which was quite distinct from the other paper mills near Wrexham (Buckley to Turkey, above).

Chirk (doubtful)

In 1812 (the first of numerous similar references) it was stated that in the vicinity of Chirk were "several paper manufactories, the Ceiriog supplying abundance of water" and that paper was made "of divers qualities, from the coarsest wrapping to the finest writing[33]." These mills have not been identified.

Sarn

The first known paper maker here was Simon Hope, about the year 1790[34]. In 1816 Mill No. 43, Sarn, was held by Benjamin Bates; it was discontinued in 1824[35].

Upper Mill, Halghton, Hanmer

Thomas Downward was a paper man of Halton in 1706[36]. In 1816 Mill No. 42, Upper Mill, was in the hands of Samuel Adams, who was probably the "late Mr. Adams, paper maker" of Hanmer, referred to in 1835[37].

Coldbach

In 1847 Mill No. 442, Coldbach, in the Wales North Collection of Excise, was held by Wilbraham and Walter Mangnall[38]. I am unable to identify this site.

Churchstoke (doubtful)

There is said to have been a paper mill near Lower Mellington, Churchstoke, Mongomeryshire, and a reference is given to a paper manufacturer residing at the Brynkin in 1841[39]. I have not been able to find confirmation of this mill.

Haverfordwest (four mills)

It is probable that papermaking was carried on in at least two mills in or near Haverfordwest before the year 1800[40]. The Hartsore paper mill, recorded in 1771, was in the parish of St. Martin, and must have been different from the paper mill in the parish of St. Thomas, mentioned in 1783; and a reference to paper mills near Haverfordwest in 1798 may relate to yet another site. The Prendergast Mills to the north of the town were probably converted to papermaking soon after 1805, and must have been one of the two Haverfordwest paper mills which were held by Charles Lloyd & Co. under the Excise Numbers 446 and 447 in 1816[41].

The last known reference to Mill No. 446 is in 1866, when it was in the hands of Benjamin Harvey & Sons[42]. Meanwhile, No. 447 appears to have been renumbered 216, for a mill bearing that Number at Millbank, Haverfordwest, was worked by Benjamin Harvey in 1842[43]; in 1866 the name of the mill was given as Prendergast and in 1876 as Cleddau[44]. In 1885 Samuel Read & Co. were making rope browns, manillas, cartridges, caps and grocery papers on one machine of 51 inches, and they were followed for a short period by D. O. Evans, the last proprietor of the Prendergast Mills[45].

Carmarthen

David Charles, paper maker at Mill No. 448, Carmarthen, is recorded from 1816[46] to 1860[47].

PAPER MILLS IN WALES

Kidwelly

A notice that this paper mill was for sale is the only known reference. It was advertised in 1765[48].

Pandy, Cadle, Llangyfelach

In 1765 the death was recorded of Thomas Jenkin of the paper mill[49]. In 1816 the mill was held by William Spencer under the Number 441, and the last known master paper maker was James West, in 1834[50].

Monk's Mill, Llandilo-talybont

In 1738 Thomas Selman was a paper man of Llandilo-talbont[51]. The last known proprietor of the mill was Thomas Rowland, in 1816, when the Excise Number was 442[52].

Ely

This large modern mill was founded in 1867, when there were two machines[53]. It is still working, under the firm of Thomas Owen & Co. Ltd.

The other mills in Glamorgan — Treforest and Bridgend — are of more recent establishment. The firms are Wiggins, Teape & Co. Ltd. and Western Board Mills Ltd. at Treforest, and the Bridgend Paper Mills Ltd., Llynfri Valley, Bridgend.

Llangenny

The first known reference to a master paper maker here is to George Window in 1790[54]. In 1816 James Window held Mill No. 440, Llangenny[55]. The last proprietor of this old mill appears to have been James Holden, recorded there in 1847[56].

Golden Grove, Llangenny

In 1851 there is a new entry of No. 440 under the name of James Window Rumsey, a maker of paper and millboard[57]. This appears to have been a new mill, which was later known as Golden Grove, mainly a millboard mill. The last known reference to No. 440 is under the firm of James Jacob & Co. who made millboards and paper from three vats up to about 1892[58].

Golden Grove, Millbrook

The first known reference to Mill No. 616, Golden Grove, is from 1826, when the master maker was James Window[59]. The mill of this Number was later called Glanaber or Millbrook Mills and from about 1876 was making boards only[60]. It was last worked by Robert H. Hawkins up to about 1934[61], and was demolished during World War II.

Millbrook

Another Millbrook millboard mill, with two vats, is recorded in 1884 and 1885. It was worked by F. C. Gwynne[62].

South Vale, Llangroyney

Llangroyney Mill, Excise Number 388, was held by William Parry and James Window in 1849[63]. From about 1886 to 1932 it was known as the Usk Paper Works, and has since been at work under the South Vale Paper Mill (1939) Ltd.

REFERENCES

1. Excise statistics concerning papermaking in Wales were usually consolidated with those relating to England. See A. H. Shorter, *Paper Mills and Paper Makers in England, 1495-1800*, The Paper Publications Society, Hilversum. Holland. 1957, pp. 72-3 and 82.
2. *Beauties of England and Wales*, XVII, Pt. I. 1812, p. 343.
3. *Excise General Letter*, October 8, 1816.
4. *Ibid.*, May 2, 1827.
5. *Ibid.*, October 8, 1816.
6. *Ibid.*, January 23, 1846.
7. *Slater's Directory*, 1850.
8. *Excise General Letters*, February 20, 1819, and May 2. 1827.
9. A. H. Shorter, *op. cit.*, p. 257.
10. *Excise General Letter*, October 8, 1816.
11. *Directory of Paper Makers*, 1910-18.
12. *Excise General Letter*, October 9, 1822.
13. *Paper Mills Directory*, 1860.
14. A. H. Shorter, *op. cit.*, p. 257.
15. *Excise General Letter*, May 3, 1821.
16. *Sun Fire Insurance Policy* No. 751625, August 8, 1803.
17. *Excise General Letter*, October 8, 1816.
18. *Ibid.*, December 1, 1842.

19. *Directory of Paper Makers*, 1890.
20. *Excise General Letters*, October 8, 1816, and June 17, 1825.
21. *Pigot's Directory*, 1818-22.
22. *Excise General Letter*, February 19, 1823.
23. *Paper Mills Directory*, 1866.
24. *Gentleman's Magazine*, 80 (2), 1810, p. 582.
25. *Excise General Letter*, October 8, 1816.
26. *London Gazette*, July 18, 1848.
27. I. Jones, *A History of Printing and Printers in Wales to 1810*, 1925, p. 124; *Excise General Letter*, October 8, 1816; and *Pigot's Directory*, 1818-20.
28. *Excise General Letter*, November 28, 1832.
29. *Pigot's Directory*, 1844.
30. *Paper Mills Directory*, 1860.
31. *Directory of Paper Makers*, 1916.
32. *Sun Fire Insurance Policy* No. 666345, April 11, 1797.
33. *Beauties of England and Wales*, XVII, Pt. I, 1812, p. 573.
34. A. H. Shorter, *op. cit.*, p. 257.
35. *Excise General Letters*, October 8, 1816, and October 21, 1824.
36. A. H. Shorter, *op. cit.*, p. 257.
37. *Excise General Letter*, October 8, 1816, and *Shrewsbury Chronicle*, April 29, 1835.
38. *Excise General Letter*, April 30, 1847.
39. *Montgomery Collections*, XL, p. 216.
40. A. H. Shorter, *op. cit.*, p. 258.
41. *Excise General Letter*, October 8, 1816.
42. *Paper Mills Directory*, 1866.
43. *Excise General Letter*, December 1, 1842.
44. *Paper Mills Directory*, 1866 and 1876.
45. *Directory of Paper Makers*, 1885 and 1895.
46. *Excise General Letter*, October 8, 1816.
47. *Paper Mills Directory*, 1860.
48. A. H. Shorter, *op. cit.*, p. 257.
49. *Ibid.*, pp. 257-8.
50. *Excise General Letters*, October 8, 1816, and January 17, 1834.
51. A. H. Shorter, *op. cit.*, p. 258.
52. *Excise General Letter*, October 8, 1816.
53. A. D. Spicer, *The Paper Trade*, 1907, p. 210.
54. A. H. Shorter, *op. cit.*, p. 256.
55. *Excise General Letter*, October 8, 1816.
56. *Ibid.*, April 30, 1847.
57. *Ibid.*, May 20, 1851.
58. *Directory of Paper Makers*, 1892.
59. *Excise General Letter*, September 13, 1826.
60. *Paper Mills Directory*, 1876.
61. *Directory of Paper Makers*, 1934.
62. *Paper Makers' Directory of All Nations*, 1884, and *Directory of Paper Makers*, 1885.
63. *Excise General Letter*, March 14, 1849.

XXXVIII

PAPER MILLS IN IRELAND

The account of the present position of the paper industry in Ireland which was given in *The Paper Maker*, March, 1963, reminded me that there appears to be scope for a full historical study of Irish paper-making. The subject might well be worked into a sizeable book which would take its proper place in a comprehensive history of the paper industry in the British Isles. There certainly seems to be consider-able material, for quite incidentally I have come across numerous references to Ireland in the course of my research on the history of paper mills in England. This article is based almost entirely upon such references and is concerned with Irish mills down to the 1880's; from that time various Directories of paper makers and paper mills began to appear regularly and much information about the modern period can easily be obtained from them. There are also the records of individual firms, articles and notes in such journals as *The Paper Maker* and *The World's Paper Trade Review*, and other modern printed sources(1). However, there must be many primary sources in Ireland, such as maps, county histories and surveys, local records, newspapers and directories, which could be systematically searched for information about Irish papermaking in earlier times.

First mills 1690

Some years ago Mr. Rhys Jenkins informed me that he knew of references to what were apparently the first attempts to establish papermaking in Ireland in the 1690's; there is mention of white paper makers, a brown paper company, and applications for patents for the manufacture of blue, purple and other papers(2). The white paper manufactory was located at Rathfarnham near Dublin, and during the next sixty years or so as many as twelve paper mills may have been at work in the vicinity of that city. A 'trial list' which gives the names, addresses and dates of many Irish paper makers between 1690 and 1800 has recently been published(3), and among the paper mills that can be identified from references during that period are the following in the Dublin area: Rathfarnham, Templeogue, Milltown, Tallaght, Kilternan, Chapelizod, Millmount, Whitechurch, Donnybrook, Newtown, Saggart, and Newbridge (Co. Kildare). By the middle of the eighteenth century there were probably half a dozen paper mills in the north of Ireland, chiefly in Antrim, and perhaps five or six in the south, principally in the Cork district.

No doubt the early Irish paper makers had to face the prospect of severe competition in the home market, especially from such well-established importers of paper as France and Holland, and in the period from the 1730's to the 1760's several of them were given financial encouragement to improve their manufacture. In 1737, for example, Parliament "granted £500 to Mr. Thomas Slater, paper maker (he having made great improvement in the writing- and printing-paper) to enable him to build a new mill," which he proposed to do "after the Dutch manner"(4). Paper makers who were at Rathfarnham, Templeogue and Tallaght in the 1740's were among those who qualified for premiums awarded by the Dublin Society(5); there were also awards to Joseph Sexton "who laid out above £1,000 in a double mill near Limerick" and Daniel Blow "who laid out £520 in such a mill near Antrim." In 1749 a parliamentary grant of £200 was made to Francis Joy as a reward for his improvements in the paper manufacture in the north of Ireland. He is said to have introduced the first paper engine (a Hollander) into Ulster(6).

Variety of paper

It is probable that most of the mills working in Ireland during the second half of the eighteenth century had only one or two vats, but a variety of papers was produced. Judging by the evidence from watermarks(7), some mills were making good quality writing and printing papers, but no doubt as in England a large proportion of the total output consisted of packing, shop and other common papers.

Labour troubles

The considerable wallpaper industry in Ireland and the papermaking industry must have been mutually beneficial during this period(8). In the eighteenth and early nineteenth centuries Irish paper makers probably had little trouble in getting a fair supply of materials for making common papers, but it seems to have been much more difficult for them to obtain sufficient linen rags and other good quality materials. From time to time rewards were offered to anyone who could increase the supply of rags; in 1753, for example, the Dublin Society announced premiums for "gathering and selling most linen rags to the paper makers in Dublin(9)." Among the other problems which Irish paper masters had to contend with were labour difficulties. One of the earliest known references to a combination of workers in the paper industry mentions an incident near Donnybrook in 1773(10), when two journeymen who had refused to enter into a combination with the other paper makers were assaulted. But despite these and other difficulties such as foreign competition and the incidence of taxation the Irish paper industry seems to have expanded appreciably if not spectacularly. At the beginning of the nineteenth century there were 17 paper mills in the county of Dublin alone(11), and no doubt by that time there were several more in Ulster and in the south(12).

Following the erection of the first Fourdrinier machines in Hertfordshire, an agreement was reached for the installation of a machine in a paper mill near Cork; unfortunately the Irish paper maker and stationer concerned went bankrupt(13). By 1824, however, Fourdrinier machines were in use in three mills in the Cork district, and there was one machine "on another construction" near Dublin(14). Although most of the Irish mills must have been quite small, there were several mills of fairly large size, including the leading mills in the Dublin area. Some indication of the numbers employed in these in the 1830's is given in statements(15) that there were about 150 people at work at Killeen and nearly 200 at the two Saggart mills; McDonnell's other mills at Old Bawn (Tallaght) had about 50 employees and the Drimnagh mill about 25.

There does not appear to be a complete Excise list of Irish paper mills comparable with that for England and Wales in 1816(16), but in various *Excise General Letters*(17) issued between 1831 and 1851 there are references to Irish mills whose Excise Numbers ranged from 1 (Roan in the Armagh Collection of Excise) to 81 (Six Miles Bridge, Limerick). This range of Numbers does not imply that there were 81 paper mills at work at one and the same time; board manufactories were included in the *Excise Letters*, and no doubt as in England the Excise Numbers of certain mills were changed from time to time and fresh Numbers were added as new mills began work or old mills recommenced after a period of idleness. The identification, mapping and description of all the Irish paper mills mentioned in the Excise records and in other documents during the first half of the nine-teenth century can only be done with the aid of large-scale maps and local sources, and this should be a fascinating task for a student working on the histori-cal geography of industry in Ireland. From what is already known about papermaking sites during this period, it is of course obvious that there were numer-ous mills in the Dublin region and in Ulster and Cork, but elsewhere there were mills about which very little seems to be known—for example those in the counties of Limerick, Waterford and Galway.

Some 40 of the Irish mills which were at work at various times during the nineteenth century have been listed(18), but there must have been many others, especially during peak periods in the number of mills at work which appear to have been reached in the 1820's and the 1830's. In 1824(19) it was stated that the total of 54 paper mills in existence was slightly decreasing, and that 47 mills were licensed; there were three makers of fine paper. In 1835(20) Ireland had 57 makers of paper and no pasteboard

Mill Number	Name or Locality	Equipment	Chief products
3	Mount Brown, Kilmainham	1 machine	browns, greys
4	Ballyclare	4 machines	printings, news
7	Antrim		browns, web printings
12	Butlerstown, Cork		browns, small hands
13	Gurth, Blarney	1 machine	browns, grocery papers
18	Madeira, Galway	closed	
31	Sally Park, Clondalkin	2 machines	printings, news, shut down
32	Newbrook, Rathfarnham	1 machine	browns, small hands, printings
36	Boldbrook, Tallaght	1 machine	browns, grocery papers
40	Old Bawn	1 machine	news, printings
41	Swift Brook, Saggart	1 machine	fine writings
42	Killeen	handmade & machine	writings, printings, news
43	Drimnagh	1 machine	grocery papers
44	Golden Bridge	closed	
52	Sallybrook, Cork	closed	
66	Edmondstown & Millmount		browns, greys
67	Glenville, Cork		browns, grocery papers
75	Killeen	handmade	book, loan, banknote paper

makers, but although the total output increased with the mechanisation of certain mills, by 1851 the number of paper mills at work was only 28(21); of the 86 beating engines enumerated in the latter year, 15 were 'silent.' Saggart and Clondalkin were easily the largest mills at that time, with 15 and 9 beating engines working; many of the other mills were very small, with only one or two engines each. Of the mills listed in 1851, the following were in the Dublin area: Ballyboden (two mills), Boldbrook, Harold's Cross, Templeogue, Old Bawn, Killeen, Drimnagh, Golden Bridge, Great Newtown, Edmondstown, Kilternan, Clondalkin, Salmon Leap and Saggart. In Antrim there were Carnanee, Milltown, Derriaghy, Dunadry and Antrim Mills. Tyrone had Donemara and Fartlaghan, and Armagh had Roan Mill. The mills in the Cork district were Transtown, Dripsey and Towerbridge, and there was one mill in Galway and one in Clare.

The decline in the number of paper mills in Ireland continued during the second half of the nineteenth century and into the twentieth. In 1876 a reliable source(22) recorded only 19 mills in the whole country, and four of these were closed or 'shut down.' In 1885 the total of mills in existence had fallen to 13 and by 1900 it was down to 9(23). The above table is an extract from the information about the mills listed in the Directory of 1876.

Some of the causes of the decrease in the number of Irish paper mills down to the twentieth century are obvious enough. In the competitive conditions of the time, the Irish papermaking industry suffered from the lack of capital in a country with a comparatively low standard of living, the lack of a major coalfield in Ireland itself, and the decline in population from 1840 on. Inevitably the casualties among the mills included many of the small units, especially those which made only common papers, and most of the really remote mills. Eventually the survivors were markedly concentrated in the more favourable areas of Dublin and the north, the parts of Ireland within which the early paper makers had established their mills. An investigation of the history of all the known mills would reveal much that is still hidden from us, and the time is ripe for this research work to be carried out.

(1) Among the secondary sources a good starting-point would be an article by H. Ewen on Paper Making in Ireland, in *Progress in Irish Printing*, Dublin, *circa* 1936.

(2) *State Papers Domestic*, 1690-92; *London Gazette*, March 12, 1694.

(3) J. W. Phillips, A Trial List of Irish Papermakers, 1690-1800, *The Library*, Fifth Ser., XIII, 1958.

(4) *The Country Journal or The Craftsman*, Dec. 3, 1737.

(5) *Newcastle Journal*, June 23, 1750.

(6) A. Atkinson, *Ireland exhibited to England . . .*, 1823. Also in the 1750's there were grants by the Parliament of Ireland to paper makers to enable them to carry on the paper manufacture. Instances are mentioned in *Gentleman's Magazine*, 21, Nov. 1751, and 27, Dec. 1757, and in *Oxford Gazette and Reading Mercury*, Nov. 26, 1753.

(7) J. W. Phillips, *op. cit.*

(8) Many details of the Irish wallpaper industry are given by A. K. Longfield, History of the Dublin Wall-Paper Industry in the Eighteenth Century, *Journal of the Royal Society of Antiquaries of Ireland*, LXXVII, 1947.

(9) *Felix Farley's Bristol Journal*, Sept. 22, 1753. Similar premiums had been offered in the 1740's. An instance is mentioned in *Gentleman's Magazine*, 18, Aug. 1748.

(10) *The Gazetteer and New Daily Advertiser*, Aug. 25, 1773.

(11) J. D'Alton, *The History of the County of Dublin*, 1838.

(12) Paper makers at Belfast and Cork, for example, are recorded in *Holden's Triennial Directory*, 1805-7. Ulster is said to have had as many as 16 paper mills. A. Atkinson, *op.cit.* This apparently refers to the very early nineteenth century.

(13) *Bath Chronicle*, May 31, 1810. The Fourdriniers also went bankrupt. The agreement between them and James Bartholomew O'Sullivan, paper maker of Cork, for the erection of a papermaking machine is further mentioned in *London Gazette*, January 19, 1813.

(14) *Eighth Report of the Commissioners of Inquiry into the Collection and Management of the Revenue arising in Ireland . . . Excise, Ireland*, 1824.

(15) J. D'Alton, *op.cit.*

(16) See A. H. Shorter, The Excise Numbers of Paper Mills in England and Wales, *The Paper Maker*, CXXXV and CXXXVI, 1958.

(17) I am grateful to the Commissioners of H.M. Customs and Excise for permission to search and to quote from their records.

(18) *World's Paper Trade Review*, 1911, kindly quoted to me by Mr. G. Roddick (North of Ireland Paper Mill, Bally-clare), Mr. D. P. Walls (Drimnagh Paper Mills Ltd.) and Mr. R. W. Horsburgh (Swift Brook Paper Mills Ltd.).

(19) *Eighth Report . . .*, as for reference 14 above.

(20) *Fourteenth Report of the Commissioners of Inquiry into the Excise Establishment—Paper*, 1835, Appendix 18.

(21) See A. H. Shorter, The Distribution of British Paper Mills in 1851, *The Paper Maker*, CXXI, 1951.

(22) *Paper Mills Directory*, 1876.

(23) *Directory of Paper Makers*.

GENERAL INDEX

Page numbers in italic refer to pictures, maps or illustrations of watermarks.

LIST OF PAPERMILLS

The numbers in brackets after the mill name refer to the numbers allocated by the Excise officials as given by Shorter and page numbers in italics refers to pictures, maps or illustrations of watermarks.